CW00392108

CHURCHILL'S
DESERT
RATS

in North Africa, Burma, Sicily and Italy

CHURCHILL'S
DESERT
RATS

in North Africa, Burma, Sicily and Italy

PATRICK DELAFORCE

Pen & Sword
MILITARY

First published in 2002 by
Sutton Publishing Limited
Republished in Great Britain in 2009 by
Pen & Sword Military
an imprint of
Pen & Sword Books Ltd
47 Church Street
Barnsley
South Yorkshire S70 2AS

ISBN 978 1 84884 039 3

A CIP catalogue record for this book is
available from the British Library

Pen
Pen & Sword /   ord Military,
Wh
Per
Remember   ublishing

For a complete list of Pen & Sword titles please contact
PEN & SWORD BOOKS LIMITED
47 Church Street, Barnsley, South Yorkshire, S70 2AS, England
E-mail: enquiries@pen-and-sword.co.uk
Website: www.pen-and-sword.co.uk

Contents

Introduction

Winston Churchill controlled the deployment of British Armed Forces throughout the Second World War. Generals decided what they wanted to do in the field but Whitehall – and that meant the Prime Minister – directed the broad strategy. Churchill took an immense interest in the widespread Middle East campaigns. He wrote that 'the Persian oilfields were a prime war factor' and 'the security of Egypt remains paramount'. The 8th Army was responsible for the land campaigns in North Africa and the 7th Armoured Division – later to be known as the Desert Rats – was the spearhead of that formation. Churchill, as his memoirs reveal, followed their successes (and their failures) with intense interest. The initial battles against Mussolini's second-class armies were completely successful, but when General Erwin Rommel took command of the joint Axis forces battles raged that went alternately to one side or the other. Churchill mentioned the division dozens of times and visited them (and the 8th Army) in Africa on two occasions.

Their emblem of a flaming scarlet desert rat (Jerboa) became famous throughout the British Army and to the war-torn British public that needed heroic symbols to keep up morale. This was the formation founded and trained by Major-General Percy Hobart in 1938 and 1939. They fought from the desert – Cairo to Tunis – then in Italy, 'Overlord' in Normandy, France, Belgium, Holland and all the way to Berlin.

Their two armoured (tank) brigades – the 4th and 7th – became famous in their own right when they became independent of the parent. When 7th Armoured Brigade sailed for Burma at the end of 1941 they kept the divisional sign but changed the Jerboa's colour to jungle green. After many vicissitudes they returned to the Middle East. Then in summer 1943 they battled their way up the east coast of Italy, through the Caesar, Gothic, Gustav and Ghengis Khan enemy defence lines to victory in Venice and Trieste.

After the capture of Tunis, 4th Armoured Brigade finally left the parent division, kept the Jerboa, now coloured black, and put his tail more aggressively over his head, instead of between his legs. They helped in Operation Husky to capture Sicily, fought in southern Italy, returned to Europe to fight – in parallel – with the main 7th Armoured Division through four countries to meet the Russians on the Baltic. Composed of Hussars, Royal Tank Regiments, Yeomanry, Royal Horse Artillery, Rifle Brigade and supporting Sappers, RASC, RAOC, REME and RAMC, the three superb Desert Rat formations took on the Axis powers (including briefly the Japanese) and fought them to a standstill.

For the first time the story of the three – scarlet, green and black Jerboas – is told by scores of combatants – troopers, gunners and infantrymen (the Queens Brigade joined them at Alamein). In one short dramatic week in North Africa they won three Victoria Crosses – it was a magnificent record and a marvellous story.

On 21 July 1945 Prime Minister Winston Churchill addressed them at the Berlin Victory Parade. 'I have a word more to say about the Desert Rats. They were the first to begin. The 11th Hussars were in action in the desert in 1940 and ever since you have kept marching steadily forward on the long road to victory. Through so many countries and changing scenes you have fought your way. . . . It is a march unsurpassed through all the story of war so far as my reading of history leads me to believe. May the fathers long tell the children about this tale.' This is their tale.

FLOREAT JERBOA

Foreword

by

Major General PAJ Cordingley DSO

Fifty years after the Desert Rats were formed in North Africa, their successors, the Red Jerboa Rats of 7th Armoured Brigade and the Black Jerboa Rats of 4th Armoured Brigade were back in the desert. This time, 1991, it was in Saudi Arabia waiting to fight the Iraqis and expel them from Kuwait.

We lived once more in the sand like our illustrious forebears. While we waited and trained, we thought of them. We asked for their advice and we tried to learn as much as possible from their exploits. Frequent letters arrived which discussed subjects from tank tactics to dust and flies to washing. I remember one day receiving a letter from an old comrade in my Regiment reminding me that if I was attacked by a Messerschmitt when in my tank, 'not to forget to zigzag'!

When our fighting came it lasted only four days. We were proud of our achievements but I hope not boastful. After all, we defeated a demoralised and technologically inferior enemy and met very few reverses. This was very similar to the opening phase in North Africa in 1940 when our forebears overcame the Italians. For neither of us could we pretend it was violent for the victors. In 1991 we had complete air supremacy and almost total domination on the ground with our superior equipment. We won because we were aggressive and used to full advantage the staggering artillery firepower available to us. Also our outstanding tanks could pick off the enemy at three thousand yards range; our infantry was well equipped and trained; we could and did fight at night. Not all of these advantages were available to our Second World War predecessors, yet they prevailed.

While we returned to our families in Europe in 1991, the 7th Armoured Division went to Cairo in 1941. But they were not destined to go home from there. Rommel had arrived in Tripoli and for the next two years the Desert Rats fought the Afrika Korps. No major battle took place without them being there: Tobruk, Sidi Rezegh where three Victoria Crosses were awarded to soldiers of the 7th Armoured Brigade, Gazala, Alam Halfa and, of course, El Alamein. But, as this fine account describes, their magnificent exploits continued in Burma, Iraq, Sicily and Italy. The story of their victorious advance across North West Europe is to be told in a later volume. Since 1991 both the Red and Black Desert Rats have returned to fight in Iraq but, surely, nothing compares to the incredible story that unfolds in this enthralling book.

I now repeat the words written by one of the original 7th Armoured Division commanders, 'So many scenes, good times and bad, savage heat and extreme cold, sand storms and rain and sunshine and perhaps too many names ...who gave their whole endeavours to their comrades and their Regiments and who died in battle.' I feel sure I speak for all present day Desert Rats when I say 'We salute you all. Floreat Jerboa.'

Patrick Cordingley
Commander 7th Armoured Brigade 1988 – 1991

CHAPTER ONE

Churchill and the Desert War

During the Twilight War between 3 September 1939 and 10 May 1940, when Nazi Germany and Fascist Italy were preparing for major Blitzkrieg operations against Britain and France, Winston Churchill was offered the Admiralty as First Lord and a seat in the War Cabinet. He noted in his memoirs:

> Should Italy become hostile our first battlefield must be the Mediterranean. . . . The British domination of the Mediterranean would inflict injuries upon an enemy Italy which might be fatal to her power of continuing the war. All her troops in Libya and in Abyssinia would be cut flowers in a vase. . . . Not to hold the Central Mediterranean would be to expose Egypt and the Canal as well as the French possessions to invasions by Italian troops with German leadership. Moreover a series of swift and striking victories in this theatre, which might be obtainable in the early weeks of a war, would have a most healthy and helpful bearing upon the main struggle with Germany.

On 10 May Holland and Belgium were overrun by the German Panzers and their formidable Stuka divebombers, and Winston Churchill became Prime Minister.

For the next four years Churchill masterminded the Mediterranean and North African campaigns, initially against the Italians and then against them under German leadership. The British 8th Army bore the brunt of the continuous land fighting and their spearhead was the 7th Armoured Division, soon to be christened the Desert Rats. His memoirs mention that formation more frequently – and with more feeling – than any other in the British Army. At the end of hostilities he addressed them in Berlin. 'Dear Desert Rats! May your glory ever shine! May your laurels never fade! May the memory of this glorious pilgrimage of war which you have made from Alamein, via the Baltic to Berlin, never die!'

In his book *The River War* as a young second lieutenant in the Twenty-First Lancers Churchill took part in the Lancers' great charge at Omdurman (south from Wadi Halfa through the Sudan to Atbara and Khartoum) in 1898. He wrote 'In one respect a cavalry charge is very like ordinary life. So long as you are all right, firmly in your saddle, your horse in hand and well armed, lots of enemies will give you a wide berth. But as soon as you have lost a stirrup, have a rein cut, have dropped your weapon, then is the moment when from all quarters enemies rush upon you.'

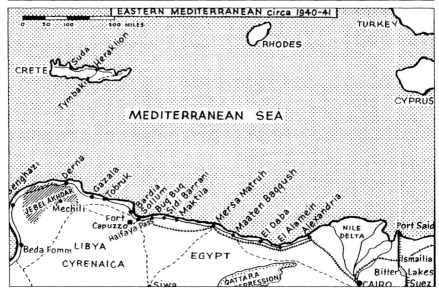

Battleground in the Eastern Mediterranean, c. 1940–1.

Rarely in the history of war have the fortunes of the opposing armies so fluctuated in the desperate four years of savage ebb and flow – Italians and Germans on the one side, British, Australian, New Zealanders, South Africans, Indians and Free French on the other. From Cairo to Sollum on the Libyan border is 500 miles, to Benghazi 750 miles and to Tunis 1,500 miles. The logistics of POL (Petrol, Oil and Lubricant), water (in flimsy jerry cans), ammunition, and food (mostly tinned) were frightening. Vast dumps were built up that changed hands frequently as advance turned into retreat. Tank tracks wore out (there were never enough tank transporters) and trucks broke down frequently. The whole of the vast campaign area was dominated by the need for ports (Bardia, Tobruk, Benghazi and Tripoli) and for control of the one major coastal road. From Tripoli eastwards the Italians had built a magnificent road through Tripolitania and Cyrenaica to the Egyptian frontier and along its 1,000 miles Italian troop garrisons were established at Benghazi, Derna, Tobruk, Bardia and Sollum.

Churchill wrote of the area west of Cairo leading to the Italian frontier wire fortifications.

> In this small but lively warfare our troops felt they had the advantage, and soon conceived themselves to be masters of the desert. Until they came up against large formed bodies or fortified posts they could go where they liked, collecting trophies from sharp encounters. When armies approach each other it makes all the difference which owns only the ground on which it stands or sleeps and which one owns all the rest. I saw this in the Boer War where we owned nothing beyond the fires of our camps and bivouacs, whereas the Boers rode where they pleased all over the country.

The historian of the 11th Hussars (Cherry Pickers) described the main battlegrounds.

The main feature of the Western desert of Egypt – and the scene of all its major battles – is the coastal plain, averaging about 30 miles in width, which runs for 300 miles from the Cairo–Alexandria road to the Cyrenaican frontier at Sollum. It is widest at the eastern end and narrows down to a matter of yards where the escarpment sweeps round to meet the sea just past Sollum. Here the barbed-wire fence rose out of the water and struggled up the steep cliff face to reach the plateau, running thence in a southerly direction as far as the wastes of the Great Sand Sea, 200 miles beyond. In 1940 up from Cairo turn westward by the aerodromes and army camps at Amariya on the outskirts of Alexandria and then pass in turn the landmarks of El Alamein (60 miles), Mersa Matruh (175 miles) and Sidi Barrani (250 miles). On the right hand are the low sand dunes and the blue waters of the Mediterranean, and away to the left the purple outlines of the escarpment rising for 600 feet to the desert plateau above. The plain carried both the railway and the one good road but the greater part of the surface was quite passable to desert-worthy vehicles, except where there were some wide patches of loose sand and when the lakes of mud came from the heavy rains of winter. It was the natural route from Libya to Egypt and the only practical one for the main armies. The desert plateau which lay to the south beyond the escarpment was a forbidding wilderness of rock and sand, marked only by an occasional well (in Arabic 'Bir') and sparse scatterings of the black tents of nomad Arabs.

Alan Moorehead, the intrepid front-line journalist who wrote *African Trilogy*, wrote of the dangers of 'the Khamseen sandstorm which blows more or less throughout the year is the most hellish wind on earth. It picks up the surface dust as fine as baking powder and blows it thickly into the air across hundreds of square miles of desert. . . . It blocked visibility down to half a dozen yards. Little crazy lines of yellow dust snaked across the road. . . . It crept up your nose and down your throat, itching unbearably and making it difficult to breathe. Sometimes a Khamseen may blow for days making you feel that you will never see light and air and feel coolness again. I hate them and I hate the desert because of them.' But Churchill with his painter's eye saw 'level plains of smooth sand, a little rosier than buff, a little paler than salmon – are interrupted only by occasional peaks of rocks – black, stark and shapeless. Rainless storms dance firelessly over the hot crisp surface of the ground. The fine sand driven by the wind, gathers into deep drifts and silts among the dark rocks of the hills, exactly as snow hangs about an Alpine summit: only it is fiery snow such as might fall in hell. The earth burns with the quenchless thirst of ages and in the steel blue sky scarcely a cloud obstructs the unrelenting triumph of the sun.'

On 10 June 1940 when Mussolini declared war on Great Britain, Churchill wrote 'Nevertheless the War Cabinet were determined to defend Egypt against all comers with whatever resources could be spared from the decisive struggle at home.'

CHAPTER TWO

Hobart's Creation – Army of the Nile

Since 1882 British troops had soldiered in leisurely fashion in Egypt. The security of the Suez Canal was a significant reason for their presence, and British administrators ensured stability even when, after the First World War, King Fuad became the sovereign. The treaty of 1936 confined British troops to the Canal Zone. Every year a cavalry regiment went from Egypt to India, while another returned to the UK and a third arrived in Egypt. The Egyptian Mobile Force (predictably nicknamed the Immobile Force) had been operative since 1936 when the 1st Battalion (Light) Royal Tank Regiment arrived for a short visit and returned in 1938 with Lieutenant-Colonel J.A.L. 'Blood' Caunter as their commanding officer. Air support consisted of RAF Audaxes, Gladiators, Harts and Blenheims.

After the Munich crisis in 1938 the Cairo Cavalry Brigade, under Brigadier H.E. Russell, formed the Matruh Mobile Force, based on the Mersa Matruh 'fortress'. Its task was to support the garrison (both British and Egyptian troops) in the 'Charing Cross' area. A stubby, bushy little tree (known as the Fig Tree) stands near the junction of the road to Sidi Barrani and the Siwa track on a plateau about 6 miles outside Mersa Matruh. Major General P.C.S. Hobart, the leading tank expert in the British Army, arrived in Egypt on 27 September 1938 to take command of all forces in the Canal Zone. He received an unfriendly greeting from the GOC, Lieutenant-General Gordon-Finlayson. 'I don't know what you've come here for and I don't want you anyway.'

The mechanisation of traditional cavalry regiments in 1936–7 was greeted with dismay by many officers, and Hobart, as one of the few professional tank experts, met deep hostility. He was a highly decorated officer, with boundless energy, many controversial ideas on military tactics, and did not suffer fools gladly. He set about transforming the Mobile Force into an efficient fighting formation, and much helped by a staff officer, Major C.M. Smith RASC, three brigades were formed: the Heavy Brigade (Lieutenant-Colonel H.R.B. Watkins) with 1st (Lieutenant-Colonel Caunter) and 6th Bns (Lieutenant-Colonel Morrogh), Royal Tank Regiment; the Light Armoured Brigade (Brigadier H.E. Russell) with 7th (Queen's Own) Hussars, 8th (King's Royal Irish) Hussars, and 11th (Prince Albert's Own) Hussars, known as the Cherry Pickers; and finally the Pivot Group (later known as the Support Group) under Lieutenant-Colonel W.H.B. Mirrlees with 3rd Regiment Royal House Artillery, 'F' Battery 4 RHA, and recently arrived from Burma 1st Bn King's Royal Rifle Corps. Hobart also commanded the Abbassia District with the main barracks area, plus three regiments of Egyptian troops. 1st RTR with 58 high mileage light tanks, 7th Hussars with two light tank squadrons and Mk IIIs, VIA and VIB and 8th Hussars with Vickers-Berthier guns mounted on 15-cwt trucks were the main strike force. 6 RTR defended Cairo with its old medium and light tanks and the 11th Hussars were the reconnaissance regiment with a mixture of Rolls-Royce and Morris armoured cars. 1st RTR had experimented for a year with a secret new device, a very powerful searchlight mounted on a tank which was meant to dazzle and confuse the enemy in night fighting. Known as Canal Defence Lights (to confuse enemy agents), the CDL was one of the mysteries of the Second World War. A whole brigade was formed in the UK for the invasion of Europe, landed in Normandy, but were never used in action. The support (pivot) group, 3 RHA, were equipped with 3.7-inch Howitzers towed by 'Dragons', which were soon replaced by the ubiquitous 25-pounders for direct anti-tank fire and for a longer-ranging indirect fire. The 1st Bn KRRC was motorised and carried into battle zones in trucks.

John Bainbridge, 6 RTR, arrived in Egypt in early 1937 on HMT *Lancashire*. 'We then entrained for Cairo and arrived at Abbassia Rail Siding. We paraded on the square of Main Barracks and were greeted by RSM Stannard, Captain Cooper, the Adjutant and Lieutenant-Colonel Morrogh the CO.' His leisurely life was soon altered 'after the arrival of Major-General PCS Hobart who came to form a Mobile Division. There was a great deal of activity, such as conferences, indoor exercises, TEWTS (tactical exercises without troops), sand table exercises, cadre courses. The wish for intensive training became infectious'. The 6 RTR Adjutant Captain, G.P.B. Roberts, frequently took out small parties into the desert and gave meticulous instruction in map reading, navigation and use of a sun compass. Seven years later in the great Victory Parade in Berlin before Winston Churchill, 3 RHA, 11th Hussars and 8th Hussars were key members of Britain's famous 7th Armoured division – the Desert Rats.

The vital Delta area was likely to be a key enemy (presumably Italian) objective on the outbreak of war. The 'Egypt War Plan' was in two phases. 'Umbrella' was the precautionary stage with all units placed at 96 hours' notice to move, and 'Scram' meant a move into the Western Desert. The new name for the Immobile Force was now the respectable 'Armoured Division Egypt'.

General Hobart wrote 'I decided to concentrate on dispersion, flexibility and mobility this season; to try and get the Division and formations well extended, really handy and under quick control. To units unused to the speed and wide frontages made possible by mechanisation these matters presented considerable difficulties. There is the isolation due to the wide intervals necessary in the desert, involving the necessity of being able to keep direction, to navigate a unit, to keep a dead reckoning, to learn to watch for small indications and to use one's eyes in spite of mirage. . . . It has not yet become instinctive for crews and commanders to get down at *every* halt and look round their vehicles *at once*. Many oil leaks, loose bolts etc would be seen and remedied and subsequent demands on fitters avoided. Crews should make it a point of honour to keep their vehicles running without outside assistance.'

Hobart devised numerous exercises, such as 'Mosquito' tactics of small, mobile harassing movements, and 'Leaguering' of triangular or square defensive positions at night with armoured vehicles on the perimeter, 'soft' in the centre. There were divisional 'recovery' exercises, others for 'B' Echelon evacuation and 'A' and 'B' echelons in refilling and replenishing.

Officers and men learned to navigate by reference to sun, compass and stars at night, plus keen observation of minor landmarks, scrub, a ruined stone hut, a wrecked car. Soon they learned to live in the desert. Each formation, however, had a navigation officer leading the way. They learned how to take up 'hull down' positions for tanks behind sand dunes, from which only their turrets would be visible to the enemy. Desert driving needed new skills; sudden hollows, sharp rocks, a boulder and deep or very soft sands were hazards. The tank squadron learned to conserve petrol, food and especially water, which was usually rationed.

The battlefields of the future lay to the west – or 'up the blue' in military vernacular. The outstanding feature of this desert expanse is the steep escarpment which, after hugging the coast in Cyrenaica, takes a mainland slant south-eastwards from Sollum. At Sollum the coast road climbed the escarpment by a series of hairpin bends, and another way up it was by the Halfaya Pass, four miles to the south-east; there the track had been demolished. Beyond that point the escarpment is a barrier to vehicles for some fifty miles, but then fades away, near Sofafi. South and west of the escarpment the desert plateau is easily traversable by all types of mechanised vehicle, although there are stretches of rocky ground that form slow going. North of the escarpment, the coastal strip varies between bushy hummocks and rocky outcrop, so that movement tends to be difficult except by a few tracks.

There were only two roads in the whole area: the coast road and a secondary one running from Matruh southward to the Siwa Oasis. The coast road was tarmac from Matruh, the railhead, along the seventy-mile stretch to Sidi Barrani, but for the next sixty miles to the frontier near Sollum it was little better than a track. On the Italian side of the frontier it was again a good tarmac road. The rain belt extended from these to some miles beyond the escarpment, so that all tracks in the area were liable to turn into quagmires.

The Egyptian Survey department under British officers had produced quite accurate 1:100,000 gridded maps. Hobart established distinctive

1 RTR Cruiser tanks on the way 'up to the Blue'. *Imperial War Museum*

beacons, painting on them map references. Made of metal (no use to Arabs as firewood) they were known as 'Hobo Beacons'. In the featureless desert occasional 'landmarks' could be found: at Gabr (a tomb), Birs (rock cisterns), Alam (small cairn) and Ghot (small depressions). Young Second Lieutenant Michael Carver, who earned 9*s* 10*d* per day, was taught by Major Donald John McLeod, 1 RTR, 'a wise charming elderly major experienced in the desert,' to drive and navigate. In turn Carver trained young officers and NCOs in navigation and 'the arts of desert life'. Lieutenant-Colonel Horace Birks (later 2 i/c 4th Armoured Brigade) wrote of Hobart's armoured division.

> The division itself was seriously short of essential equipment even for communication purposes. There was no such thing as telephone communication in advance of Divisional Headquarters, and as, for security reasons, wireless communication was limited to urgent operational messages, all communications, including orders, had to be delivered by liaison officers in trucks – who frequently took a day to reach their destination.
>
> Transport was reduced to the bare minimum to maintain units in their operational positions, and deliveries were necessarily limited to petrol for machines, hard rations for the troops, and water at the rate of half a gallon per head per day, which included that required for vehicles and loss in transit. For weeks, forward troops existed on biscuits, bully, limited tinned rations and a pint of tea in the morning and in the evening. With the shade temperature ranging between 80° and 100°, living conditions for the troops, who had little or no shade, were extremely severe.
>
> Workshops were at Alexandria and Cairo, and the forward delivery point at Matruh, not less than a hundred miles from forward units – all replacements having to journey by stages and be driven by spare crews forward from Matruh. The position of the wounded was even grimmer, for until they could be got back to Sidi Barrani they, too, had to be laboriously staged from post to post.

1 RTR Cruiser tanks, Abbasia, May 1940. *Imperial War Museum*

> Air support consisted of a flight of three Lysanders, which had a fighter cover of three Gladiators – until one was lost, when the remaining two were withdrawn. Instructions from GHQ at Cairo restricted the use of 25-pounder ammunition to two rounds per gun per day and other ammunition was only to be expended if a good dividend could be expected.

Meanwhile new or newish equipment arrived. 7th Hussars had three squadrons of light tanks and passed on their 'rejects' to 8th Hussars and to 6 RTR to replace their Ford 15-cwt 'pick-ups'. But 6 RTR also received their first new A-9 Cruiser tanks with a 2-pdr gun, three .303 MGs, a crew of 6, weight 12 tons and a maximum speed of 25 mph.

All vehicles including tanks were fitted with sand filters and improved water pumps; use of the sun-compass was taught and guns and radios were calibrated. John Bainbridge 6 RTR wrote 'All ranks became fanatical about training and volunteered to devote most of their leisure time to practising and becoming more efficient.' Even the regimental cooks became skilled marksmen. Tanks were loaded on to railway flats to reduce transport and track usage. 'My regiment 6 RTR became a very formidable, fit, well trained fighting unit and sent instructors to 7th Hussars for driving and maintenance of their tanks.' Sergeant Alec Lewis RASC noted that 'Div HQ was administered at the old Renault Depot and the Chief Clerk was WO1 "Dolly" Gray.' Hours of work were from 8 to 12 noon and from 1700 to 1900 hrs.

> Nobody in Cairo seemed to work in the afternoons. The majority of troops wore their 'blues' when off duty in the city. Very smart they were too. The 11th Hussars in their 'Cherry Picker' maroon trousers, the 'Tankies' in their navy blue uniforms and berets, the gunners

with their dress caps, blues and red braid, the Rifle Brigade and the KRRCs in their dark green tunics and black facings. Hobart immediately launched divisional exercises in the desert around Gerawia, ten miles east of Mersa Matruh. There were few tanks available, out of date and their track mileage was restricted.

When 6 RTR received some A-9 Cruiser tanks in exchange for their old medium tanks they were delighted. The old Mark VI and VIB light tanks were soon to be in action.

In the summer of 1939 General 'Copper' Gordon-Finlayson handed over command of all British troops in Egypt to General 'Jumbo' Maitland Wilson. Both disliked Hobart and his total disregard of orders from GOC HQ. 'Hobo' was determined to exercise all his divisional troops as thoroughly and as often as possible. 'Jumbo' Wilson watched the end of the exercises in July and according to Michael Carver 'appeared impressed with the division's achievements, although appalled by the lack of equipment and their poor state'. Hobart then left for leave in the UK, but was recalled on the outbreak of war and moved the Mobile Division rapidly out to Mersa Matruh to repel a possible invasion.

On 23 and 24 August 1939 Operations 'Umbrella' and 'Scram' were ordered as the war clouds gathered over Europe and Benito Mussolini made even more belligerent speeches. The bulk of the division moved to Mersa Matruh and 11th Hussars, a squadron of 1 RTR and a battery of 3 RHA moved westwards to the Sidi Barrani area. 7th Hussars were cheered when the regimental band appeared in its war paint with four Bofors 2 pdr Anti-

2 RTR tanks arrive in Egypt, 1940. *Imperial War Museum*

tank guns mounted on a 3-ton chassis. And four days after the outbreak of war HM King Farouk, King of Egypt inspected the armoured division defending 'his' country. Hobart then initiated a series of ambitious exercises leading to a major clash with General Wilson.

1 RTR 'war' diary shows that the exercises included TEWTS; simulated attacks on convoys; training in navigation and battle drill; RAF lectures on aircraft recognition; training in (a) advance to contact (b) unit change of direction (c) W/T control, jamming frequencies, changing from W/T to R/T. There were night training exercises, forming brigade leaguer at night, use of CDL searchlights, and action to be taken on Alarms. Hobart had produced a first-class, trained fighting division and was summarily 'sacked' in November 1939.

As Hobart's car drove the mile and a half to the airstrip from his HQ, the route was lined by men of the division; gunners, rifles, cavalry and tankmen, all cheering their general in a spontaneous and unforgettable farewell. Major-General O'Connor, GOC 8th Infantry Division at Matruh, wrote 'It [the 7th] was the best trained division I have ever seen.'

At the end of 1939 Major-General O'Moore Creagh MC, a cavalry officer, became the new divisional commander. The Mobile Division officially became 7th Armoured Division on 16 February 1940. The Light Armoured Brigade became 7th Armoured Brigade under Brigadier Hugh Russell, and the Heavy Armoured Brigade became 4th Armoured Brigade under Brigadier 'Blood' Caunter (the nickname derived from his favourite oath 'buckets of blood'). 1 RTR changed places with 7th Hussars. Soon the tough, wiry, leaping little desert rat called the Jerboa was selected to become the divisional sign. Lieutenant-Colonel Horace Birks became GSO1. The Pivot/Support Group consisted of 3 and 4 RHA plus the motorised infantry of 1st KRRC and 2nd Rifle Brigade under Brigadier 'Strafer' Gott. Each tank regiment now had fifty-two tanks, but when fifty-seven of the new A-9 tanks went out on two divisional exercises in February, their engines tended to seize up as they had not been 'run in' properly. There were no spares available; Hobart would never have allowed such a stupid mistake to occur.

Fortunately for Hobart and the British Army, he was rescued from the obscure and absurd ranks of 'Dad's Army', the Home Guard, by Winston Churchill. He wrote to the CIGS General Ironside. 'I think very highly of this officer and I am not at all impressed by the prejudices against him in certain quarters. Such prejudices attach frequently to persons of strong personality and original views. In this case General Hobart's original views have been only too tragically borne out. The neglect by the General Staff even to devise proper patterns of tanks before the war has robbed us of all the fruits of this invention. These fruits have been reaped by the enemy, with terrible consequences. We should therefore remember that this was an officer who had the root of the matter in him, and also vision.' Churchill was referring to the successful tank use by the Germans in their Panzer Blitzkrieg tactics in the spring and summer of 1940.

Winston Churchill had been informed by British intelligence services that Marshal Graziani's Italian Army consisted in Tripolitania of 6 metropolitan and 2 militia divisions, in Cyrenaica 2 metropolitan and 2 militia divisions plus 3 frontier force divisions. The 15 divisions totalled 215,000 troops. Against them were some 50,000 Allied troops consisting of the 7th Armoured Division, two-thirds of the 4th Indian Division, one-third of the New Zealand Division plus 14 British battalions and 2 regiments of Royal Artillery ungrouped with higher formations. The Italians also had air superiority.

CHAPTER THREE

The Cherry Picker War

The 11th Hussars (Prince Albert's Own) sailed for Egypt on HMT *Neuralia* in November 1934. The following year they became one of the founding members of the British 'Mobile Force' formed from the Cairo Cavalry Brigade (which although cruelly nicknamed the 'Immobile Force' became under Major General Hobart's driving personality an efficient armoured division). Quite soon they were driving their 1920–4 vintage Rolls-Royce-armoured cars quite confidently on 200-mile journeys from Cairo to the desert oases of Baharia and Siwa and back again. Some of their young or youngish leaders survived all or most of the bitter desert fighting still to come – John Combe 'C' Squadron, Jack Leetham 'A' Squadron, Payne-Gallwey (a Grand National jockey) 'C' Squadron, Bill Wainman 'A' Squadron, John Lawson 'A' Squadron and Harry Petch. A full establishment consisted of 23 officers and 408 other ranks. The fighting vehicles were 34 Rolls-Royces (lightly armoured, crew of three with a ball-mounted Vickers MG mounted in the turret) and 5 Crossleys with wireless (replaced in 1938). The three squadrons, 'A', 'B' and 'C', each had an HQ and three (later four) troops of armoured cars. Training exercises took place and vehicle maintenance (cleaning oil filters, lifting cylinder heads, mending punctures, track cleaning) was vital. So too was the art of defensive driving: avoiding soft sand traps and wadis. The 11th Hussars spent 1936–8 in Palestine helping deal with the Arab rebellion, by escorting convoys day and night, with many minor skirmishes. At the outbreak of war in September 1939 Mussolini pounced on Albania and soon 11th Hussars were told 'Mobilise and prepare to move at once.' Lieutenant-Colonel John Combe led the Cherry Pickers from Helmieh, 9 miles north of Cairo, off to Mersa Matruh for 'special training'.

Alan Moorehead, writing despatches for the London *Daily Express*, noted 'Units were seldom diverted to places in the desert. They were simply ordered to proceed on a compass bearing to a certain point and there camp down. Except in action there was wireless silence and communications were kept up by a few light aircraft and motorcyclists . . . desert warfare resembled war at sea. Men moved by compass. No position was static. There were few if any forts to be held. Each truck or tank was as individual as a destroyer and each squadron of tanks or guns made great sweeps across the desert as a battle-squadron at sea will vanish over the horizon; one did not occupy the desert any more than one occupied the sea. One simply took up a position for a day or a week and patrolled about it with Bren gun carriers and light armoured vehicles. There were no trenches. There was no front line. We might patrol five hundred miles into Libya and call the country ours. The Italians might as easily have patrolled as far into the Egyptian desert without being seen. Desert forces must be mobile. They were seeking not the conquest of territory but combat with the enemy. We hunted men, not land.'

General Wavell, GOC Middle East, Commander of the British forces in Egypt, Palestine and Cyprus, knew that his first priority was to guard against Marshal Graziani's huge army, behind the frontier barbed-wire fence, launching a sudden invasion of Egypt. The Italians had at least 6 divisions, 200 tanks, strong artillery and airforce support and presented a major threat. Mersa Matruh was the westerly defensive position of the British Army, reached by road and rail, 200 miles west of Alexandria. A metalled road continued west to Sidi Barrani, then there was a gap of fifty miles of desert before the Italian frontier fence was reached.

Lieutenant-Colonel John Combe had made sure during the phoney war that desert navigation and radio discipline were of a high order. But recognising that many armoured-car troops, even single cars, could be patrolling in isolation, he ensured that the Ford utility truck in each squadron was converted into an emergency ambulance and that the LAD (Light Aid Detachment) of fitters and ordnance workshop lorries operated well forward with the squadrons. On 1 May 1940, Major-General O'Moore-Creagh, GOC of the Mobile Division, now officially 7th Armoured Division, sent his covering forces up to the Cyrenaican frontier. The 11th Hussars were now up to full strength with drafts of seventy-four men of the Northamptonshire and Gloucestershire Yeomanry and fifty-five Rhodesians. The first patrols from Sidi Barrani to Sollum and 40 miles to the south showed no enemy movements. By then the Crossleys had been replaced by Morris cars and the elderly Rolls-Royces had an enlarged two-man turret, bringing crew strength to four and additional armament of a .55 Boyes anti-tank rifle and a Bren MG.

For the next six months the Cherry Pickers were the 'eyes' of the British Army in North Africa. Churchill wrote

Within twenty four hours of the outbreak of war [with Italy] the 11th Hussars crossed the frontier, took the Italians, who had not heard that war had been declared, by surprise, and captured prisoners. The next night, 12th June, they had a similar success and on 14th June with the 7th Hussars and one company of the 60th Rifles, captured the frontier forts at Capuzzo and Maddalena taking 220 prisoners. On the 16th they raided deeper, destroyed twelve tanks, intercepted a convoy on the Tobruk–Bardia road and captured a general. In this small but lively warfare our troops felt they had the advantage and soon conceived themselves to be masters of the desert. Until they came up against large formed bodies or fortified posts they could go where they liked, collecting trophies from sharp encounters.

Major General O'Moore-Creagh had set the 11th Hussars the task of 'dominating' the frontier between Fort Capuzzo and Fort Maddalena to the south – a distance of some 75 miles. Major Blakiston-Houston OC 'A' Squadron and Major Miller OC 'B' Squadron were at Dar El Hamra, 27 miles from Fort Maddalena, and Major Payne-Gallwey OC 'C' Squadron was in front of the 7th Armoured Division Support Group near Sollum. In addition to delaying the inevitable Italian advance, a key task was for the armoured cars to destroy the barbed-wire fencing, penetrate into Italian territory and harass communications along the Italian-built road through Bardia towards Tobruk.

It was in fact a traditional light cavalry role. Lieutenant-Colonel John Combe had already built experimental sections of wire with cemented posts in the ground. By pushing, almost rocking, with the armoured bonnets of the Rolls-Royces the posts and wire could be flattened and destroyed. The whole regiment was in action during the night of 11 June. 'B' Squadron gathered in fifty-two prisoners, nine Breda automatics and sixty rifles. The next night 'C' Squadron made a determined raid inland through the wire to Sidi Azeiz, and on the 13th 'A' Squadron captured and burned two forts at Sidi Omar (south-west of Capuzzo) and their No. 4 Troop tackled Fort Maddalena. The Italians reacted sharply with fire from twelve machine guns and, for the first time, the Regia Aeronautica (Italian airforce) was in action. No fewer than six Caproni bombers and nine Fiat fighters chased the impudent Cherry Picker troop back across the frontier. Their 28-shot Bren guns were no great deterrent, but the car commanders learned to watch the bombs falling in the air and so take evasive action.

Brigadier Caunter's 4th Armoured Brigade now had 11th Hussars under command who were tasked (with 7th Hussars) to capture the forts of Maddalena, Capuzzo and Sidi Azeiz on the 14th. A flight of Blenheim bombers softened up the former as the garrison of eighteen (with twelve machine guns) surrendered without a fight. Sidi Azeiz put up a stiff fight and many of 7th Hussar light tanks were blown up or immobilised in the middle of a hidden minefield. Fort Capuzzo fell easily enough to inaccurate Blenheim bombing and a few 2-pounder shells from 7th Hussar Cruiser tanks. Alan Moorehead visited it. 'Wrecking parties went into the fort each night to deal with ammunition stores and vehicles the Italians left behind. It was little more than four white stone walls with crenellated battlement enclosing a central courtyard. A typical desert post valuable at keeping Arab tribesmen at bay. In modern warfare its walls crumpled under even the lightest shell.' The Italians had laid extensive minefields across roads and around fortified positions. For the first time 'B' Squadron encountered Italian L-3 tanks near Sidi Azeiz; Second Lieutenant Halliday knocked out one (a thinly armoured Fiat-Ansolda 'carri veloce', a veritable death-trap) with a Boyes anti-tank rifle. The other five scuttled away 'like a lot of little pigs'.

Brigadier Caunter now ordered 11th Hussars to isolate and harass the defences of Bardia, a little seaport hanging from the cliffs, 10 miles north of Fort Capuzzo. The little battle of Nezuet Ghirba took place on the 16th when 'C' Squadron encountered two reinforcing Italian columns moving towards Fort Capuzzo: the first of 12 L-3 tanks and 30 lorries, and the second of 17 L-3 tanks and 300 infantry. Major Miller's two isolated troops were at risk and they were ordered to withdraw, while RHA anti-tank guns were brought up to help. Second Lieutenant W.H.V. Gape had meanwhile attacked one column with his two cars and machine-gunned the Italian lorries. The twelve escorting L-3 tanks then had a running fight in which two were destroyed and one Rolls-Royce car damaged. Gape was in trouble but Second Lieutenant G.E.C. Diers' troop suddenly arrived to help and promptly knocked out an L-3. Lieutenant-Colonel Combe then concentrated all available Cherry Picker cars plus Major Delmé Seymour-Evans' mixed cruiser squadron 7th Hussars and an RHA anti-tank troop. The Italian groups had now met and concentrated their infantry and lorries into a solid square with the L-3s ranged along the flanks – classic Waterloo tactics of infantry squares receiving a cavalry charge. The five 7th Hussar Cruiser tanks in line ahead went for the Italian square, and the RHA fired at it from the right flank. Seven L-3s were shot to pieces, and despite brave fire from four Eritrean-manned field guns a massed close-range battle took place. The Cherry Pickers rounded up a dozen lorries, 100 POWs and captured 5 more L-3s in the ensuing mêlée.

By early afternoon it was all over. Two companies of Italian tanks and a motorised battery of guns had been utterly destroyed. An infantry battalion too was destroyed with over 100 prisoners. There were no Hussar casualties. John Combe won the first of his two DSOs, Lieutenant Gape the Military Cross, and Major Seymour-Evans a Bar to his MC won in Palestine. On the same day Payne-Gallwey's 'C' Squadron laid an ambush 20 miles behind the enemy lines on the edge of an escarpment overlooking the main road to Tobruk. They halted a convoy with a cut-down telegraph pole and then came another convoy. By the end of the morning of the 15th 40 lorries were burned, 100 POWs brought in, including a general, his staff officer, and 2 lady friends. A handsome Lancia staff car contained marked maps of the Bardia defences. In the afternoon Italian fighter planes scored hits on one car without causing casualties. By dawn on the 17th Payne-Gallwey's squadron were back across the frontier with their prisoners, including Generale di Corpo Lastucci, Engineer-in-Chief of the Italian Tenth Army. When 7th Hussars were withdrawn to rest, the 11th were the only British troops operating inside Italian territory.

Midsummer in the desert brings intense heat and frequent burning Khamseen dust storms. These started on 19 June, and the heat and consequent lack of water reduced military activities. In the deep south Major Blakiston-Houston's 'A' squadron encountered tanks, infantry and artillery around El Gubi near Gabr Saleh.

The regimental history records two problems.

On 25th June the Khamseen blew its very worst. It was the hottest day the 11th Hussars had yet experienced. The growing air attacks which the squadrons were now drawing down [on them] each day. Together the two seemed calculated to defeat every attempt they made to carry on. Colonel John Combe travelling around his scattered squadrons was horrified to find the men becoming really frightened of their continual thirst under the piercing heat. The armoured cars became too hot to touch and the exhausted crews lay sweating underneath them. One patrol now would alone use more water than the daily allowance for a whole troop.

The first casualties occurred on the 21st. Sergeant Major Howarth's troop of 'A' Squadron was attacked near El Gubi, and he and three troopers were taken prisoner and flown back direct to Marshal Balbo, and a week later Trooper Muscatelli died of his wounds trying to tow a damaged car to safety. The regiment then concentrated at Fort Maddalena, and in early July moved to Bir Sheferzen south of Sidi Omar. During the month the heat and dust storms continued but short leave to Cairo or the seaside at Buqbuq was possible. Major Blakiston-Houston OC 'A' Squadron wrote home and described a typical day 40 miles into enemy territory and 40 miles from any other troops. Reveille was at 0530 hrs. They moved to a new bit of desert at 0615 hrs. Patrols went out at dawn. 'We settled down to cook and eat our breakfast. We all lived with our crews.' Soon after 0900 hrs a visit was made by 'Big Barney', a three-engined Italian bomber which flew along the main track, Trigh el Abd. Patrols reported on the wireless at half past each hour. The cars not on patrol were well covered with camel thorn as camouflage. At about 1245 hrs there was a cold midday meal of onions, cheese and army biscuits and tea or bully beef and army biscuits. After lunch they slept or read until 1600 hrs.

> Then I stripped and washed and probably also washed my shirt and trousers and socks. The evening meal was bully stew and tinned fruit or pancake and sausages with biscuits or bread, and tea. A wireless operator would tune to the overseas service of the BBC. Then a whisky and water at about 8 p.m. Then return some five miles to our refuelling station where we slept the night. The evenings were very pleasant and cool. Moving to night leaguer we kept a very sharp lookout in case anyone was waiting for us.

A particularly bad day for the Hussars was 26 July. In a variety of actions near Gambut, halfway between Bardia and Tobruk, half of 'C' Squadron were killed, wounded or taken prisoner. Some were attacked by tanks, some by aircraft, some by anti-tank guns. Lieutenant Tommy Pitman, Second Lieutenant Jenson, Sergeant Kynes, Corporal Dayman and ten others were captured, Sergeant Mines died of wounds in Tobruk Hospital, and Sergeant Whitehorse was killed in action.

During August patrolling the frontier was based from Gabr Saleh with a squadron in action, while the other was out of the line at Buqbuq or the seaside village of Maaten Mohamed. Sergeant Hutchinson won the DCM on 24 August when Lieutenant John Poston (destined later to become General Montgomery's ADC) with 'A' Squadron No. 1 troop was bombed and machine-gunned for much of the day south of Gabr Saleh. Marshal Graziani's slow, ponderous move eastwards started on 13 September with spectacular artillery bombardments on the empty barracks at Musaid and at

Cherry Pickers (11th Hussars) on patrol. *Imperial War Museum*

Sollum. On the way to Halfaya Pass RAF Blenheims, Gladiators and a few Hurricanes from the air, and RHA batteries from the ground, did much damage. Brigadier 'Strafer' Gott's 7th Armoured Division support group (Rifle Brigade, Coldstream Guards, RHA and of course the Cherry Pickers) could not hold up a force of five divisions for long. On 16 September the Italians reached Sidi Barrani and then Maktila. And that was that. Civil engineering was now the order of the day. Italian engineers gapped the roadless 50 miles between Sidi Barrani and the frontier, laid water pipes and built large supply dumps. The Italians had suffered 3,500 casualties (including 700 POWs), 150 vehicles destroyed and the British lost 150 since the advance started (11th Hussars 8 casualties). For the rest of September the Cherry Pickers had actions each day, 'B' Squadron on the coast road and eastern exits from Sidi Barrani, 'A' on the escarpment on the left flank, and 'C' and RHQ manned the centre. The enemy was consolidating his defences with a series of regular forts.

General Wavell sent a despatch to the Secretary of State for War in London. 'The 11th Hussars, the armoured car regiment, was continuously in the front line and usually behind that of the enemy, during the whole period; its tireless and daring search for information and constant harassing of the enemy showed a spirit and efficiency worthy of the best traditions of this fine regiment.'

After the war the Italian General Cadorna told (Major General) John Combe that having no armoured cars and confronted by his brigadiers complaining 'We cannot move because of these 11th Hussars', a whole air squadron was employed to try to spoil (with some success) the Cherry Picker 'mosquito'-like tactics.

One squadron at a time was now attached to the famous Jock [Campbell] columns of armoured cars, RHA artillery and lorried infantry. The 70-mile strip of no man's land between Sofafi and Sidi Barrani had to be controlled and dominated. The other squadrons kept up their patrolling activities throughout October and November. A new squadron 'D' was now formed by the arrival of ten RAF Rolls-Royce-armoured cars [No. 2 RAF Armoured Car Company] released from duties in Palestine guarding the Iraq oil pipelines. And on the night of 7/8 December the Battle of Sidi Barrani started.

CHAPTER FOUR

Operation Compass

Despite the successful retreat and evacuation of 338,000 British and French troops from Dunkirk, the brilliant air defence by the RAF 'Few' in the Battle of Britain, the apparent delays, even cancellation of Adolf Hitler's Operation Sea Lion (the invasion of Britain), the demoralising French surrender and the terrible autumn Luftwaffe Blitz of British cities, Winston Churchill remained unbowed and indomitable. Under immense pressure he still plotted and controlled the strategy and tactics in the Mediterranean and the Middle East. Mussolini had strong troop garrisons in Abyssinia, Eritrea and Somaliland, and in July and August Italian forces threatened action against Khartoum in the Sudan, Nairobi in Kenya and, to Churchill's anger and mortification, drove the British, Indian and East African forces out of British Somaliland. Churchill wrote 'There was much jubilation in Italy, Mussolini exulted in the prospects of his attack in the Nile Valley.' General Sir Archibald Wavell was now Commander-in-Chief Middle East – an immense responsibility – and on 8 August 1940 was called back to London for a conference to establish priorities. Churchill wrote 'The command in the Middle East at that time comprised an extraordinary amalgam of military, political, diplomatic and administrative problems of extreme complexity.' To Churchill there appeared to be 20,000 troops 'idle' in Kenya, large forces also 'idle' in Palestine (including the British Yeomanry Cavalry Division, Australians and New Zealanders) – but only two divisions in the vital Delta of the Nile theatre. He was convinced that a major invasion of Egypt from Libya was imminent and reinforcements were urgently required.

The 2nd and 7th RTR plus 3rd Hussars reached Port Said on 24 September. The 2nd RTR had mainly A-13s, but some were A-9 and A-10 tanks. The 7th RTR had slow heavy infantry support tanks called Matildas, the first to arrive in the Middle East. The 3rd Hussars still had light tanks only. The next month Lieutenant-Colonel A.C. Harcourt's 2nd RTR joined 4th Armoured Brigade and 3rd Hussars joined 7th Armoured Brigade – two welcome additions to the Desert Rats. Major-General O'Moore-Creagh transferred the 'B' Squadron of Cruiser tanks to 3rd Hussars, swapping their 'B' Squadron for light tanks. 7 RTR under Lieutenant-Colonel R.M. Jerram trained with various infantry brigades. All the troops of the Army of the Nile enjoyed the delights of Cairo. Roy Farran, 3rd Hussars, wrote:

Like most of the young officers in Cairo we had very little work to do. With the threat of battle over our shoulders we overspent our incomes with a reckless, gay abandon in the cabarets and fleshpots of Cairo. There was something about Cairo that drew us like a magnet from our tents near Almaczar. Sometimes we tried to stay in the mess but soon after dinner we would gaze at the bright lights behind the palm trees, hear the faint strains of Arab music borne upon the evening breeze and scent the hot smell of jasmine or jackala trees. It was irresistible. Sometimes gaily, and sometimes sadly we would ring up for a taxi and be whisked off for another night of merry-making. After a drink at the Continental where one could meet at some time or another every officer in the Middle East, we would dine on the Roof Garden where one could see a floor show or St James where a film could be seen from the dining room. We would be led in a cabaret to the best table by the dance floor where we would sing and dance and carouse with the girls until the small hours of the morning . . . those careless reckless days at the beginning of the war. Officially we were allowed four days leave in the Delta in every three months. It was rare for anyone to return to the desert with a single penny of his three months' pay. It was rare to be completely sober in those four days. We knew that perhaps death and certainly boredom lay before us.

Despite the frivolity of the Cairo scene, intense training – Hobart's legacy – continued in the desert. Cyril Joly, a young 2 RTR troop commander, described some of the problems.

The great handicap which we all had to overcome was that there were too many things to think about at the same time. A course had to be set either by the troop commander or, more usually, by his conforming to the movements of the squadron or regimental navigator. The enemy had to be found and identified. The other two tanks had to be instructed about their formation or chivvied if they failed to keep in place. The driver had to be given his orders about his direction and speed, the gunner warned about the target and which gun to use, the loader-operator told to load the gun. The correct information had to be passed over the wireless to the squadron commander. If these things were not done properly, or if they were done at the wrong time, the whole manoeuvre or battle was liable to fail at the crucial moment, with men's lives lost and valuable tanks destroyed. It was a matter of practice and more practice and practice whenever possible. It was a question of lengthy discussion about the action that each tank would take in certain eventualities, of careful planning of the use of ground or the mutual support that might be given by other troops or even other arms, such as the infantry and guns.

Gradually one gained more confidence. Navigation or map-reading became less of a problem. We evolved certain simple drills which covered most of the troop's tactics. One learnt where to look for the enemy and quick methods of identifying him. Orders and information, which earlier one had hesitated in passing, one now gave out almost unconsciously. One soon had no difficulty in remembering the correct wireless procedure and, in fact, learnt also new, abbreviated and simplified methods. We all acquired a great deal of confidence in each other, and so made ourselves into a really effective fighting machine.

At the same time the training within the crew improved. Though the tank broke down just as frequently, we mended it more quickly. As my ability to judge the distance to each target – always difficult in the peculiar condition of light and ground in the desert – improved, so, with the improvement of the gunner's shooting, we were able to hit our targets sooner in each action.

By the autumn of 1940 desert dress had become more unorthodox and more colourful. Brigadier Jock Campbell, CO of the Desert Rat Support Group, was usually dressed in light cord trousers, suede desert boots (nicknamed brothel creepers), a silk neckerchief and in the desert winter, a goatskin coat from Persia or Afghanistan. When Captain Clay, 2nd Royal Gloucester Hussars, was captured by the Italians in 1941 he wore no badges of rank, but a golf jacket, a pink shirt into which was tucked a yellow silk scarf, a pair of green corduroys and an expensive pair of suede boots.

2 RTR at Mersa Matruh, 1940. *Major Norman Plough*

Mufflers were often blue, red or yellow, and green or magenta cap-comforters or balaclava helmets were also worn. The warm UK-made khaki battledress, issued to 2 and 7 RTR, 3rd Hussars, ideal for the desert winter, was much envied by the 'old' desert hands.

Churchill wanted the key Mersa Matruh position fortified 'completely and with the utmost speed'. The 'Cherry Picker War' chapter ends with a kind of 'limbo' war around Mersa Matruh. The Duce took a fateful decision to attack Greece on 15 October, although the invasion was halted ignominiously soon afterwards. Churchill was determined to help.

> The collapse of Greece without any effort by us will have a deadly effect on Turkey and on the future of the war. .·. . No one will thank us for sitting tight in Egypt with ever growing forces [53,000 reinforcements to the Army of the Delta before the end of 1940] while Greek situation and all that hangs on it is cast away. Loss of Athens far greater injury than Kenya and Khartoum.

To Churchill's great surprise Anthony Eden, who was on the Middle East War Committee, had brought back, on 8 November, a secret plan hatched by Generals Wavell and Wilson – Operation 'Compass'. Marshal Graziani's Italian army, 80,000 strong, which had crossed the Italian frontier was spread over a 50-mile front with a number of fortified camps. Between Sofafi on the southern flank and the next camp at Nibeiwa was a gap of over 20 miles. The 7th Armoured Division would lead 4th Indian Division and 16th British Infantry Brigade through the gap and attack the Nibeiwa and

Tummar Camps from the rear and contain and surround the two Sofafi camps and the one at Maktila on the coast. A move of all the best troops available over 70 miles on two successive nights across the open desert was very risky. 'The prize was worthy of the hazard. The arrival of our vanguard on the sea at Buqbuq would cut the communications of Marshal Graziani's army. Attacked by surprise from the rear they might well be forced as a result of vigorous fighting into mass surrenders. In this case the Italian front would be irretrievably broken. . . . We were all delighted. I purred like six cats,' wrote Churchill. Alan Moorhead described the camps:

> As desert architecture goes these camps were pretty lavish affairs. The general design was usually on a convenient rise perhaps half a mile or a mile square surrounded with a stone wall. Inside the Italians had established messes, hospitals and sleeping quarters by scraping holes in the sand and rock, putting a stone wall round the holes and surmounting the tops with camouflaged canvas. Outside the camps they built watching posts by digging holes in the desert. Minefields were embedded on the eastern, northern and southern approaches. Rough, incredibly dusty tracks linked one camp with another. Sidi Barrani had in addition to its ring of outlying camps, two lines of fortifications where they had dug anti-tank traps and furnished niches for machine-guns, anti-tank guns and artillery. Each camp was reckoned to have about 3,000 men with a very high rate of firepower.

Major-General Richard O'Connor was summoned to Cairo by General Maitland Wilson to assume command of all forces there for the planned 'Five Day Raid', later to be called Operation Compass, initially to protect

2 RTR at Mersa Matruh, 1940. *Major Norman Plough*

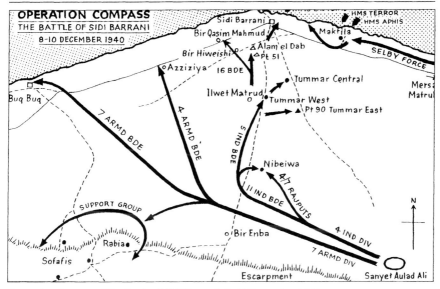

Operation Compass. The Battle of Sidi Barrani, 8–10 December 1940.

Egypt from Italian attack. O'Connor with First World War decorations of DSO and Bar, MC and nine mentions in despatches had a brilliant service career of thirty years. Small, quiet, bird-like with a clear, light voice, he was highly professional. He would take clear risks to reconnoitre enemy territory often well behind their lines.

The Cherry Pickers had suffered persistent casualties in their daring forays, and to add weight and additional protection they needed mobile artillery, signallers and sappers to lift mines. Small forces of mixed arms were now formed to intrude into the enemy positions and inflict damage. Lieutenant-Colonel 'Jock' Campbell, RHA, was the first commander of the first 'Jock column' probing the Italian defences on the frontier, harassing the rear areas and communications, lifting mines and taking prisoners for identification. In the limbo war preceding Operation Compass, the Jock columns were invaluable.

O'Connor instituted two detailed training exercises on fortified locations, 'replicas' of the Italian camps at Nibeiwa and Tummar. His plans for Compass involved the Royal Navy monitors, *Ladybird, Terror* and *Aphis*, bombarding coastal defences between Sidi Barrani and Maktila and spirited RAF bombing attacks on the Italian camps.

Intense secrecy was observed in Whitehall, but it was much more difficult in Cairo, teeming with enemy agents. Moreover 5,000 vehicles containing the attacking forces (7th Armoured Division, 4th Indian Division and Selby force – some of the Mersa Matruh garrison, 3rd Bn Coldstream Guards, some artillery and MG support) moved across the desert through the night of the 7th as secretly as possible to the assembly areas. Lieutenant Cyril Joly,

A Cruiser A–13, 2 RTR, December 1940. *Major Norman Plough*

2 RTR, wrote 'The second exercise started on 7th December. The same routine was to be followed and we expected to return after three days and to settle down again to the interminable waiting.' But it was the real thing. The secret passwords were 7 Dec/Churchill; 8 Dec/Valour; 9 Dec/Violence; 10 Dec/O'Connor; 11 Dec/Tidworth; 12 Dec/Warminster; 13 Dec/John O'Groats; 14 Dec/Land's End. The 4th Indian Division (which included two British battalions and 16th British Brigade) backed by the forty-eight powerful Matilda (Infantry) tanks of 7 RTR had the main task of breaking through and capturing the Italian camps. 'Selby' Force, starting from Mersa Matruh, followed the coast road west to tackle Maktila 60 miles away. The 7th Armoured Division would break through the Enba gap, with 4th Armoured Brigade heading north to Azziziya and 7th Armoured Brigade north-west to Buqbuq and if possible, west to Sollum and Halfaya Pass. Barry Pitt's *Crucible of War, Western Desert 1940–1941* gives a superb account of the battle. By the evening of 10 December 20,000 Italian POWs had been taken. O'Connor was naturally delighted that in the main, the complex plans had worked. However, to his dismay, on the following morning General Maitland Wilson 'confiscated' the 4th Indian Division to strengthen the defences in the Sudan.

General O'Connor then directed the Cherry Pickers and 7th Armoured Brigade towards Buqbuq. General Gallini and many Italian prisoners were taken when Maktila fell to Selby Force spearheaded by Cruiser tanks of 6 RTR and Matildas of 7 RTR. Meanwhile, Winston Churchill was amused

A-15 Crusader, 2 RTR. *Major Norman Plough*

A-9 Cruiser, 2 RTR. *Major Norman Plough*

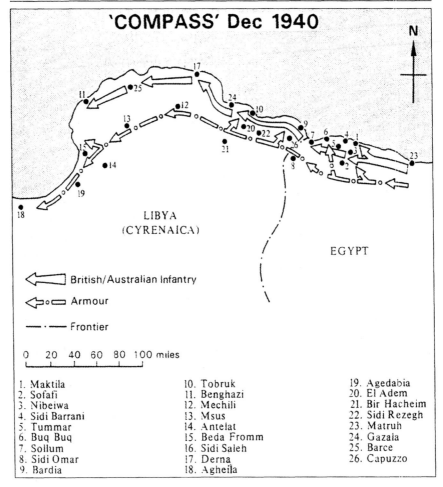

Operation Compass, December 1940.

by a message from a 7th Armoured Brigade tank commander: 'Have arrived at the second "B" in Buqbuq.' Churchill wrote:

> From December 11th onwards the action consisted of a pursuit of the Italian fugitives by the 7th Armoured Division followed by the 16th British (Motorised) Infantry Brigade [and the newly arrived] 6th Australian division. On December 12th I could tell the House of Commons that the whole coastal region around Buqbuq and Sidi Barrani was in the hands of British and Imperial troops and that 7,000 prisoners had already reached Mersa Matruh. . . . The best part of three Italian divisions including numerous Blackshirt formations have been either destroyed or captured.

The Italian 64th Catanazaro Division under General Amico put up a fight among the sand dunes, salt pans and mudflats on the way to Sollum. The 3rd Hussars, in their first action in the desert, encountered the Catanazaro

'COMPASS' Dec 1940

N

LIBYA
(CYRENAICA)

EGYPT

⇐▭ British/Australian Infantry

⇐o▭ Armour

—·— Frontier

0   20   40   60   80   100 miles

1. Maktila
2. Sofafi
3. Nibeiwa
4. Sidi Barrani
5. Tummar
6. Buq Buq
7. Sollum
8. Sidi Omar
9. Bardia
10. Tobruk
11. Benghazi
12. Mechili
13. Msus
14. Antelat
15. Beda Fromm
16. Sidi Saleh
17. Derna
18. Agheila
19. Agedabia
20. El Adem
21. Bir Hacheim
22. Sidi Rezegh
23. Matruh
24. Gazala
25. Barce
26. Capuzzo

Division in a defensive position with thirty-five guns covering the east and twenty-five guns the south. 'A' Squadron's light tanks were trapped in the salt marshes. Captain Tom Somerville, the RMO, bravely rescued and operated on several of the Hussar casualties under intense fire and was awarded the DSO. The Italian gunners fought throughout the afternoon in the battle of Buqbuq and eventually 'B' Squadron's Cruiser tanks got the upper hand. Cruiser tanks of 8th Hussars had outflanked the Italian defences on the western seaward side and the Cherry Pickers had cut the coast road to the south.

The Italians lost 1,000 killed in action, 4,500 taken prisoner and 65 guns were captured. By the end of the third day of battle another 14,000 POWs and 68 guns had been captured. One report stated 'twenty acres of officers and about a hundred acres of men'. Lieutenant-Colonel Alec Gatehouse, 2 i/c 7th Armoured Brigade, wrote 'No defeated army has ever co-operated with its opponents to the extent that the Italians did on this day. They assembled their own lorries, refuelled them with their own fuel and drove them full of their own prisoners to Maktila and they came back for more – all without escort of any kind!' But the CO 2 RTR, Lieutenant-Colonel John Brown, was killed in action near the shattered village of Sidi Barrani. By the night of the 13th allied casualties totalled 133 killed in action, 387 wounded and 8 missing. Horace Birk's force (Birkforce) consisting of 7th Hussars, half of 11th Hussars, two batteries of RHA and Lieutenant-Colonel John Combe, CO 11th Hussars (Combeforce) with 2 RTR, half of 11th Hussars and two batteries of RHA crossed the Libyan frontier at midnight on 13 December. Their RV was an area 20 miles west of Bardia. The Regia Aeronautica caught Combeforce working their way down the escarpment and wrecked seven vehicles and caused seven casualties. During the day the unfortunate Cherry Pickers were bombed and machine-gunned over twenty times. But 2 RTR pressed on down the escarpment and cut off Bardia. General O'Connor ordered 7th Armoured Brigade to capture Sollum and get between Fort Capuzzo and the coast, holding back any Italian reinforcements trying to retreat into Sollum (commanded by General Bergonzoli). This 7th Armoured Brigade failed to do. General O'Connor was furious since night marches were considered less important than tank maintenance, refuelling and evening meals.

General Bergonzoli had a garrison of 45,000 men with about 400 guns. The 18-mile perimeter around Bardia had a strong double barbed-wire fence, a four-foot-deep anti-tank ditch, many natural wadis and scores of artillery and MG strongholds, plus six well-dispersed minefields. He had a dozen M-13 tanks and a hundred of the modest little L-3s. General O'Connor sent 4th Armoured Brigade back to deal with the Sidi Omar garrison in the south on the 16th, while 7th Armoured Brigade surrounded Bardia waiting for the 6th Australian Division to come up from the Delta. Major Pat Hobart (the famous Major-General's nephew) commanded 'C' Squadron 2 RTR and wrote this account of the 'glorious gallop' that took Sidi Omar.

Sollum. *Major Norman Plough*

We drove around to avoid the enemy shelling while the 25 pounders did their bombardment, then formed up in line and advanced at full speed on the fort in what I imagined to be the best traditions of the *arme blanche*. The enemy must have suffered pretty severely from the attentions of the RHA, for in we went unscathed, with every gun and machine-gun firing. My orders to the squadron were to drive straight through the perimeter, doing as much destruction as possible, out the other side, and then to return again and rally back on the near side. I was in the centre of the squadron line, and in an excess of zeal and enthusiasm charged the fort itself. The outer wall was built of solid blocks of stone, and in breaking it I knocked off my nearside idler, so that I found myself inside the courtyard of the two-storey fort, with an immobilised tank. . . . There were some hectic minutes, particularly as my second-in-command, David Wilkie, was shelling the fort from outside with his close support tank. During this time I had inadvertently left my No. 9 set switched to "send", so that all my frenzied orders and exhortations to my crew were going out over the regimental net – which caused considerable pleasure to my brother officers, later embarrassment to me.

Major Stuart Pitman quoted advice given to an officer of the 7th Hussars (part of 4th Armoured Brigade in 1940): 'The battle always looks like a muddle, It often is but the actual business of fighting is easy enough. You go in, you come out, you go in again, and you keep on doing it, till they break or you are dead.' These were wonderful dashing cavalry tactics perhaps reminiscent of Waterloo, and certainly appropriate against the rather amateurish Italian armies. But when the Afrika Korps appeared it became a recipe for disaster.

The 7th Hussars and 'B' Squadron 3rd Hussars joined in the fun, and the battle was over in ten minutes; 900 Italian POWs were taken and 50 killed in action, but the Fascist gunners, with their guns sited on the east flank, fired resolutely to little avail. Two batteries of 4 RHA had pounded the little white 'Beau Geste' fort as the main attack came in from the west and south.

General O'Connor and Major General I. Mackay, GOC 6th Australian Division, had served together in Palestine and now planned the major onslaught on Bardia. Most of 7th Armoured Division celebrated Christmas with salt water laced with rum, bully beef and biscuits.

The Australian troops received a Christmas 'comforts' parcel that contained plum pudding, tinned cream, cake, fruit, cheese and some canned beer. The Italian garrison of Bardia had every luxury, pasta dishes with rich sauces and much Chianti. Dawn on 3 January 1941 was zero hour for the Australian attack on Bardia along with twenty-two powerful Matilda tanks of Lieutenant-Colonel Jerram's 7th RTR. Every night Air Commodore Collishaw's RAF bombers were over the little port and HMS *Terror* and *Aphis* bombarded from the sea. The 4th Armoured Brigade and Combeforce patrolled outside the western perimeter and 7th Armoured Brigade controlled the Sollum sector to the east. The Western Desert Force, under General O'Connor, was now re-named XIII Corps in the midst of heavy rain, icy winds, sleet, yellow fog and intense cold. Some 11,500 sleeveless leather jackets had been rushed up from Cairo for the mid-winter attacks. General Mackay's plan was for a 120-gun barrage with the main weight on a 800-yard stretch around Sidi Azeiz to the west, and a feint attack from the south. Three Royal Naval battleships and four destroyers arrived offshore to pound the north side of Bardia.

The Sollum Pass. *Major Norman Plough*

Tobruk, January 1941. *Major Norman Plough*

The Australian brigades fought superbly and the 7 RTR Matildas gave excellent support. By 5 January an unbelievable total of 45,000 POWs and 462 guns were taken. 6 RTR made an incursion in the northern sector and one tank commander had a batch of 1,500 Italians surrender to him. The Australian casualties were 130 killed in action and 326 wounded, but 'Electric Whiskers', General Bergonzoli, escaped on foot to Tobruk.

General O'Connor now made plans to capture Tobruk. The town, perched on a spit of white cliffs that formed the seaward flank of the harbour, was double the size of Bardia. It was the most valuable harbour between Alexandria and Benghazi and was a key supply point for any army (Italian, British or later German). The garrison of 25,000 was surrounded by two perimeters of defences, the outer of 30 miles, the inner of 19 miles with wire, defence posts and minefields. Italian naval forces were established there and from the *San Giorgio* cruiser several large naval guns had been brought ashore. The Italian garrison were seasoned troops and well dug in, commanded by an admiral.

O'Connor's combination of Australian infantry and British armour was about to be tested again. The 7th Armoured Brigade and the Support Group encircled Tobruk to the west and 4th Armoured Brigade moved west from Trigh Capuzzo to El Adem and drove the enemy into the perimeter defences. These moves were completed on the 6th and the next day the indomitable Australians (with their faithful 7 RTR Matildas) were in place.

O'Connor's main problem was that of logistics and supplies. The 7th Armoured Division FSD (Supply Points) Nos 4 and 5 were 100 and 70 miles behind the front lines. The 16th British Brigade set up No. 8 in the small Sollum port. Unfortunately, Bardia's port facilities had been totally smashed up by the RAF and Royal Navy. Moreover, most of the tanks of 7th Armoured Division were on their last legs with very high track mileages and limited repair facilities.

The attack on Tobruk went in on 21 January and was a repeat performance of Derna, but against more determined opposition. The 7th Armoured Division and the Support Group contained the outer perimeter while the Australians, with 7 RTR Matilda support under heavy artillery barrages, fought their way doggedly through the defences. Forts Pilastrino and Solaro held out for a while. Ammiraglio Vietina and 27,000 prisoners, 230 guns and 200 vehicles were captured, but again General Bergonzoli escaped. In the port area a power station was in working order, one or more jetties were usable, and two water distilleries and sub-artesian wells could produce 40,000 gallons of slightly brackish water. The enemy airfields contained hundreds of wrecked aircraft mainly destroyed by the RAF with some help from the Long-Range Desert Group activities.

O'Connor now directed the Australians towards Derna, a small port, 100 miles along the coast westwards from Tobruk. 'Derna,' wrote Alan Moorehead, 'was an oasis of banana plantations and pomegranate groves, of lush gardens and leafy trees. A fresh mountain wind blew and with it came heavy rain and hailstones . . . green valleys and hilltops dotted with shepherds' flocks and neat white colonial homesteads.' Mussolini had settled 90,000 Italian emigrant families in the lush plateau of the Jebel Akhdar. The Wadi Derna to the east of the town was a long, deep, formidable 'tank-trap', and the 19th Australian Brigade was held up for four days by heavy Italian shelling. However, on the 30th the garrison slipped away into the Green Mountains of the 2,500-ft high Jebel Akhdar. In effect this was the end of Operation Compass – a successful extended 'Five-Day Raid'.

CHAPTER FIVE

Triumph at Beda Fomm

Deserted, beautiful Cyrene fell on 3 February 1941 and Barce was found empty on the 7th. General O'Connor was anxious to trap the Italian General Babini's XX Corps, known to be in the Mechili area (50 miles south-west of Derna), and then head south and west through Msus and Antelat to cut the main road leading to Benghazi. General Creagh, GOC 7th Armoured Division, was entrusted with the specific task of the destruction of General Babini's forces (reinforced by 150 M-13 tanks). So 7th Armoured Brigade moved westwards and encountered Italian defences at Martuba (south-east of Derna) and 4th Armoured Brigade were soon south of Mechili. Since mid-January the Cherry Pickers had patrols past Bomba and between Derna and Chaulan.

The 6 RTR and 8th Hussars, because of tank losses and mechanical troubles, were returned to Cairo and their surviving tanks were handed over to 2 RTR and 7th Hussars. The 3rd Hussars were lent to 4th Armoured Brigade. General Creagh had a total of eighty light thin-skinned Vickers tanks – no use in a tank battle – and only 40 A-9, A-10 or A-13 Cruiser tanks armed with 2 pounders. On 24 January a brisk tank battle took place north-east of Mechili when nine Italian M-13s were knocked out by 2 RTR for the loss of a cruiser and six light tanks of 7th Hussars. O'Connor assumed that 4th Armoured Brigade had been sitting across General Babini's escape route.

Generals O'Connor and Creagh were 'very disappointed indeed' at this mistake. 'Pip' Roberts, who was Brigade Major of 4th Armoured Brigade, wrote:

> All round Mechili was very bad tank country particularly to the NW which would be the line of retreat of the Italians. The main problem was a series of steep rocky wadis which were virtually impassable. We waited around making faces at the Italians and awaiting the arrival of the Support Group because it was clearly an infantry operation and in addition more guns were required. The night before the Support Group arrived (held up for want of petrol) the Italians slipped away and they used a new, and good road not marked on the map. The fact that we, 4th Armoured Brigade had let them get away was not well received by our superiors and Horace Birks got a black mark! Brigadier 'Blood' Caunter then returned to take command. The pursuit of the Italians was called off on 29th January and 4th Armoured returned to Mechili.

The historian of the 2nd Bn Rifle Brigade wrote:

> We were told no move before the 15th. Every truck had its bonnet open. Washing operations (one gallon a day) were in progress. Hair was being cut, vehicles were being unloaded. Hugo Garmoyle went on leave, Callum Renton having actually taken over command. The Adjutant

2 RTR tank at the Derna Pass. *Major Norman Plough*

had already been overtaken by piles of paper. Then General Wilson drove up. The enemy were showing signs of quitting Benghazi, of giving up Cyrenaica altogether. The plan was to send an armoured force straight across the desert for a good 150 miles to cut the road from Benghazi to Tripoli where it ran along the Gulf of Sirte. The Battalion would take part in this gallop. There was no time to lose.

'A' and 'C' Squadrons of the Cherry Pickers led at dawn, followed by the 50 cruiser and 95 light tanks of 3rd Hussars (on loan), 7th Hussars and 2 RTR, and then 2nd Rifle Brigade, 4 RHA and a battery of 106 RHA anti-tank guns. Lieutenant Cyril Joly leading 2 RTR wrote: 'For mile after mile I was faced with a vista of huge, forbidding rocks and boulders through which I had to pick my way carefully to avoid the risk of shedding a track. All the time I was being nagged and harried by the CO [Lieutenant-Colonel Sandy Harcourt] to speed up and press on.' By 1530 hrs the Cherry Pickers had pushed the Italian rearguard out of Msus fort [80 miles south-west of Mechili]. Major-General Creagh realised that wheels would reach the coast before tracks and formed Combeforce under Lieutenant-Colonel John Combe, 11th Hussars plus 2nd Rifle Brigade and 4 RHA. They set off for Antelat [40 miles south-west of Msus].

By midday on 5 February the Cherry Pickers had reached the road at Sidi Saleh, 10 miles south of Beda Fomm. Two hours later a company of 2nd Rifle Brigade was in place across the road and two more companies

An A-9 casualty at Beda Fomm, 2 RTR. *Major Norman Plough*

screened the 4 RHA gun positions under the expert direction of Jock Campbell. Brigadier Caunter ordered 7th Hussars and 'A' Squadron 2 RTR (with six fast A-13 tanks) to make an interception near Beda Fomm, 10 miles north of Combeforce. The Hussars caught and destroyed a transport column and Major Gerald Strong led 'A' Squadron 2 RTR at their top speed of nearly 30 mph in its race for the road coming into action just before 1800 hrs against an infantry column. Trooper E. Hughes saw two enemy M-13 medium tanks, and captured them *on foot* by single-handedly jumping on to each tank in turn, opening the flap and forcing the crew to surrender at pistol point.

During the night of the 5th/6th sporadic actions continued, and in pouring rain at daylight the Beroaglicii units with a few light L-3 tanks attacked the Rifle Brigade/Cherry Picker roadblock. Two half-hearted assaults were beaten off. Seven miles north of the roadblock were the only landmarks, a white tomb-like Mosque on a low ridge (the Pimple) and two windmills. The light tanks of 3rd and 7th Hussars were harassing the long flanks of Bergonzoli's retreating Tenth Army, but the nineteen 2 RTR Cruiser tanks now did serious damage. Two miles north of the Pimple Major Jim Richardson, Major G.T. Strong, Lieutenant Norman Plough and Trooper 'Topper' Brown (who fired 112 rounds of 2-pounder shells and knocked out at least ten M-13s) were some of the many heroes.

Lieutenant Farran, 3rd Hussars, wrote

Jim Richardson put his eight Cruiser tanks around the pimple-shaped mound on which stood the mosque of Beda Fomm, he broke up wave after wave of Italian tanks. The M-13s were coming in along the line of the road in batches of thirty tanks, but each time their attack met disaster when they encountered the cruisers around the mosque. Their crews were brave enough but their tactics were almost too crude to be sane.

One problem was that many of the Italian tank commanders fired (most inaccurately) on the move. 2 RTR had sited hull-down positions and probably accounted for 100 Italian tanks in the three-day battle. However, the Italian artillery knocked out four of 2 RTR's tanks. Ammunition ran out and supply lorries arrived at 1300 hrs on the 7th and 2 RTR were down to ten effective cruisers.

The Pimple changed hands several times and 2nd Rifle Brigade had trouble checking infiltration through the sand dunes along the seashore. The 4 RHA were magnificent. Major Loder-Symonds's guns knocked out half a dozen Italian tanks, but by mid-afternoon the crisis point of the battle came. The 7th and 3rd Hussars were chewing up the columns of advancing infantry, but were vulnerable to the M-13 cruisers. Ammunition for tanks and 25-pounders was running short. The RHA forward observation post was knocked out. And in the nick of time 1 RTR Cruiser tanks, under Major George Hynes, reached a mill where 7th Hussars and 2 RTR tanks were refuelling and taking aboard ammunition. Lieutenant-Colonel James

After the battle. *Major Norman Plough*

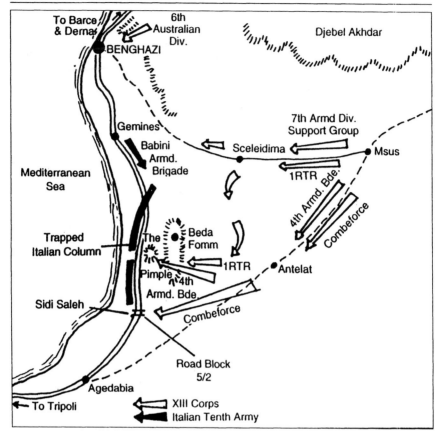

The Action at Beda Fomm, February 1941.

Culverwell, CO 1 RTR, and their 2 i/c Major 'Buster' Brown were determined to get into the action. Hynes surveyed the scene.

> It was the most wonderful sight it has ever been my lot to see. For miles in each direction the road was packed tight with lorries and guns and cars and buses and tanks – everything you can think of. We fired everything we had at them and the whole road began to seethe like an ant's nest, with Italians running in all directions. They fought back at us with their guns and we got several hits but no harm was done.

Major Burton, 106 anti-tank battery commander, watched the last of his portee-mounted (converted truck) gun crews wiped out by machine-gun fire. With his batman and battery cook, he drove the portee into the shelter of a dune, checked sights, traverse wheels and ammunition and then proceeded to destroy five M-13s in a fury of fire.

Lieutenant Cyril Joly, 2 RTR,

> For a time [7th February] there was silence on both sides. For all the efforts of the previous day the Italian column still looked huge and threatening. I watched with apprehension the

The Advance through
Cyrenaica.

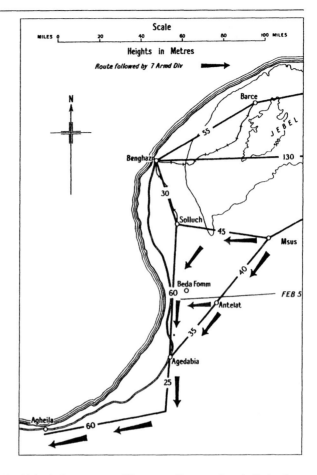

movements of the mass of vehicles before me. . . . We were well outnumbered. Each of us knew by what slim margin we still held dominance over the battlefield. Gradually I became aware of a startling change. First one and then another white flag appeared in the host of vehicles. More and more became visible, until the whole column was a forest of waving banners.

General Tellera had been wounded and died. General Cona, General Bignani, General Negroni, General Bardini, General Giuliano, with scores of brigadiers and colonels, became prisoners. And *Barba Elettrica*, Bergonzoli himself was finally captured. He told Alan Moorehead,

> You were here too soon, that is all. But we gave battle at once. And always, here as everywhere else, we were grossly outnumbered. So when our second attack was unable to prevail we had no choice but to make an honourable surrender.

Lt Roy Farran, 3rd Hussars,

> For ten miles as far as the eye could see there was a mass of abandoned lorries and tanks. The enemy had panicked in the night after his vehicles had got stuck in soft sand during an

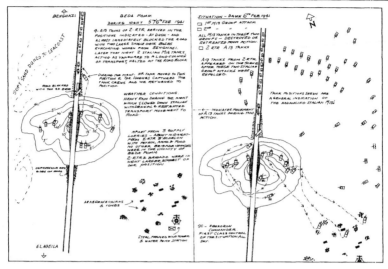

Major Norman Plough's map of the Battle of Beda Fomm, 5–6 February 1941.

attempt to wriggle past us down the coast leaving their lorries, guns and tanks, almost all undamaged, they had bolted down to the beaches. It was a glorious victory. The Italian Army of Cyrenaica was completely smashed.

To the victors the spoils. For the next three days the Hussars, RTR, RB and RHA rounded up prisoners and towed in captured transport. There were bottles of wine, boxes of chocolates, tins of fruit, china plates, silver cutlery. Everyone wore clean Italian shirts, every officer had a civilian car, every soldier had a motorcycle. The fitters found tools they had only dreamed of. The doctors had medical equipment up to the standard of a Harley Street clinic. Brand-new watches, Zeiss binoculars, dainty little Beretta automatics, superb cameras. Roy Farran wrote 'We were so drunk with success that we thought it the end of the war and frivolously talked of policing Libya until the Germans surrendered.'

General O'Connor had sent 7th Armoured Support Group forward. Lieutenant Crankshaw, 'C' Squadron 11th Hussars, took Agedabia, 20 miles south, and moved on to the fort and barracks of El Agheila on the border between Tripolitania and Cyrenaica, and Benghazi fell on 9 February. Brigadier 'Red Robby', the dynamic Australian who had pushed his troops from Barce, El Abiar, Regima and Benina airport, accepted the surrender of the town from the mayor in pouring rain and hail on a bleak windy morning. The posters of Mussolini had been defaced. Graziani's HQ had been in the Hotel Berenice.

Tobruk was now operating as a port and Benghazi soon would be. General Maitland Wilson was appointed governor of Cyrenaica installed at Barce. O'Connor felt his troops could push on to Tripoli. But in Wavell's HQ office in Cairo was a huge map of Greece. So no Tripoli.

CHAPTER SIX

1 RTR in Tobruk –
on Loan to the Australians

'In two months', Churchill wrote, 'the Army of the Nile had advanced 500 miles, had destroyed an Italian Army of more than nine divisions and had captured 130,000 prisoners, 400 tanks and 1,290 guns. The conquest of Cyrenaica was complete.' The whole of 7th Armoured Division could only muster twelve cruiser and forty light tanks fit for another 100 miles. Bedecked with flags they returned triumphant to Cairo, reached on 23 February 1941, leaving its few tanks behind. The base workshops slowly, very slowly, started to re-equip the division. Churchill wrote:

> At the end of February the 7th British Armoured division had been withdrawn to Egypt to rest and refit. This famous unit had rendered the highest service. Its tanks had travelled far and were largely used up. Its numbers had shrunk by fighting and wear and tear. Still there was a core of the most experienced hard-bitten, desert-worthy fighting men, the like of whom could not be found by us. It was a pity not to keep in being the nucleus of this unique organisation and rebuild its strength by drafts of officers and men arriving trained, fresh and keen from England and to send up to them the pick of whatever new tanks or spare parts could be found. Thus the 7th Armoured Division would have preserved a continuity of life and been resuscitated in strength.

Churchill and Wavell had turned their attentions to the desperate need to help the gallant Greek Army stave off Mussolini's unwarranted attack. British and Commonwealth forces were deployed (including 3 RTR) and another sinister threat appeared. The Chiefs of Staff sent a telegram to Wavell. 'In view of arrival of German armoured formations and aircraft in Tripolitania, the question of defence commitments in Egypt and Cyrenaica has been considered here.' General Erwin Rommel arrived in Tripoli on 12 February with his personal staff. On 17 March Generals Wavell and Dill visited Antelat and the key Agheila defile. Rommel's mainly Italian forces, but with a German panzer-tank brigade, launched their attack on 31 March, and swept aside (with their 120 Mark III and Mark IV tanks) the brigade of 2nd Armoured Division in front of them. One brigade of their two tank regiments had been sent to Greece. The other had fifty-two Cruiser tanks (half were in workshops), including 6 RTR equipped with captured Italian M-13 tanks. The 3rd Hussars were re-equipping with M-13s when Rommel's attack went in.

Lieutenant Roy Farran wrote:

An air of panic, even of terror and of lost confidence, ran through the whole army, which had apparently been surprised by a strong German attack along the coast on the 29th March. We heard pitiful tales of the failure of our much-vaunted Cruiser tanks in action against German Mark IIIs. . . . The tale of the next seven days is perhaps one of the most inglorious in the history of the British Army. . . . The Brigade began their headlong retreat on the 1st April.

Through Antelat and Msus (where most of the diesel-run M-13s were destroyed through lack of fuel), under Stuka dive-bombing, through the Jebel to the coast road (Divisional HQ were captured at Mekili), to Derna and Gazala to Tobruk. It did not help that Generals O'Connor and Neame were captured on 6 April (without any escort). The 9th Australian Division was withdrawing eastwards along the coastal road, commanded by a very resolute GOC, Major-General L.J. Morshead. Mechili was taken by the DAK (Deutsch Afrika Korps) on 8 April. On the same day Wavell flew into Tobruk and gave orders for the defence of the fortress. The 9th Australian Division had arrived there and a brigade group of 7th Australian Division arrived from Egypt, escorted by the Royal Navy. With them on a large freighter SS *Thurland Castle* came 'B' and 'C' Squadrons 1st RTR with twenty Mark VIB light tanks and sixteen A9 and A10 Cruiser tanks, plus four Matildas of 4 RTR. Lieutenant-Colonel Culverwell was CO 1 RTR, but was replaced on 24 April by Lieutenant-Colonel 'Buster' Brown.

There were a number of Desert Rat units involved in the first great siege of Tobruk. In addition to 1 RTR, the Chestnut and Rocket troops of 1 RHA, some Cherry Pickers, 51st Field Regiment (Corps troops allocated to 7th Armoured Division). During the siege they came under command of 'Ming the Merciless', the nickname for Major-General Morshead. After the siege 1 RTR and 1 RHA reverted to the Desert Rats. Among other British troops serving in Tobruk were the machine-gunners of the Royal Northumberland Fusiliers, 51st Heavy AA Regiment – a total of 8,000 British supporting the 15,000 Australians. Lord Haw-Haw, the renegade 'German' radio broadcaster, nicknamed the defenders 'the rats of Tobruk', but this was not a direct reference to the Desert Rats of 7th Armoured.

The Cherry Pickers, by chance, had a small detachment in Tobruk. On about 8 April Lieutenant Pat Stewart had taken two Marmon-Harringtons to have their Breda AA MGs fitted in the ordnance depot. The job was incomplete when the siege of Tobruk started. A light truck with Sergeants Corcoran and Jones was marooned while on a visit to draw stores. The Cherry Pickers joined the 3rd Hussar group who used them in an AA role, and the new Bredas were frequently in action against Junkers 87, low-flying Messerschmitt 109s and Stuka divebombers. Later they were assigned to protect the aerodrome as the RAF started to fly out their surviving Hurricanes. The two Marmon-Harringtons were in action every day, but Stewart and the cars were shipped back to Alexandria on landing craft tanks after a month of non-stop action.

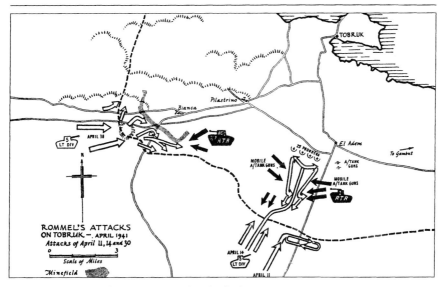

Rommel's attacks on Tobruk, 11, 14 and 30 April 1941.

There are several excellent first-hand reports and diaries from various British 'rats of Tobruk', including three from 1 RTR. Major Ray Leakey commanded 'C' Squadron, Major George Hynes 'B' Squadron, Lieutenant John Wollaston was Intelligence Officer and Unit Navigator and Lieutenant J.I. Bouverie-Brine served with 'B' Squadron and kept a daily diary. He noted that 'In early March '41 we were ordered "post haste" to Greece and within 24 hours the Regiment was stowed in SS *Thurland Castle*. . . . However less than an hour before we sailed the news was announced that Greece had fallen and we were now going to Tobruk at once, which we did.'

Rommel's Operation Sonnenblume (Sunflower) had pushed General Johannes Streich, 5th Leichte (Light) Division, later to be reorganised as 21st Panzer Division, up to the 30-mile perimeter of Tobruk. Their first attack on 11 April on the south-west along the track to hill Point 209 fizzled out. Two days later Streich sent in a more determined attack, the Brescia Division and 5th Light that breached the perimeter to almost 2 miles' depth. Major Ray Leakey wrote 'here for the first time my Regiment fought against German tanks'. 1 RTR had fifteen cruisers and fifteen more light tanks and engaged fifteen German Mark IIIs. 'C' Squadron had a major engagement and anti-tank guns of 1 RHA helped repel the German attack. Lieutenant Wollaston, 1 RTR, found a German tank captain's diary. 'He was amazed at the anti-tank fire . . . 38 [German] tanks went into action and 17 were disabled. 2 officers were killed and 7 wounded.'

On 15 April Rommel himself directed another major attack commanded by Oberst Ponath. In the three-day battle the Italian Ariete Division lost 1,500 prisoners and 90 out of 100 light tanks. The Luftwaffe Stukas dive-bombed the harbour frequently, but the British heavy ack-ack guns took a considerable toll. Churchill was watching the battle arena from London and wrote to the CIGS on 18 April:

> After the capture of Benghazi on 6th February, the 7th Armoured Division which had done so much good hard service was ordered back to Cairo to refit. This involved a journey of over 400 miles and must have completed the wearing out of many of the tanks. It was an act of improvidence to send the whole division all this way back in view of the fact that German elements were already reported in Tripoli. The whole of the tanks in this division could not have been all simultaneously in a condition of needing prolonged heavy repairs. Workshops should have been improvised at the front for lighter repairs and servicing personnel sent forward. . . . After their journey back at least 114 cruisers and 48 I tanks, total 162, entered the workshops in Egypt and are still there.

The Greek Government surrendered on 25 April and the British forces, including 3 RTR, fought a determined retreat south to Piraeus. Five days later a major attack against Tobruk started on 1 May. Major Walter Benzie became OC, 'C' Squadron, and Major 'Buster' Brown became CO, 1 RTR. During the day's fighting Major George Hynes, 'B' Squadron, had his A-10 cruiser hit and 'brewed up'; so did Lieutenant-Colonel Brown's and Lieutenant Wollaston's tanks. Tobruk had efficient tank-repair workshops and, surprisingly, produced twelve new A-13 tanks for 'C' Squadron. Major Benzie used to go around the various Australian battalions holding the perimeter offering the service of 1 RTR tanks. Several four-tank raids were organised with Benzie and Leakey taking it in turns to lead them. Soon, however, petrol rationing prevented activities except in an emergency, so the intrepid pair 'joined' the infantry of 2/23 Australian battalion.

Churchill's response to the humiliating retreat from Benghazi up to Tobruk and the equally tragic withdrawal from Greece (and later Crete) was magnificent. By 28 April Wavell had been informed of the imminent arrival in the Delta of 300 new tanks and over 50 Hurricane fighters. Wavell decided to launch Operation Brevity at dawn on 15 May. It was a three-pronged counter-attack on Halfaya Pass, Sollum, Musaid, Fort Capuzzo and, if successful, on to Bardia and perhaps the relief of Tobruk. Wavell sent a telegram on the 13th to Churchill ending: 'If successful will consider combined action by Gott's force and Tobruk garrison to drive enemy west of Tobruk'. Brigadier 'Strafer' Gott's force on the frontier comprised 7th Armoured Division Support Group, plus 2 RTR (Lieutenant-Colonel R.F.E. Chute in command) and 4 RTR that formed 7th Armoured Brigade. The 2 RTR was equipped with twenty-nine reconditioned Cruiser tanks, A-9s and A-10s. The 4 RTR (Lieutenant-Colonel W. O'Carroll) was to lead the 22nd Guards Brigade attack on the fortified posts with its twenty-six Matilda tanks. The three-pronged attack, with 2nd Bn Rifle Brigade supported by artillery, advanced on the coast road towards Sollum, the 22 Guards Brigade and 4 RTR in the centre driving along the edge of the escarpment above Halfaya Pass, then on to Fort Capuzzo. The 7th Armoured Brigade Group were to screen the slower-moving forces on their right.

1 RTR tanks in Tobruk. *Imperial War Museum*

The German commander, Oberst von Herff, put up such a spirited resistance that by the morning of 17 May, after 160 casualties, 5 Matildas destroyed and 13 damaged, the British forces were back where they had started, apart from the temporary capture of Halfaya Pass. The 2 RTR had two encounters with German tank groups and had to withdraw to Sidi Suleiman with 22 cruisers in shaky condition. The British infantry (1st Durham Light Infantry) who had reached Fort Capuzzo were pushed back to Musaid with heavy losses. Operation Brevity was a minor disaster, but Churchill wrote optimistically on the 17th to Wavell: 'You have taken the offensive, advanced 30 miles, have captured Halfaya and Sollum, have taken 500 German prisoners and inflicted heavy losses in men and tanks on the enemy. For this 20 'I' tanks and 1,000–1,500 casualties do not seem to be at all too heavy a cost.'

Ten days later von Herff sent seventy Panzers and infantry to retake Halfaya Pass and installed a line of dug-in 88mm anti-tank strongposts to hold it. Meanwhile, Churchill was by now well aware that British and American tanks and their commanders' tactics, appeared to be inferior to those of the DAK. Perhaps too the organisation of a British armoured division may have been faulty. On 16 May he sent a note to the CIGS:

> You tell me that the total number of Cruiser tanks in a brigade of the 7th Armoured Division is 210 (including 20 per cent reserves) and that of the I Brigade 200 I tanks – say 400 heavy tanks in the 7th Armoured Division. We must try to compare like with like. I am told that the German principle is two light tanks to every heavy; thus there would be in a German armoured division about 135 heavy tanks, ie fewer heavy tanks than one of our tank brigades. What is the additional outfit of our armoured brigades in light tanks?

The first great siege of Tobruk was a magnificent defensive action by the Commonwealth garrison under Ming the Merciless. The assorted Desert Rat formations among the defenders contributed greatly to the main Australian effort. Stuka bombing continued non-stop, but after the determined DAK attacks in April and early May, Rommel contained the perimeter, and tried to deny the night-run supply convoys by the gallant Royal Navy. Eventually, on 21 November, the breakout from Tobruk achieved great acclaim. By then the British 70th Division had taken over from the Australian. Among the survivors of the garrison were two squadrons of 1 RTR with their rather battered Cruiser tanks. The Desert Rats had played a small but significant role.

Alan Moorehead, journalist and author, drove into Tobruk and wrote:

> As you wind down from the El Adem crossroads the scarred white village breaks suddenly into view. It had the appearance of utter dreariness and monotony as though the very earth itself was tired. Every foot of dust was touched in some way by high explosive. The sand was full of shrapnel and broken bits of metal. Countless thousands of shells, bombs and bullets had fallen here among the rusting barbed wire, the dug-outs and the dust-coloured trucks. You could distinguish the men of Tobruk from the other soldiers. Their clothing, their skin and especially their faces, were stained the same colour as the earth. They moved slowly and precisely with an absolute economy of effort. They were lean and hard and their lips were drawn tightly together against the dust. They seemed to fit perfectly into the landscape and it was impossible to say whether their morale was good or bad, whether they were tired after so many months of bombing and shelling and isolation or merely indifferent. . . . Of the high excitement and heroism that had held this place for nine months, there was no sign whatsoever. There were no flags, no bands, no marching men. The war seemed to have reduced nearly everything to a neutral dust. Except for the lines of crosses in the cemetery.

CHAPTER SEVEN

Operation Battleaxe

Under 'Ming the Merciless' the Australian and British defenders of Tobruk passed most of May and June 1941 without any major attacks. Rommel's forces surrounding Tobruk included the Italian Ariete tank Division, Brescia and Pavia Italian infantry divisions boosted by German rifle companies in the salient inside the perimeter. With the arrival of the 300 new tanks (Winston Churchill called them 'Tiger Cubs') Wavell, with much hesitancy, decided, after the failure of Operation Brevity, to mount a more substantial attack, and wrote, on 28 May, to the CIGS (General Dill) in London. 'All available armoured strength which will be the deciding factor, is being put into Operation "Battleaxe". Various difficulties are delaying reconstitution of 7th Armoured Division. Earliest date for beginning of forward move from [Mersa] Matruh will be 7th June, and may be later.'

Intelligence information revealed that Rommel's DAK had now been reinforced by the powerful 15th Panzer Division. Benghazi was a vital supply port for Rommel's desert army and his German tank force now numbered 200. Wavell told London that the British and South African armoured cars were powerless against the German eight-wheeled armoured cars; and suffered heavily from Luftwaffe fighters; that the Infantry (Matilda) tanks were too slow for battle in the desert and were being hammered by the powerful 88mm anti-tank guns; that the British Cruiser tanks were unreliable technically and had little advantage in power or speed over German medium tanks. 'All the above factors may limit our success,' Churchill wrote, 'The extra fortnight that had passed before the Tiger Cubs could be assimilated by the 7th Armoured division made me fear that the 15th Panzers would all have reached Rommel.'

Rommel had salvaged from abandoned Italian and British equipment, guns, some tanks, lorries, cars and motorcycles, now all newly painted with the Afrika Korps insignia of palm tree and swastika. The DAK had parity in the number of tanks, but a clear advantage in anti-tank guns. Their dozen 88mm anti-aircraft guns used in an anti-tank role could pierce even the thick armour of the Matilda I tank at ranges up to 2,000 yards. Of the total of 143 anti-tank guns, 54 were the long-barrelled 50mm Pak 38, which at 1,000 yards range had a penetration 40 per cent better than the British tank 2-pounder gun. Rommel insisted that his anti-tank gunners *operated in close combination with their Panzer tanks both in*

An M–3 medium tank with sunshield. *Major Norman Plough*

attack and defence. The British usually relied on their 25-pounder field guns to knock out either by direct or indirect fire the powerful German anti-tank guns. The latter were often screened or dug in to make them more difficult targets. Another distinct advantage for the DAK was their very efficient and daring tank repair units which at night roamed the battlefields. They took away and repaired not only Axis equipment but British tanks, guns and lorries either knocked out or fuelless. The famous, brand-new Tiger Cubs numbered 135 Matildas, 82 Cruisers (including 50 new Mark IV Crusaders) and 21 light tanks. When the SS *Empire Song* was mined and sunk, 57 Tiger Cubs went down with her.

The 7th Armoured Division had been reconstituted and re-equipped and was commanded by Major-General O'Moore-Creagh. The 4th Armoured Brigade consisted of 4th and 7th RTR, both with Matilda 'I' tanks under Brigadier Alec Gatehouse. 7th Armoured Brigade had 2nd and 6th RTR with a mixture of old cruisers and new Crusaders. The Cherry Pickers skirmished ahead as usual. Harry Buckledee, 11th Hussars, recalled: 'Fighter aircraft were our greatest hazard. With the Italians it was their CR 42s firing .5 inch armour-piercing bullets which penetrated our armour plating. Against the Germans it was the

Messerschmitt 109 and 110.' The 1 KRRC and 2nd Rifle Brigade were the motorised infantry, 1st, 3rd, 4th and 106 RHA were the artillery units – the whole support group commanded by Brigadier 'Jock' Campbell RHA. Major-General F.W. Messervy commanded the 4th Indian Division – also taking part in Operation Battleaxe with four British and three Indian battalions.

The Desert Rats' quota of Tiger Cubs had many mechanical faults, and many were without wireless sets. The division had been without tanks for four months and badly needed extra desert training. Moreover, the Desert Rats' two brigades lacked their usual third tank regiment. Churchill and the British public were anxious for a desert victory and Wavell was under constant pressure to launch a major attack.

Brigadier Alec Gatehouse related:

At the final conference when orders were given for Operation Battleaxe, I pointed out to General Beresford-Peirse, the XIII Corps Commander, that I was clear as to his intention but that I wanted an elucidation of his term 'Rally-forward'. As used by the Royal Armoured Corps, after the capture of any objective the tanks should *not* be kept hanging about on the objective, but that in half an hour after the capture, infantry should have organised their defences *including anti-tank* defence. The tanks could then 'Forward-Rally' viz go to a rallying position behind but close to the infantry so that they could intervene if the infantry were threatened by enemy tanks. The General insisted that tanks should 'rally forward' *between* the enemy and our own infantry. From the RTR point of view that would be suicidal if a tank with a minor defect such as faulty petrol pump, broken bogey, etc could not be worked on by the fitters in such a position. If Rommel counter-attacked

A 2 RTR squadron mess, July 1941. *Major Norman Plough*

successfully any such tank might be lost to the enemy. In Gatehouse's opinion a large majority of the British tanks were presented to Rommel by faulty 'direction', and could have been saved based on *accepted* armoured training being utilised.

There were many examples, unfortunately, of faulty tank tactics, many inflicted on the hapless tank battalions by ignorant or stubborn Army or Corps commanders. Lieutenant-Colonel 'Pip' Roberts, who was GSO2 and HQ 7th Armoured Division, wrote:

The operation was to start, and did start, on 14th June. 7th Armoured Division consisted of 4th Armoured Brigade (4 and 7 RTR equipped with Matildas), 7th Armoured Brigade (2 RTR equipped with A-9s and A-10s and 6 RTR equipped with Crusaders) and the Support Group 1 KRRC, 2 RB and 4 RHA, together with the King's Dragoon Guards (Armoured Cars) and additional artillery. On our right was 4th Indian Division with, under command, 22nd Guards Brigade. In broad outline the plan was as follows: in the first stage 4th Indian Division were to capture the area Halfaya-Sollum-Capuzzo, and for this task they were to have under command 4th Armoured Brigade, temporarily detached from 7th Armoured Division. In this first stage 7th Armoured Division (less 4th Armoured Brigade) was to protect the southern flank of 4th Indian Division and to do this were to capture Hafid Ridge, as a first objective.

In the second stage, 4th Armoured Brigade would return to 7th Armoured Division who were then to make an exploiting drive for Tobruk.

For the first stage Dickie Creagh gave 7th Armoured Brigade the task of securing Hafid Ridge, just on the west side of the frontier wire, and the Support Group was to protect the left and rear against a wide outflanking movement.

HQ 7th Armoured Division had moved on 14th June further forward nearer the scene of operations. On the 15th, the day started misty and in places foggy. A Tac HQ was formed to keep up with the battle but bore little relation in composition to the Tac HQ of later years; it consisted of about a third of the Main HQ and led by the large ACVI, with the General, GSO1 and GSO2, then ACV II (Intelligence and Spare), then a small ACV as rear link to Corps, a number of liaison officers in scout cars or trucks, numerous signal vehicles and some supply lorries. In ACV1, the General and the G1 sat mostly on the top with a map board between them and I (as G2) sat inside, glued to the wireless.

The preliminary advance up to the frontier wire had no sooner started than the poor visibility started disorganising things. The 11th Hussars who were in front and to the left of 2 RTR, the leading armoured regiment, were reporting their leading squadron in a certain position; 7th Armoured Brigade doubted this, as 2 RTR had reported themselves in the same position. Noel Wall (7th Hussars) was BM 7th Armoured Brigade and was a particular friend of mine. I urged him to try to sort this little problem out, as if we were at sixes and sevens regarding locations before any fighting had begun we were going to be in real trouble later.

At about 10am Noel reported that Hafid Ridge was taken; I said, 'Are you sure?' and he replied, 'Yes. Hafid Ridge [he used a codeword] is well and truly ours.'

I reported this to the General, but said I was checking with 11th Hussars. The 11th Hussars did not agree as they maintained that their leading squadron had just been heavily fired on from Hafid Ridge and the squadron commander was trying to contact the CO of 2 RTR. Visibility was now improving and although we never really decided which ridge was Hafid, we in future accepted that the ridge occupied by the enemy was that ridge.

From now on until the late afternoon very little happened. Later in the morning the squadron of 2nd RTR put in an attack on Hafid supported by an RHA battery, but had to withdraw as they were faced with further guns in depth and could not remain in such an isolated position. Around 2pm Rikki Richards (G1) was pressing the General to press Hugh Russell (commander 7th Armoured Brigade) to do something; but the General would not have him harassed.

Our Tac HQ sat where it was; we couldn't see any bit of the battle and nothing happened until 5.30pm. Why Dickie Creagh did not go forward and see for himself I do not know.

Then, as a result of report that the enemy was withdrawing from the Hafid Ridge, 6 RTR was launched to attack it. We waited anxiously in the ACVI to hear the result, but it was sometime before we could get any information. At last we knew that 6 RTR had had to withdraw after heavy casualties. The fact was that the German withdrawal was a trap; many anti-tank guns had been left in concealed positions around knocked-out vehicles and held their fire until the tanks were within 'killing' distance and quickly knocked out eleven, with others disabled.

The history of 6 RTR recounts during Battleaxe that

Supported on the right flank by 2 RTR, the regiment went into battle with 51 A-15 Crusader tanks at Hafid Ridge on 15th June. Simultaneously attacks were made upon enemy occupied Halfaya Pass and Fort Capuzzo which were held by infantry in well prepared positions. 'B' Squadron advanced over the ridge and disaster fell upon them. Reports were received of extremely heavy casualties, no more was heard of them. Only two tanks survived. The squadron ran into a line of [anti-]tank guns concealed behind dummy vehicles. The Germans true to form, counter-attacked. 'C' Squadron reported 35 tanks advancing from the SE. 6 RTR only had 20 tanks battleworthy. A long-range duel developed. Our 2 pdrs were hopelessly out-gunned by the German 75mms. By nightfall the strength was down to 15 tanks. By dawn on the 16th 21 tanks commanded by Major R.I.S.C. Jones moved off with a mobile gun column towards Hafid Ridge, reported by 11th Hussars still held by the Germans. In the Sidi Omar area actions continued all morning. Two pounder and BESA fire caused much damage among MET. . . . On the evening of 17th the Germans advanced on 6 RTR [strength only 11 tanks] and 2 RTR. Fanning out into the lines both units were forced to retire firing as they went. Within 15 minutes 6 RTR only had five tanks left. Although 2nd Tanks fought a magnificent

6 RTR light tanks go into action near Mersa Matruh. *Imperial War Museum*

rearguard action until nightfall, they were unable to hold up the rapid German advance. They occupied Sidi Suleiman and the remains of 6 RTR returned to the Charing Cross area. In the Bir Sidi Ali area 6 RTR were brought up to strength with more Crusader tanks.

Rommel's battle was a brilliant defensive operation. As Major-General Creagh admitted 'His policy was to draw our tanks on to his guns and then to counter-attack them with tanks.' At Fort Capuzzo and Hafid Ridge a pretended 'withdrawal' helped lure the tanks of 7th Armoured on to the powerful anti-tank screen.

The Cherry Pickers were soon based on Sidi Omar on the left/western flank to protect Brigadier Russell's 7th Armoured Brigade's flank and rear. By 0900 hrs on 15th they had swept round to the west of Fort Capuzzo and reached the Hafid Ridge. The historian of the 11th Hussars wrote:

'A' Squadron were just in time to see two long columns of Rommel's tanks moving down from the north to reinforce Hafid Ridge, and to wireless back the news to brigade headquarters.

There now followed the decisive stage of the day's fighting. Twice within the next hour the British tanks tried gallantly to rush the enemy positions on the ridge, and twice they came within inches of success. Then, with the afternoon, the new arrivals entered on the field – a fresh battalion of tanks hurriedly summoned from Tobruk – and in the face of superior numbers Russell's regiments were forced to withdraw with heavy losses. By then the Guards Brigade, after a very long approach march from Sofafi, had successfully captured Fort Capuzzo and taken several hundred prisoners; but on the right wing the Indians' advance had run into the fiercest opposition. After long hours of bitter fighting Sollum still remained in German hands when at last darkness closed in upon the ravaged desert.

'A' Squadron were set upon by seven Messerschmitt 110s that annihilated No. 4 troop. Then just before darkness No. 5 troop observed a column of thirty German tanks moving south on Sidi Omar and No. 1 troop spotted another German tank column driving from Hafid Ridge towards the frontier. This much fought-over ridge consisted of three gentle crests, and between them lay a screen of anti-tank guns including four 88mms. That first night 2 RTR strength was down to nineteen tanks having started with thirty-eight and 6 RTR were reduced to eighteen.

The 4 RTR, under Lieutenant-Colonel O'Carroll, were in action all day, supporting, with their Matildas, two troops escorting the Indian battalions on the coast road attacking the fort of Halfaya Pass, one squadron with the Camerons tackling the garrison at the top of the pass and the rest with 7 RTR supporting the 22nd Guards Brigade towards Capuzzo and Sollum. Point 206, strongly defended, was bypassed and Capuzzo was reached at midday, but in counter-attacks 7 RTR lost nine Matildas. Of the 100 Matildas that went into action on the morning of the 15th only 37 were 'runners' at nightfall, although the fitters added another 11 by the following morning. Churchill wrote of the first day, 'At first things went reasonably well', and of the second,

No progress was made. Halfaya and Sollum held firm against us. In the afternoon strong forces of enemy tanks appeared moving with the clear intention of outflanking our attack from the west. The 7th Armoured Brigade moved to deal with this threat. They engaged the enemy near Sidi Omar and were forced to withdraw. The flank of the main attack, which it was their task to protect, was thereby imperilled.

Lieutenant P.F. Stewart, 11th Hussars, was watching the battle:

We got shelled from the outskirts of the battle and beat it with dust from shells whipping up round our heels. From some way back – where we still got shelled – we watched the smoke of battle ebb and clear and the noise die away. We saw about 50 vehicles, guns and infantry, line up. . . . Suddenly our own tanks came down . . . and waded into this lot who retreated, leaving any amount of kit behind and one or two lorries burning. I was asked by the tank major to go forward and reconnoitre for anti-tank guns. . . . I saw the whole column had moved back a bit and that there was a mass of men moving about.

I was then joined by two gunner Observation Posts who were, as usual, completely without fear. They proceeded to shell the concentration to hell, so I went forward again, only to run into about 50 tanks coming down from the north. They halted and I was having a good look when shells arrived really close. My driver tried to engage the gear without declutching, and finally started with a jerk which almost broke my neck. Got back to the OPs who were still merrily shelling away at the column at Sidi Omar.

The sheer weight of the Panzer counter-attack carried them right to the frontier fence by Sidi Omar and were eventually halted by the RHA anti-tank gunfire. The 4 RTR Matildas managed to retain control of Point 206. The 2 RTR lost five cruisers who charged together on the Hafid Ridge and were never seen again. They had no radios and never heard the order to retire and regroup.

On the second day of Battleaxe Rommel pushed his 5th Light Division, now commanded by General Lieutenant von Ravenstein, on the road from Tobruk towards Sidi Azeiz, while Neumann-Sylkow's 15th Panzer were partly in reserve, partly fighting around Capuzzo. Here for once Rommel's tactics either failed or were ignored. He did not believe that armour should fight armour. His Panzers' task was to find weak places in the enemy's defences – probably infantry positions – attack in force, break through and wipe out all their thin-skinned echelons. The main purpose of Rommel's artillery and anti-tank guns was to fight and destroy British tanks. His panzer grenadiers (lorried or track-carried infantry) would capture their enemies' artillery positions. At Capuzzo on the second day, two columns, totalling eighty Panzer tanks, attacked in parallel. A barrage of RHA 25 pounders and anti-tank guns, with 4th Armoured Brigade Matildas in hull-down positions, fought an excellent defensive battle. By noon 15th Panzer drew back having had their tank strength reduced to thirty. Al Halfaya Pass was still held by the German Commander, Bach. On the west and southwest flanks 7th Armoured Brigade, 2 RTR and 6 RTR, had mixed fortunes against 5th Light Division. The British cruisers smashed a large column of Echelon transport, but the two RTR regiments were pushed aside – a gap of 6 miles – while von Ravenstein, with Mark IV Panzers, first mauled 6 RTR, who had only nine remaining cruisers, then turned north-east to tackle 2 RTR until darkness intervened.

By nightfall 7th Armoured Brigade only had twenty-five tanks left in action. The Panzers were equipped with 75mm guns that could fire high explosive shells to hit at 3,000 yards, which would seriously damage a British Cruiser tank and certainly knocked out unprotected 25-pounder guns and crews. During the day 7th Armoured Brigade had seven cruisers knocked out and a further sixteen disabled by hits. At first light 2 RTR withdrew to Bir Kireigat. Lieutenant P.F. Stewart, 11th Hussars, watched the battle at dusk:

> The gunners on my left were showing remarkable courage and audacity, above all the 2 pounders on portees which stuck it nobly till the last moment against special detachments of tanks which came out to deal with them. The main body went NE and in the gathering dusk a tremendous tank battle took place which was fascinating even if a little dangerous to watch. One could see the tracer hitting the ground and rebounding high into the air, and hear the constant sound of the movement and noise of the guns. I saw the head of their column turn back and as night came down finally I went right forward and watched them leaguering.

Churchill wrote about the final day of Battleaxe – 17 June:

> Everything went wrong. Capuzzo was taken from the Guards Brigade by a considerable force with 100 tanks. The 7th Armoured Brigade with only about 20 Cruiser tanks now in action had spent the night near Sidi Suleiman. The enemy force which had forced them back overnight from Sidi Omar, made towards Halfaya and threatened to cut off the Guards Brigade. To deal with this threat General Creagh proposed an attack with the 7th Armoured Brigade from the south, while the 4th Armoured Brigade, to be relieved of its task of co-operating with the Guards Brigade, attacked from the north.

Rommel wrote afterwards in the Rommel papers after the previous day's battle between 5th Light and 7th Armoured tanks:

> This was the turning point of the battle. I immediately ordered the 15th Panzer Division to disengage all its mobile forces as quickly as possible and leaving only the essential minimum to hold the position north of Capuzzo, to go forward on the northern flank of the victorious 5th Light Division towards Sidi Suleiman. The decisive moment had come.

The Panzers moved at 0430 hrs and seventy-five German tanks with strong artillery support moved to within 10 miles of Halfaya Pass. The 4th Indian Division had been pushed out of Sollum, and General Messervy ordered a complete withdrawal to the coastal plain. Wavell had flown in to see the state of the battle and confirmed Messervy's decision.

The 22nd Guards Brigade was nearly trapped at Capuzzo, and Creagh ordered the 4th Armoured's surviving Matildas and 7th Armoured Crusaders with the Support Group's 25 pounders to fight a final defensive battle for six hours, to buy time for the 4th Indian to retreat from Capuzzo and Halfaya. By mid-afternoon Rommel was furious to find that his trap had failed. Moreover, the RAF bombers and fighters covered XIII Corps' retreat. '"Battleaxe" became a byword for blundering,' wrote Liddell Hart afterwards. Lieutenant-Colonel (later Field-Marshal) Carver wrote in his history of 4th Armoured Brigade:

It was a complete failure. The unreliable painfully slow Matildas were never designed to operate as Cruiser tanks. Many broke down on their way to their objectives: many more were knocked out by 88s before they knew what had hit them. On our left 7th Armoured Brigade were having an equally bad time against German Mark IIIs and 88s, 6 RTR in particular suffering heavy losses at Hafid Ridge. The attack was a complete failure and only saved from turning to disaster by the brilliant work of 4 RHA under command of Jock Campbell.

Wavell's despatch written after Battleaxe stated, 'The main cause of our failure was undoubtedly the difficulty in combining the action of cruiser and 'I' tanks, the cramping effect on manoeuvre of having only two regiments in each armoured brigade and the lack of training in the 7th Armoured Division.' In fact, the Matilda 'I' tanks were allotted to the infantry commanders at the outset and rarely did they fight in combination with the Cruisers.

After Battleaxe the Cherry Pickers spent three months back in the Delta equipping with new Humber cars with a neat turret, heavier armour, 7.92mm MG, a 15mm BESA machine-gun, but with a badly underpowered engine and a crew of three; there were three cars to a troop, but still no match for a German 6- or 8-wheeler armoured car. Brigadier 'Strafer' Gott, 7th Armoured Support Group, wrote that 'The respite you provided has enabled the Army of the Nile to become once again strong, well trained and ready. You can look back on the summer of 1941 as a time when you gave valuable assistance towards our ultimate victory.' The British and Indians suffered 1,000 casualties in the three-day battle: 122 killed in action, 588 wounded, 259 missing. No fewer than fifty-eight Matildas and twenty-nine Cruisers were lost, and despite optimistic claims, the Panzers recovered all their tanks except a dozen destroyed on the battlefield. General Wavell telegrammed the Prime Minster on 21 June 1941. 'Am very sorry for failure of 'Battleaxe' and loss of so many Tiger Cubs. . . . I was over-optimistic and should have advised you that 7th Armoured Division required more training before going into battle. . . .' Churchill sent Wavell to command in the Indian theatre, and replaced him with General Claude Auchinleck.

CHAPTER EIGHT

Operation Crusader

Rommel's Axis forces had won a decisive victory in the short battle of Operation Battleaxe. For a variety of reasons he chose not to exploit his success. The vigorous and continuing defence of Tobruk athwart his line of supply and communication was a constant threat and thorn in his side. For the time being he established a defensive ring from Sidi Omar to the top of Halfaya Pass, while 7th Armoured and 4th Indian Divisions withdrew to Alexandria and Cairo. Rommel's experienced 5th Leicht Division, now equipped with newly arrived medium Mark III Panzer tanks, was renamed 21st Panzer Division. The 90th Light Division arrived in North Africa without tanks and with little transport, but the DAK had increased its strength of the dominating 88mm anti-tank guns to thirty-five. Three untried Italian divisions brought the strength of the Axis forces up to three German and six Italian divisions.

The arrival of General Auchinleck on 5 July 1941 brought about many changes. The 8th Army now comprised XIII Corps under Lieutenant-General Godwin Austin and the new XXX Corps under Lieutenant-General Norrie. Auchinleck's commander in the field was Lieutenant-General Sir Alan Cunningham who had been so successful in the Abyssinian campaign. Originally a gunner and GOC of an infantry division, he had little experience of armoured warfare. 7th Armoured Division had a new GOC in Major-General 'Strafer' Gott, a dynamic, popular and brave leader, but obviously not experienced at commanding what was for Operation Crusader the size of a Panzer Corps. For some reason nine armoured regiments were grouped into *three* armoured brigades – an unwieldy operation for a new divisional commander to control; plus the support group of 3 and 4 RHA, 1st KRRC, 2nd Rifle Brigade and 60th Field Regiment RA. The 4th Armoured Brigade (8th Hussars, 3rd and 5th RTR plus 2 RHA and 2nd Scots Guards) had a strength of 166 Stuart tanks commanded by Brigadier Alec Gatehouse. The 7th Armoured Brigade, commanded by Brigadier G.M.O. Davy, was composed of 129 Crusaders and older Cruiser tanks of 7th Hussars, 2nd and 6th RTR. The newcomers, 22nd Armoured Brigade, had arrived at Port Tewfik on 5 October 1941 as part of 1st Armoured Division; they had been training in the UK since the outbreak of war. Brigadier Scott-Cockburn commanded 3rd and 4th County of London Yeomanry (CLY) and 2nd Royal Gloucestershire Hussars (RGH) equipped with the fast new Crusader A-15 cruisers – 158 of them. Their 2-pounder guns could fire AP shot but not HE, a serious disadvantage in the desert. Desert modifications were carried out in the ordnance workshops at Wardian near Alexandria. On 20 October their tanks, on railway flats, moved west to the Charing Cross railhead south-west of Mersah Matruh. In a heavy rainstorm early on 18 November this 'virgin' brigade crossed the frontier into Libya.

Meanwhile holding the line were, predictably, the Cherry Pickers plus Brigadier Gott's 7th Armoured Division Support Group. They held the high ground between Buqbuq and Sofafi. The Cherry Pickers watched a 25-mile front from Sheferzen in the south to the edge of the escarpment by Halfaya Pass. Lieutenant P.F. Stewart's remarkable diary reveals their patrol activities.

Out on patrol I do the last guard always in order to wake the men up, and I have seen the gradual recession of the moon and each day the north-east whiten and the stars become ineffectual. These nights I find a constant strain, especially after the wearying vigil of the day. We jolt back our few miles and leaguer. The men gather together, talking in low voices and then go to bed. Sgt Lamb and I stand and talk and drink whisky long after the others have slept. We discuss incidents and emotions, childhood and the Army, and then go to bed in our turn. I glance at the clear skies, the bright stars with the white floss of the Milky Way flung across them, and slip between my blankets. I always dream, waking suddenly in unjustifiable fears, sitting up, wondering where I am, what relation the cars have to each other, in which direction they are pointing.

Usually at 4.30 I am woken, feeling horribly tired, and hurry into my clothes, finding my groundsheet has slipped from my greatcoat which is wet with dew. How I long then for my three-quarters of an hour to be finished, listening for each sound, imagining each bush into a man, a machine. Eventually there is the faintest perceptible light, the least bright stars go out. I look at my watch; it is 5 o'clock. Another quarter of an hour and there is a dim visibility all round.

I rouse my wireless operator to make his hourly call, and rouse the men – whose reactions are always the same. Some come quickly to their senses; some merely turn over; others groan, moan, grunt and cough. The silence I have so strictly reserved to listen for enemy approach is shattered by a host of little sounds, people putting on their boots, the scratch of a match, the noise of folded blankets. I wonder desperately how I shall ever hear anything, neglectful of the fact that I can hear an enemy tank ten miles away and recognise the sound. We stand about till it is light enough to move – ten minutes or so in which to smoke a cigarette – and then go cautiously up to the day position, with the constant apprehension that *they* may have laid up for us in the night and with the determination not be caught. And then another day of watching.

Sergeant Jake Wardrop, 5 RTR, noted in his diary:

The big experiment of guns, tanks and infantry was proving a huge success, by this time we were operating like clockwork. It was good to watch the guns getting into action. They travelled about two thousand yards behind us, but up in front with the forward tanks there was an officer [FOO] of the Artillery [usually RHA] in a tank who was in touch with the guns on the air [by wireless]. When we met any trouble, the CO would take a quick look at it and pass a message to the gunner officer to take it on and that was enough. The CO was then free to direct the tanks . . . the whole operation took about three minutes and they [the enemy] didn't like it at all. The 25-pounder is known as the 'daisy cutter' as it bursts along the deck.

Liddell Hart in his classic book *The Tanks* noted:

There was no realisation that the [German] 88mm gun had been the chief instrument in Rommel's defensive tactics. The higher headquarters discredited the reports that this anti-aircraft gun was being used in an anti-tank role. Six months later [after Battleaxe] and after further heavy losses from its fire, they were then slow to believe that it could be used *except* in an emplacement and were thus caught unawares by the next development in Rommel's defensive tactics of using it as a mobile anti-tank gun.

German Army Planning Staff in July 1941 produced 'Plan Orient' to win supremacy in the Middle East. They assumed that the Russian campaign, Operation Barbarossa, would be over in the autumn – the North African operation was not important to them. The DAK role in the summer and autumn of 1941 was to be purely defensive – *except that Tobruk was to be taken.* German forces had only been sent to Greece and North Africa to stop the humiliating defeats of their Italian allies. Rommel's requirements in a minor theatre of war were only grudgingly met. During August a third of all the supplies to the DAK across the Mediterranean were lost, and by October two-thirds were lost – courtesy of the Royal Navy and the Royal Air Force. Rommel, that great 'chancer', knew of the supply risks behind him and trusted that his efficient supply echelons would continue to 'provide'.

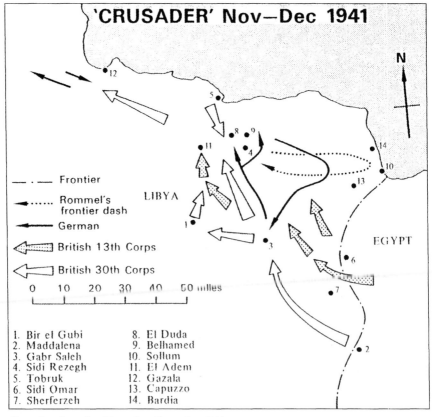

Operation Crusader, November–December 1941.

The plan for Operation Crusader was ambitious – to destroy the enemy forces in eastern Cyrenaica, relieve Tobruk, occupy Tripolitania and perhaps even more. The unwieldy 7th Armoured Division was part of XXX Corps' task to capture the airfields of Sidi Rezegh and El Adem, 25 and 20 miles respectively south-west and south of Tobruk, both situated on an escarpment. The Tobruk garrison would then make a determined sortie to link up with XXX Corps and force the Axis forces to retreat westwards. The total British tank strength had built up to 774, with 455 in 7th Armoured Division, and 210 'I' Matildas supporting the infantry formations. British Intelligence assessed the Axis tank strength at 388, but in fact it was now 558 of which two-thirds were German Panzers.

Rommel's staff had planned their attack, code operation 'Winter Battle' to start on 23 November, but they were forestalled by the 8th Army's D-Day of the 18th.

The 7th Armoured Division's three-pronged attack would advance north-west in a semi-circle towards Tobruk, with 4th Armoured Brigade on the right, 7th in the centre and 22nd on the left.

4th Armoured Brigade in Crusader

After passing through the frontier wire, a brief skirmish took place at Bir Sciafsciuf, but on the 19th the brigade, with their 164 Stuarts, met the whole weight of 15th Panzer Division at Gabr Taieb el Essem, north-west of Scheferzen. For two days a fierce battle ensued with 8th Hussars having heavy casualties. At the end of the 20th the enemy were reinforced by 21 Panzer Division.

Corporal Fred Dale, 3 Tp 'A' 3 RTR, wrote:

We got in sight of the coast by mid-day when the Squadron Leader reported over the wireless that a tank column were crossing our front and turning towards us, the approaching tanks were the 15th and 21st Panzer Divisions. When the battle started we were firing at Mk3 and Mk4 German tanks and we were outgunned. We were told to fall back to the other squadrons, our tank was now firing over the engine, then there was a big bang, we had been hit in the engine. This was extremely lucky. If we had been hit in the turret, I would not be writing this! The crew of a knocked out MkIV German tank, 150 yards away came over to look at us, as our tank now in flames, the ammunition began to explode.

The following morning they were rescued by the Indian Division.

Sergeant, Jake Wardrop, 5 RTR, wrote in his diary:

As soon as the fun began we fanned out to see what was happening. On the wireless there were ten tanks here, ten there, then someone would report another twenty-five. We took on the 21st Panzer Division that morning on 20th November – Cambrai day! And we got into line and advanced to the fray. We held them for about an hour and during that time 3rd Tanks and 8th Hussars were pushing in from the left and right and shooting them up from the sides. They turned and ran for it leaving nine behind. The great thing about this scrap was the fact that we had fought back the crack German division and they had bigger guns and thicker tanks. The losses were heavy, we had six killed in the Squadron, ten wounded while most of the tanks had been hit and some were ready to be written off.

Both 3rd and 5th RTR chased back 25 miles to the Trigh el Abd where 8th Hussars were being hammered at Gabr Saleh, losing twenty tanks. The brigade claimed to have knocked out between nineteen and twenty-six tanks, but in fact only three had been destroyed and four had been disabled.

The German Battlegroup Stephan (part of 21st Panzers), consisting of eighty-five MkIII and MkIV Panzers, plus thirty-five MkII Panzers with a strong artillery group of 105mm howitzers and 88mm anti-tank guns, were sent at 1145 hrs on the 20th to destroy the British forces north-east of Gabr Saleh. Five hours later they encountered the fifty Stuarts of 8th Hussars deploying to meet them. It was the first 'large' tank *v.* tank battle in the desert. The Germans had the firepower and numbers, the Stuarts the speed and manoeuvrability of their Honeys. Much later in the battle the Honeys of 5 RTR joined in the battle. Alan Moorehead wrote:

> What a moment it was. These light Honeys with their two-pounder 37 millimetre gun, their ugly box-shaped turrets; their little waving pennants had never seen the battle before. They had come straight from the steel mills of America to the desert and now for the first time we were going to see if they were good or bad or just more tanks.

Brigadier Gatehouse (and the USA military attaché, Colonel Bonnet Fellers) were watching the battlefield.

> At his command the Honeys did something that tanks don't do in the desert any more. They charged. It was novel, reckless, unexpected, impetuous and terrific. They charged straight into the curtain of dust and fire that hid the German tanks and guns. They charged at speeds of nearly forty miles per hour and some of them came right out the other side of the German lines. Then they turned and charged straight back again. Dust, smoke, burning oil, exploding shell and debris filled the air.

The 7th Armoured Brigade, 7th Hussars, 2 and 6 RTR, had a smoother passage as the central column of 129 mixed Cruisers of the attack. They leaguered on the night of the 19th 20 miles south of Sidi Rezegh where a motor track went down two escarpments towards the Tobruk perimeter, only 12 miles beyond Sidi Rezegh. The next day 2 RTR led but boggy ground – after the heavy rainstorms – meant that a detour west was needed. At 1500 hrs 6 RTR took the lead and soon over-ran the airfield 2 miles from Sidi Rezegh capturing nineteen enemy aircraft. 'C' Squadron 2 RTR were ordered up to destroy them. Major M.F.S. Rudkin wrote 'The crews enjoyed themselves smashing everything they could with sledgehammers and pickaxes. About 11.20pm when the leaguer had settled down for the night, the tanks refuelled and the crews fed, the sound of diesel lorries could be heard a few hundred yards to the north.' The Germans were very active during the night bringing up and digging in guns. On the 20th a hail of fire fell on 2 RTR on the ridge behind the airfield and 6 RTR on the southern edge. Lieutenant Jackson led a troop of 6 RTR and Lieutenant Titlestad a troop of 2 RTR to try to knock out some of the enemy MGs and anti-tank guns. Casualties forced both regiments to withdraw a short distance. 7th Armoured Division Support

Group, under Brigadier Jock Campbell (3 RHA, 4 RHA, 1st KRRC, 2 RB and 60th Field Regt RA), arrived to help secure the airfield. The 5th South African Brigade was hurrying up to join in.

Through the frontier wire on the 19th, 22nd Armoured Brigade placed 3rd CLY to the right, 4th CLY to the left and 2nd RGH in the centre. The approach march of 80 miles had caused mechanical breakdowns among the 163 Crusaders that had set out. But by noon 2 RGH had penetrated the defence lines of the Italian Ariete Division holding Bir el Gubi. Despite warnings from the Cherry Picker screen, 4 CLY came up on the left in 'the nearest thing to a cavalry charge seen during the war'. Viscount Cranley (ex-Life Guards, then a CLY squadron commander) continued: 'The enemy seemed somewhat daunted by this spirited, if not very professional attack and were coming out of their trenches in considerable numbers offering to surrender.' The brigade had knocked out 34 M-13 tanks, 12 Italian guns and taken over 200 Bersaglieri prisoners. The Gubi defences had been well prepared. By 1630 hrs the RGH and 4 CLY had run into trouble against Italian artillery and minefields, and 3 CLY, who attacked Gubi from the north-west, suffered heavily from a counter-attack by the Italian 132nd Tank Regiment. That evening the brigade had lost half their tanks, about fifty to the Ariete and over thirty to mechanical faults and breakdowns. 'C' Squadron 4 CLY lost eight out of eleven Crusaders with twenty-one casualties (4 killed in action, 17 taken prisoner). 2 RGH lost over twenty during the day. R. Godwin, 'H' Squadron RGH, commented:

> We lost six officers, 42 men killed or wounded including the CO, Colonel Birley, and our tank strength fell to 19. 'H' Sqn lost 3 tanks but we dealt with 6 Italian M-13s. We had no experience of battle, neither had our Regular Army leader who had spent years on theoretical TEWTS, possibly with horses. We now made what amounted to a cavalry charge on these prepared Italian anti-tank positions. We went in at Regimental strength and by dark we were reduced to about squadron strength . . . we were 'green' and without infantry support to take prisoners; the Italian anti-tank gunners reassumed their positions, went into action again, putting us in a crossfire position.

The Axis wireless communiqué that night claimed 'the annihilation of the British 22nd Armoured Brigade'. However the battered brigade was ordered east to join up with 4th Armoured Brigade.

Rommel ordered the Italian Ariete Division to attack the newly arrived South African Brigade and break through them to join the German forces at Sidi Rezegh. Lieutenant Stewart, 11th Hussars, was involved, arriving in the middle of the Ariete/South African battle:

> It was a huge lake of mud . . . in the middle M.13 tanks stuck, wrecked and ablaze. . . . Italians, some lying, some kneeling, crouched as if to escape notice, some advancing to be captured. I took on three when someone opened up on me, fortunately without harm, the bullet hitting the front of the turret below my face. Then there was a crash and 2-pounder shell hit the side of my car, not coming through and not touching a single one of the men who were clinging to it. [There would have been nine in all on board by this time.] I moved . . . and sailed cheerfully in past a thin, single line of men in tiny pits to find myself among

the South Africans. Glad to be alive and mildly stimulated we made tea, mended the car and handed over our prisoners.

By this time on the 21st both 4th and 22nd Armoured Brigades were in contact with the enemy around Gabr Saleh. General Cunningham had approved General Norrie, XXX Corps Commander's plan to push on to Tobruk without waiting for the 1st South African Division to come up. The Tobruk Garrison (70th Division) were ordered to break out on the 21st at dawn while the Desert Rats Support Group and 7th Armoured Brigade struck north from Sidi Rezegh to link up. At the same time Brigadier Davy had to send 7th Hussars and 2 RTR to fend off two large German armoured columns approaching from the south-east, leaving only 6 RTR to join the Support Group's attack. Lieutenant-Colonel Lister, their CO, Major Warren, the 2 i/c, both squadron commanders 'B' and 'C' were killed in the RTR's 'Charge of the Light Brigade' in their attack north to meet the Tobruk force at El Duda. By the end of the day 6 RTR were reduced to only seventeen tanks under command of Captain Longworth, 'A' Squadron. They had suffered heavily, but the 7th Hussars had been overwhelmed in a fierce fight with 21st Panzer Division.

Lieutenant-Colonel Byass had taken the 7th Hussars south-east to intercept a German force of about fifty tanks which were accompanied and sometimes preceded by anti-tank guns mingled with captured British trucks and lorries. Soon 'A' Squadron was overwhelmed, 'B' was heavily engaged and had considerable casualties. By 1800 hrs Major Fosdick, with only ten old veteran A-10 tanks, had survived and leaguered at Bir Sidi Reghem el Gharbi. Sixteen Hussars had been killed, including the CO, about thirty wounded and another thirty missing.

2 RTR, under Lieutenant-Colonel Chute, tackled about 100 tanks of 15th Panzer Division; he ordered Major Woollcombe, OC 'B' Squadron, and Major Rudkin, OC 'C' Squadron, to make a converging attack from the right and left flank. This is Rudkin's account of the action:

Before fire could be opened, the enemy sighted us and at once turned about and retired at high speed. Many of the enemy tanks were MkII's, though there were large numbers of MkIII's and IV's in the rear. 'B' and 'C' Squadrons at once gave chase and slowly closed the gap between the two forces. At this stage 'A' Squadron also joined the chase between 'C' Squadron on the left and 'B' Squadron on the right. Some excellent shooting was had by all and a total of fifteen enemy tanks were knocked out, many of the crews being overrun and captured. Enemy fire was poor, and it was obvious that they were not adept at firing on the move, because what return of fire there was, was extremely inaccurate. Had our tanks been fitted with stabilisers, there is little doubt that many more enemy tanks would have been knocked out. However, the chase covered about two miles but was called off when the enemy were seen to retire behind a screen of 88mm guns and other tanks in hull-down positions. This action, which was most successful, raised morale to a very high level, as only one of our tanks had been hit and the crew of this escaped unhurt.

By nightfall 7th Armoured Brigade had only ten 7th Hussar 'runners', six of 2 RTR, one of 6 RTR and three of Brigade HQ – many of these had been hit several times. The brigade fitters worked through the night and had twenty-eight 'runners' by the dawn. But during the 21st and 22nd Rommel had reinforced the Sidi Rezegh area and the tide was turning in his favour.

The first battle for Sidi Rezegh produced – uniquely and incredibly – three Victoria Crosses for the Desert Rats. The 3rd RHA anti-tank guns, many on portees, were supporting 2nd Rifle Brigade on the southern escarpment at Sidi Rezegh. The RA historian wrote 'Sixteen tanks appeared over a ridge moving slowly westwards about 800 yards away into the valley to the north-east. The two 2-pounders on the ridge to the north under command of 2/Lt Ward Gunn, 3 RHA opened fire on them.' One of Gunn's guns was soon put out of action, and when the crew of the second had all been killed or wounded the driver began backing the portee away. The battery commander, Major Bernard Pinney, arrived on the scene. Pinney, Ward Gunn and the wounded driver cleared the 2-pounders. Ward Gunn fired between 40 and 50 rounds at a range of about 800 yards. Two enemy tanks were hit and set on fire and others damaged before he fell dead, shot through the forehead. The motorised infantry of the 7th Armoured Support Group were in action almost non-stop. Three companies of 1st King's Royal Rifle Corps, with tanks on each flank and carrier platoons in front, launched an early morning attack on the south of the airfield against Axis infantry well dug in along the line of the escarpment ahead. Rifleman John Beeley in the final assault, with all but one of his officers killed and many ORs of his company, got to his feet and with a Bren gun ran thirty yards towards a strong anti-tank gun post (with two MGs) and killed all seven of the defenders. Beeley was killed by a grenade and won a posthumous VC.

Lieutenant-Colonel Pete Pyman, who later commanded 3 RTR, was at Major-General 'Strafer' Gott's 7th Armoured Division HQ and wrote the following account of Operation Crusader:

I do not believe that the first battle of Sidi Rezegh will ever be told with complete accuracy. All the confusions of a battle, that came to be known as the Battle of the Whirlwind, can never be unfolded now. Yet, historically, it is most important; it was our first great tank *v.* tank battle. Hitherto, from Cambrai onwards – around the anniversary of which Sidi Rezegh was fought – armour had often, virtually unchallenged, dominated a battlefield. At Sidi Rezegh both sides had large armoured forces, highly trained and of comparable strength and equipment. A great armoured clash was bound to ensue and it was right that the Royal Tank Regiment should be present in great strength.

The compass of the battlefield was immense, as the British approach march of 100 miles behind the German outposts shows. But, oddly enough, the territorial key to the battle was quite small, because he who held the escarpment in the area of Sidi Rezegh at the end must win the battle.

The whole battleground was open negotiable desert, but large areas, sometimes flooded and intersected with wadis, sometimes strewn with boulders, scarred with hummocks, soft sand patches and escarpments, greatly reduced the speed of the best cross-country vehicles. Mirage and heavy dust created by continuous movement always made friend extremely difficult to distinguish from foe, and wherever there was fighting there was thick haze. Command and control by wireless from higher headquarters – the only possible means where the distances were so great – was far from perfect, as indeed was the instrument by which that control was exercised. Daylight was comparatively short and night time was bitterly cold.

I was with Strafer Gott for the first four days of the battle. We were mainly with the headquarters of the various brigades in the Sidi Rezegh area. We spent a lot of the time together in his tank. I don't wish to justify the original deployment of 7th Armoured Divison: but I know that once Gott had established 7th Support Group and 7th Armoured Brigade at Sidi Rezegh, his one constant resolve was to concentrate all his armour there.

Several times he nearly did it, but somehow a combination of the enemy, the ground, confusion in dust and interference in communications, always upset his aim. Nights and days slipped by and casualties rose steadily through the Division.

At last, on the afternoon of November 22, the vital concentration was effected. Gott and I were with headquarters of 7th Support Group on the southern edge of Sidi Rezegh airfield. It had been a difficult day with continuous heavy pressure coming against the Support Group precariously holding the centre of our position . . .

The wounded Jock Campbell was rushing around in an open car amidst a shower of bullets inspiring all with acts of great gallantry and with exhortations in the brusque language of the polo ground. Gott stood by his tank – as a symbol of his intention to stand – serious face but calm and collected. He was waiting for the arrival of 4th Armoured Brigade, his last reserve. The strain must have been great, because our force was diminishing visibly as emplacements lapsed into silence and tanks burst into flames. The 2nd and 6th RTR had mere cadres left and the 3rd and 4th CLY, after all their heavy fighting, starting at El Gubi, had become sadly depleted.

Eventually, Alec Gatehouse appeared out of the dust from the south leading the 4th Armoured Brigade with 3rd and 5th RTR at the front. Brief verbal orders from Gott soon saw Gatehouse putting into effect a heavy flank attack with his force of over a hundred Stuart tanks. For a brief while we felt this stroke might win the day.

Brigadier Jock Campbell, RHA, won the Victoria Cross at Sidi Rezegh and urged 2 RTR into the highly confused battle, in his efforts to save 7th Armoured Division Support Group from being overwhelmed. Major Rudkin, OC 'C' Squadron, wrote:

Brigadier Campbell seized Major Rudkin's arm and said 'See that. Attack – and I like speed.' Within three minutes the squadron in line moved off and advanced towards the enemy tanks, Brigadier Campbell travelling with the leading tanks in his staff car. He stood up, waving flags and encouraging the tanks on. The enemy, on seeing this squadron at once wheeled left to about 1,200 yards, during which time enemy shells and tank fire were directed against our tanks. Deeming the distance now close enough for an effective shoot, the squadron slowed down and halted. Brigadier Campbell was very angry, apparently expecting the tanks to carry out a cavalry charge against the enemy, who outnumbered us by more than two to one. . . . One of our tanks had its gun damaged and reversed about 200 yards to put it right. Brigadier Campbell drove over to it, got out of his car, and, livid with rage, threw stones at it, shouting at it to get back into action. After about five minutes, the squadron withdrew about 200 yards by reversing, as the enemy fire was heavy. As 1,400 yards was beyond effective 2-pounder range, the tanks ceased fire, the enemy following suit. Brigadier Campbell drove back to his HQ.

The Squadron had no communications with Support Group or anyone else. The wireless was only netted to all tanks in the squadron. So the squadron was in no position to receive orders from Support Group HQ, being placed about halfway between the Support Group and the enemy forces. The Squadron second-in-command, Captain Plough, was therefore sent back to receive orders. When he reported at the HQ, Brigadier Campbell was still extremely angry that the squadron had not charged right into the enemy. Captain Plough explained that we would have achieved nothing and that it would have been suicide. Whereupon Brigadier Campbell replied, 'That's what you are soldiers for – to die.' He then gave orders that the squadron would hold their present position at all costs. If any tank withdrew a yard, he said, he had given orders for his guns to open fire on it. For the next two hours, the squadron remained in position, praying that the enemy would not advance and feeling more frightened of 'Jock' Campbell and his guns than they did of the enemy. Ammunition was running low and the whole position was most uncomfortable. Eventually a portion of A1 Echelon managed to get through and dump ammunition on the ground, from which each tank in turn refilled.

Just as the last troop of tanks was refilling with ammunition, a lot of firing started up behind in the area of the aerodrome. On looking round, Major Rudkin could see a force of about 80 enemy tanks attacking Support Group from the west, and it had already advanced to within a few hundred yards of the aerodrome. The guns of the Support Group were firing at them over open sights at about 600 yards range. Without waiting for orders, the squadron immediately about turned and joined in the battle on the high ground at the north edge of the aerodrome. The whole scene was like an artist's impression of a battlefield. All 16 enemy aircraft on the landing ground, which we had destroyed three days previously, had caught fire and had destroyed several of our guns which had been in position under or behind the aircraft. Several enemy tanks were ablaze. Round the blazing aircraft were 25-pounders and anti-tank guns firing over open sights.

General Cunningham's orders to 22nd Armoured Brigade were now drastically altered. Instead of joining the forces around Sidi Rezegh airfield their seventy-nine Crusaders were ordered to move as fast as possible eastwards to reinforce Brigadier Gatehouse's brigade of Honeys. The breakout by 70th British Division and 32 Tank Brigade (thirty-two Cruisers and sixty Matildas) was not successful. Rommel himself was personally directing the battle alongside four 88mm anti-tank guns which he had rushed across from Gambut. The five German/Italian defence posts called 'Butch', 'Jill', 'Jack', 'Tiger' and 'Tugun' were protected by minefields, wire and anti-tank ditches and proved difficult to take or bypass.

By mid-afternoon it was clear that El Duda would not be reached, indeed it was doubtful whether the key Sidi Rezegh airfield area could be held. General Auchinleck's final despatch, written later, follows:

> The enemy as was to be expected, reacted at once to the threat to Sidi Rezegh and his armoured divisions evaded [*sic*] the 4th and 22nd Armoured Brigades. The whole of the enemy armour then combined to drive us from this vital area and to prevent help reaching the [7th Armoured Division] Support Group and the 7th Armoured Brigade which were isolated there. Neither of these formations was designed to carry out a prolonged defence and it is greatly to their credit that they managed to do so, unaided, throughout the 21st.

Rommel managed to concentrate his forces. Major General 'Strafer' Gott, GOC, 7th Armoured Division, was fighting two quite separate battles, 30 miles apart. He could not exercise close control as a result. Brigadiers Gatehouse (4th Brigade) and Scott-Cockburn (22nd Brigade) spent the night of the 21st preparing battle positions for the morrow. To their surprise at dawn on the next day the Afrika Korps was seen at speed in the far distance heading north-west. Despite a vigorous pursuit in which 22nd Armoured Brigade ran foul of 15th Panzer's 88mms, it appeared that a great victory had been won.

General Auchinleck's despatch continued 'Next day [22nd] all three armoured brigades joined in the defence of the area. But our tanks and anti-tank guns were no match for the Germans, although they were fought with great gallantry and on the evening of the 22nd the XXXth Corps was compelled to retire having lost two thirds of its tanks and leaving the garrison of Tobruk with a huge salient to defend.' By daybreak on the 23rd, 22nd Armoured Brigade were down to fifteen tanks and 4th Armoured Brigade was widely scattered.

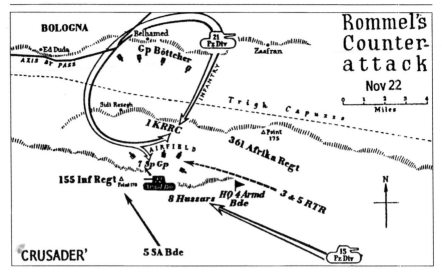

Rommel's Counter Attack, 22 November 1941.

Just before dusk on the 22nd Oberstleutnant Cramer was leading Panzer Regiment 8 of Neumann-Sylkow's 15th Panzer Division, and by sheer bad luck chanced on Brigade HQ of 4th Armoured. The Panzers put on their headlights, surrounding the British in leaguer and captured Brigadier Gatehouse's 2 i/c (Gatehouse was away), 17 officers and 150 other ranks. In addition an armoured command vehicle and no fewer than 35 AFVs, including tanks, armoured cars, guns and self-propelled guns, were captured. According to German sources most of them were from 8th Hussars. It was a humiliating blow. On their way Panzer Regiment 8 brushed aside some 5 RTR tanks trying to rescue Brigade HQ.

General Auchinleck's final despatch continues the story. 'On the 23rd Rommel practically annihilated the 5th South African Infantry Brigade, one of the *only* two infantry brigades General Norrie had under command. Then on the 24th with his armoured divisions he made a powerful stroke to the frontier.' The 'AUK' then made the point that enemy tank losses had been *grossly* exaggerated, 'he had at least as many tanks as we had, and better, and was in a position to recover more from the battlefield, which remained in his hands.'

Many of the shattered tank regiments of 7th Armoured Division were now reduced to a composite squadron. Major Yule commanded 2 RTR's only squadron. The 7th Hussar's only ten tanks were split up, some going to HQ 7th Armoured Division, others to 22nd Armoured Brigade. A composite regiment of 22nd Armoured Brigade had thirty-three tanks under Major J. Dickens, 3rd CLY, and on 23 November (with 'C' Battery 4 RHA), they were ordered to protect the rearguard withdrawal of the 5th South African Brigade against some seventy tanks of 15th Panzer Division.

On 23 November 5th RTR were inactive all day on the southern edge of the battle area. At 1000 hrs Lieutenant-Colonel Drew, their CO, informed Brigadier Gatehouse (whose HQ was near the 8th Hussars) 'that the South Africans were engaged about 5 miles to the NW, suggested we [5 RTR] should move forward to their assistance. Answer was to wait where we were until further orders owing to the threat from the south. The Bn with 2 RHA in support remained in this area until about 1615 hrs. During this period the Bn was ordered to the assistance of the South Africans on three occasions and on each occasion the order was cancelled.' At the time 5 RTR, with twenty-three battleworthy tanks, was the stronger of the two regiments in 4th Armoured Brigade. The South African Brigade suffered heavily from lack of tank support.

Three times that morning the South Africans and the 22nd flung back savage attacks before the afternoon brought unexpected enemy reinforcements. By nightfall both brigades were almost wiped out, having claimed to have knocked out fifty-two of the DAK and Ariete M-13s. Sunday 23 November was *Totensonntag*, when German protestants prayed for the souls of the dead.

Over seventy Panzers had been knocked out during the *Totensonntag* day of furious fighting. Panzer Regiment 8, Reconnaissance Battalion 33 and Rifle Regiment 115 had been decimated. General von Ravenstein's 21 Panzer Division now had only nineteen Mk II and IIIs and only one Mk IV battleworthy and 15 Panzer Division had suffered badly on the 23rd. Rommel now made his famous and bold 'Dash for the Wire' aiming for Sidi Omar and Halfaya Pass, to cut off the New Zealander and Indian formations around

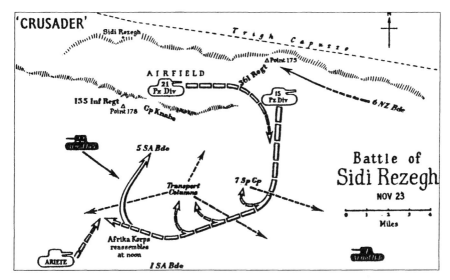

The First Battle of Sidi Rezegh, 23 November 1941.

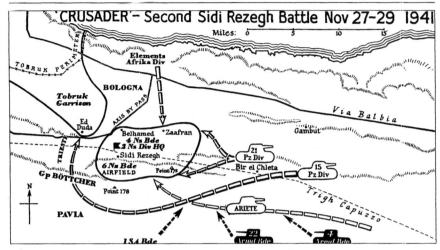

Operation Crusader. The Second Battle of Sidi Rezgh, 27–9 November 1941.

Bardia and Sollum. The three Axis armoured divisions (with Ariete) smashed every formation in their way through Bir Berraneb, Bir Taieb el Esem and Gabr Saleh. They crashed through South African and British echelons and supply columns, pushing aside XXX Corps HQ, 7th Armoured Division's surviving units, 1st South African Division and spreading chaos under Erwin Rommel's eager eye in his Mammoth command (a captured British HQ vehicle possibly belonging to General O'Connor). 'Rommel's Swan' or 'the Matruh Stakes' were other terms used for this depressing scenario. Alexander Clifford and Alan Moorehead were caught up in the 'Gazala Gallop':

> We were being followed and fast. So the hue and cry went on again. Occasionally vehicles around us ran on to mines or were hit by shells or were simply fired by their bewildered drivers who believed the enemy to be upon them. Everyone ran to their places and the stampede began again. All day for nine hours we ran. It was the contagion of bewilderment and fear and ignorance. Rumour spread at every halt, no man had orders.

General Auchinleck relieved General Cunningham on 26 November and appointed General Neil Ritchie in his place. By the following day 7th Armoured Division, by dint of excellent recovery work on the battlefields, had retrieved and repaired 119 battleworthy tanks, 77 Honeys to Gatehouse's 4th Armoured Brigade and 42 assorted cruisers to 22nd Armoured Brigade. 7th Armoured Brigade – tankless – were reformed in the New Year and sent to fight in Burma.

By the morning of the 27th the 100 7th Armoured Division tanks were harrying the Axis supply columns and threatening to cut off the rear of Rommel's leading units. His great advance had petered out. During the night the New Zealand 4 and 6 Brigades, pushing west from Gambut, had captured Sidi Rezegh (a large bare patch of desert now littered with the debris of war) and linked up at El Duda with the Tobruk Garrison.

A captured A–15 tank used by the Germans. *Major Norman Plough*

Oberleutnant Heinz Schmidt, commanding rearguard units of 15th Panzer noted that 'The desert was alive with small mobile columns of the enemy – "Jock" columns they were called which were a nuisance as mosquitoes are but in the end no more violent in their sting!' There were isolated successes. On 30 November 5 RTR with their twenty-six Stuarts fell on an Italian tank group and knocked out thirteen M-13s and five light tanks without loss to themselves. From 28 November to 1 December Major General Freyberg's New Zealand Division, with 4 RTR Matildas and RHA support, spent three days locked in combat with Rommel's Panzers who had retreated from the 'Wire'. By 1 December the New Zealanders were in desperate straits with not much help from the British armour or the South African brigade. Rommel reckoned that during twelve days the Axis troops had destroyed 814 enemy AFVs, shot down 127 aircraft and taken prisoner 9,000, including three generals (two brigadiers and a full colonel actually). Rommel thought he had won. He even proposed a second 'Dash to the Wire' with battlegroups heading for Bardia and Sidi Azeiz, although his staff brought him up to date – 142 Panzer tanks, 25 armoured cars, 390 lorries destroyed and nearly 4,000 casualties incurred.

Sidi Rezegh had been recaptured, but the 6th New Zealand Brigade was crippled and the New Zealanders suffered 3,000 casualties. Tobruk was once again isolated. But behind him Rommel was told of the ravages the British Navy had been making on seaborne supplies; nearly 60,000 tons had been sunk in November. He was told categorically no more men, or tanks, or aircraft, little ammunition and only 2,500 tons of fuel. Two of his key commanders were out of action – von Ravenstein captured and the faithful Walther Neumann-Sylkow was badly wounded and died in Derna Hospital. On 15 December 15th Panzer, still full of fight, beat back a XXX Corps attack at Alam Hanza.

Towards the end of Crusader, Alan Moorehead and Alexander Clifford, with Randolph Churchill, visited the Sidi Rezegh battlefield. According to Alan Moorehead:

> Every few hundred yards there were graves – the dead man's belt or perhaps his helmet flung down on top of the fresh earth and over it a cross made of bits of packing case. Sometimes there were mingled German and British graves as though the men had gone down together, still locked in fighting. Sometimes the dead were laid alongside the blackened hulks of their burnt out tanks. The tanks themselves still smouldered and smelt evilly. Their interior fittings had been dragged out like the entrails of some wounded animal.

Churchill wrote, 'Here then we reached a moment of relief. The German records show the gloom that had descended on military circles in Rome.' He gave praise to the Desert Rats. 'Rommel fought his way back to Sidi Rezegh, attacked in the flank by the reorganised 7th Armoured Division.' During the night of 16/17 December Rommel sent the Afrika Korps and the Italian armour diagonally south-west to Mechili and Msus and the Italian infantry west along the coast roads – in full and well organised retreat.

Operation Crusader was over, although the retreating Axis forces twice mauled 22nd Armoured Brigade (plus 3 RTR), once at Antelat and on 28 and 29 December, knocking out *sixty* tanks around Agedabia. Rommel had not been defeated. It was simply that his lines of communication were too long and his vital trans-Mediterranean supplies were so reduced as to force a retreat.

Final Casualty Figures for Operation Crusader

	Killed	Wounded	Missing	Total
Commonwealth	2,900	7,300	7,500	17,700
German	1,200	3,300	10,100	14,600
Italian	1,100	2,800	19,800	23,700
Axis losses	2,300	6,100	29,900	38,300

Alan Moorehead wrote:

> It was very near the point where one side or the other must collapse through sheer exhaustion. Some five or six hundred tanks had fought one another to destruction or impotency. Just a few were left on either side. The hard armoured coating of both armies was destroyed. The softer slower infantry was exposed at last and left to decide the battle. The Eighth Army had come out of its mortal crisis and had gathered its second wind. The first stage of the battle was over. No one could say clearly yet who had won. British, Germans and Italians lay around Tobruk too exhausted to go on, almost too tired to pick up the spoils of war.

CHAPTER NINE

The Green Jerboa Desert Rats in Burma

At the end of 1941 it was known that 7th Armoured Brigade, under the command of Brigadier J. Anstice DSO, was destined for the Far East theatre of war. The brigade, soon to wear the Jerboa divisional sign, but with the background colour changed to jungle green, was composed of 7th Queen's Own Hussars (CO Lieutenant-Colonel F.R.C. Fosdick, 2 i/c Major Roland Younger), 2nd Bn Royal Tank Regt (initially CO Lieutenant-Colonel R.F. Chute DSO, and in March 1942, Lieutenant-Colonel G.F. Yule), the 414 Battery RHA (Essex Yeomanry) 25-pounder guns, plus RAOC and RASC support troops. Equipped with fairly new American Stuart (Honey) light tanks (37mm AP gun and two .30 MGs) they set sail, with their 115 tanks aboard 7 transport ships. The 'A' vehicles were in HMT *Mariso*, HMT *Birch Bank*, HMT *African Prince* and HMT *Trojan*. Most personnel of 2 RTR were aboard HMT *Ascanius*. It was to be a voyage of 4,600 miles through the Suez Canal and Red Sea to Aden, and eventually across the Indian Ocean to Rangoon. Initially they were destined for Singapore, but Malaya was attacked by the Japanese at the same time as Pearl Harbor on 7 December, and by mid-January 1942 the situation in Johore was desperate. Their convoy was then routed to Java and Winston Churchill wrote to the US President: 'General Wavell has very rightly diverted our Armoured Brigade which should reach there [Rangoon] on the 20th instant' [February].

The Japanese had started their advance towards Burma from Siam [Thailand] on 16 January, took Kawkareik and captured Moulmein, 100 miles due east of Rangoon across the Gulf of Martaban. The Burma Rifles garrison mostly escaped from Moulmein by ferry on 21 January. Captain James Lunt had recently joined the Burma Rifles. He had arrived in Rangoon in March 1939 and quickly found that the Burmese were

a jolly crew until they were crossed or became panicky when they could be both treacherous and brutally cruel. No Burmese worth his salt ever became truly reconciled to foreign rule. Unfortunately it had been Indian soldiers and in their train tens of thousands of Indian coolies and moneylenders, who had played the principal part in conquering Burma for the British. The great British trading houses controlled the timber, mines and oil, Indians and Chinese the rice trade and the Chinese were the traders and entrepreneurs. The dentists were Japanese doubling up as spies!

Tanks negotiating a Burmese river. *Major Norman Plough*

It was definitely not good tank country. The country has two substantial rivers running north and south, the great Irrawaddy and, 50 miles to the east, the Sittang. The few roads and tracks went through rice paddy fields, underwater in the rainy season and baked hard in summer (but with many banks and obstructions). And beyond the paddy fields was the jungle, almost impenetrable for tanks.

Captain James Lunt described the retreat between Kyaikto and Mokpalin on the east side of the Sittang River:

The single track, unsurfaced, pock-marked with bomb craters, barely wide enough for one vehicle to pass another, with those carrying wounded to be given priority, was hedged in by jungle so thick that men easily became lost if they wandered far from the track. Control over any sub-unit much larger than platoon was virtually impossible. There were no 'walkie-talkies' and communications depended mostly on 'runners' many of whom lost their way. It was blazingly hot and water bottles were soon emptied. No one knew anything about the enemy but rumours abounded, last night he had been howling round the flanks, making the night hideous with his yells and mortar bombs; today he had simply vanished into thin air.

The breakdown in communications meant that Division HQ was out of touch with its own brigade and with Burma Army HQ.

The three British-Indian brigades of 17th Division were forced back from the River Bilin line 70 miles north-west of Moulmein and fought their way through dense jungle and rubber plantations to Kyaikto. Their opponents were the Japanese 213 and 214 infantry regiments who reached Mokpalin 3 miles south of the huge 500-yard long vital bridge across the River Sittang. The 46th and 16th Brigades were surrounded, and the bridgehead defenders were attacked by the Japanese 215th Infantry Regiment suddenly appearing from the right flank. By a whole series of tragic decisions, disaster occurred. Brigadier Taffy Davies, Chief of Staff to Lieutenant-General T.J. Hutton, GOC Burma, wrote that

> A terrible decision had to be made by [Major-General Jacky] Smythe [GOC 17th Division]. If he blew the bridge, he sacrificed the bulk of his division. If he failed to blow the bridge and it was secured intact by the enemy the way to Rangoon lay open with nothing interposing. General Smythe blew the bridge. In my opinion a heroic and inevitable decision.

It was blown on 23 February and of the original 12 battalions only 80 British officers, 69 Indian and Gurkha officers and 3,335 other ranks escaped. Churchill wrote 'this was a major disaster.'

On 16 February Churchill wrote to Sir R. Dorman-Smith, Governor of Burma. 'Now that Singapore has fallen more weight will assuredly be put into the attack upon you. Substantial reinforcements including the Armoured Brigade and two additional squadrons of Hurricanes should reach you soon. I regard Burma and contact with China as the most important feature in the whole [Eastern] theatre of war. All good wishes.' Apart from the survivors of the 17th Division there was only the 1st Burma Division left to try and retain the whole of Burma. The 7th Armoured Brigade convoy arrived in Rangoon harbour two days before the disaster of the Sittang bridge. Churchill went on to write in his memoirs: 'There was now only the defence line of the Pegu river between the Japanese and Rangoon. Here the remnants of the 17th Division with their 1,400 rifles and a few machine guns were joined by three British battalions from India and by 7th British Armoured Brigade, newly arrived from the Middle East on their way to Java. *This brigade played an invaluable part in all the later fighting.'*

Brigadier Anstice had flown on ahead, met the convoy on arrival and told his senior officers that the Japanese did not have an adequate anti-tank gun, and their Type 94 Tankette, Type 95 light tanks were few in numbers and of poor quality. All the Burmese dock labourers had fled after days of Japanese bombing, and the unloading of tanks, lorries, guns, ammunition and other supplies was undertaken by the troops. Captain Reverend Metcalfe, the 7th Hussars' chaplain, promptly visited Rangoon Zoo in search of fresh meat. He found a boa constrictor, a crocodile and a lively orangutan. But abandoned RAF lorries and plenty of cigarettes and spirits from bonded warehouses along the docks were soon 'discovered'. Sergeant Ken Chadwick, historian of 2 RTR, wrote 'Although Rangoon harbour was deserted of civilians and dockers, the town became our OFP, NAAFI and Woolworth's in our first week ashore.' Initially the brigade leaguer was in a large rubber plantation 15 miles north of Rangoon.

The Japanese XV Army, under General Iida, consisted of two divisions, the 33rd and 55th Infantry, who, thwarted by the demolitions of the key Sittang bridge had moved north to Kunzeik and Donzayit respectively without any opposition. Then they crossed the River Sittang by ferry heading west and south towards Rangoon. The remnants of the 17th Indian Division were reforming around Pegu. The Armoured Brigade was soon in action. 'B' Squadron 2 RTR (OC Major J. Bonham-Carter) was hurried forward on 23 February to Waw, 20 miles north-east of Pegu and 'C' Squadron (OC Major M.F.S. Rudkin) took over two days later. He burned the deserted village in order to defend a wooden bridge. The following night a KOYLI sergeant, disguised as a Burmese, escaped from the Sittang debacle, and told Rudkin that two Japanese forces were on the move to outflank Waw. An hour later several hundred Japanese arrived at the canal, so Rudkin ordered the bridge to be blown. The next day 'A' Squadron (OC Major N.H. Bourne), patrolling with the Cameronians north of Payagyi, killed fourteen Burmese 'dacoits' armed with Japanese weapons. On 1 March 'B' Squadron moved towards Tazon, and 'C' Squadron towards Waw. Battalion HQ moved to Payagyi, newly equipped with No. 19 wireless sets. The next day Second Lieutenant Yates's troop patrolled an irrigation canal and came under heavy fire from 75mm guns that knocked out two Stuart tanks, killing two troopers and wounding another in a third tank. Troopers Brown and James distinguished themselves. With the West Yorkshires, 2 RTR were in action on the 2nd to try to recapture Waw village, but were not successful. The Japanese resumed their offensive on the night of 3/4 March, and Major Rudkin's squadron were vigorously attacked at first light in heavy mist. Their tanks were surrounded and over-run with yelling Japanese who advanced right up to the tanks, some carrying explosives attached to long poles which they attempted to drop into the turrets. However, the Stuarts MGs and the tank commanders' Tommy guns produced deadly fire. Fortunately, 7th Hussars, who were due to relieve 2 RTR, were now quite close. Major Rudkin wrote:

I therefore gave orders for each tank to find its own way back to RHQ across country. The going was extremely bad and obstacles were tackled for which the tanks could never have been designed. It was a nightmare journey as one could not pick one's route owing to the mist, and the odd sniper who infiltrated across the road behind us kept the heads of the tank commanders down. By a miracle every tank arrived back safely although the crews were bruised and shaken.

Major G.C. Davies-Gilbert, OC 'B' Squadron 7th Hussars, arrived in Payagyi to find the Japanese had already arrived there. Lieutenant G.S.B.

Waw on fire. *Major Norman Plough*

Palmer, a troop leader, wrote 'In thick mist with visibility down to ten yards, wireless communications were appalling. Squadron HQ behind us and the crossroads was under attack from enemy ambush, the first of many we were to be involved in during the next few months.' A small Japanese spotter plane flew over at 500 feet and circled. 'Very soon we came under heavy mortar and artillery fire which was very accurate. One troop leader Lt Patterson and his driver were minor casualties. About 1100 I took up a position on the Payagyi crossroads to keep the village under observation. It was now appallingly hot. The crews could not dismount. We felt like fried eggs in a pan.' 'A' Squadron, under Major C.T. Llewellen Palmer, helped their infantry clear Japanese infiltrators from a wood, and two Type 95 Japanese tanks appeared in the areas and were engaged by Captain Marcus Fox. 'They appeared to be very lonely and untrained, and obviously did not know what to do, remaining stationary in the middle of an open field. They were knocked out immediately before they knew we were there. Their tanks were very much the same as the Honey (Stuart) and obviously copied from an American design; indeed they carried cans of American oil.'

Colonel Fosdick, CO 7th Hussars, had his Stuart tank hit by anti-tank fire which blew off a track, and a 'B' Squadron tank was also hit and disabled. Major Davies-Gilbert sent Lieutenant Palmer and his troop to assist 7th Hussars RHQ and all three tanks were hit repeatedly by four anti-tank guns man-handled into position in the night. Captain Shorten, the FOO of the Essex Yeomanry, put down a 'stonk' on the enemy, and Lieutenant M.M.

Stanley-Evans, 'A' Squadron, with a company of West Yorkshire infantry, mounted an attack which captured the Japanese anti-tank guns, inflicting heavy casualties. Soon three Type 95 Japanese tanks approached and were engaged by Lieutenants Barton and Stanley-Evans's troops from hull-down positions. Two Type 95s were knocked out at 1,000 yards range and the third abandoned by its crew. This success for the 7th Hussars was saddened by the death of Lieutenant Glendinning by a stray shell on the afternoon of 6 March. The 7th Hussars were ordered to retire through Pegu to rejoin the rest of 7th Armoured Brigade at Hlegu.

Lieutenant G.S.B. Palmer wrote:

We arrived in the town as darkness was falling. The town had been severely bombed and the whole place was blazing from end to end. However, we were lucky as the only bridge was still standing. Meanwhile the enemy had erected a road block three miles south west of the town and we halted while 'A' Squadron moved down to the block to ascertain its strength. Apparently it was quite impossible to get through and probes were made in various directions to get round the flanks but all were considered impossible.

Colonel Fosdick decided to move the regiment closer to the road block and leaguer for the night. While we were going into harbour Bill Kevill-Davies was killed by small-arms fire. He was buried in the leaguer which was an extremely sticky area in the heart of the enemy positions. As a night attack was expected we had to stay in the tanks and spent one of the most harassing nights I can remember in the war. Dawn was most welcome. In fact the only trouble we had was from a most searching mortar fire that continued spasmodically throughout the night. The 'B' vehicles, however, did suffer considerably. An 'O' group first thing in the morning decided that the block should be cleared by a company of infantry supported by one troop. I was the lucky individual selected to support this attack.

We set off after 7 a.m., and as we reached the road we were submerged by a panic-stricken mob of fugitives in complete disarray. They looked like wrecking the whole operation and it was impossible to move without running them down. Eventually I had to threaten to open fire, but the Japs did the job for me.

We had Noel Shorten of the Essex Yeomanry with us as OP and moved towards the road block with Sergeant Davis leading the way. On coming round a bend we suddenly came up against the road block which consisted of two lorries drawn across the road and another obstruction some 300 yards farther down the road. The country on either side was heavily wooded and there was no way round. We succeeded in partly moving the lorries with the tanks and immediately came under a hail of small-arms fire.

We took up a fire position and gave the whole area a ten minute pasting with the Brownings. While this was going on the infantry most gallantly cleared the block and the Essex Yeomanry put down a concentration on the area.

In the middle of all this I suddenly saw a bottle hit the side of Davis's tank and burst into flames – some kind of molotov cocktail. No damage was done and we shuffled forward, constantly changing, and eventually having Corporal Barr's tank knocked out, again by a molotov cocktail, although he and his crew got clear. My radio aerial was shot away and I lost contact with the regiment. I signalled to Noel that I would push on to the next block. We moved fast under heavy fire and were relieved to find it clear. As we passed through my tank was hit by an HE shell which exploded in my valise on the outside of the tank. I was mortified to see my bedding and spare kit disintegrate in all directions.

The infantry had given us most gallant support and cleared the jungle on either side. The company commander had been severely wounded during the engagement. Having got through the road block I had not a clue what was going on and decided to push on with my troop until I could rig an emergency aerial. We stopped a few miles up the road where we linked up with a patrol of 2 RTR and also with John Parry's troop which had escorted a brigadier through the block the previous night. I still could not contact squadron HQ and was getting very worried when suddenly the first of the column started to come through. The squadron had got out of a sticky position very lightly with only one man killed and few wounded.

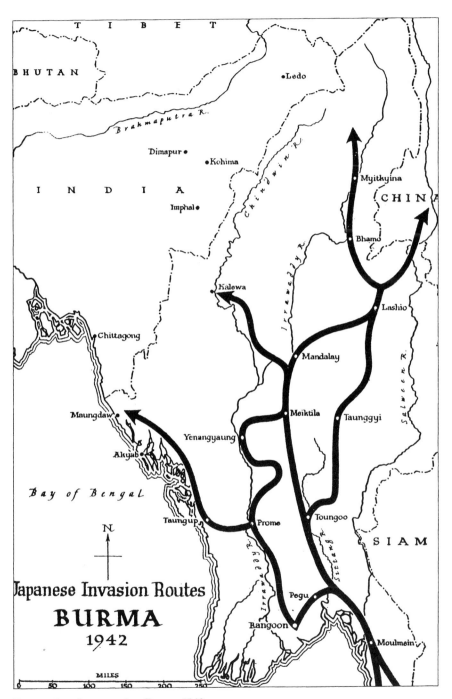

Japanese invasion routes into Burma, 1942.

Captain Reverend Metcalfe, chaplain 7th Hussars, was awarded an immediate DSO. In Pegu the Cameronians and West Yorkshires suffered casualties in their rearguard action. In their combined RAP Metcalfe and Padre Funnell had been helping the wounded all day under vigorous Japanese sniper fire. A convoy of wounded in ambulances and lorries set off with a rearguard of Cameronians under Major Magnus Grey. Metcalfe wrote:

> Heavy Jap fire compelled us to take cover under the last few lorries of the convoy, all of which were quickly put out of action. Retreating down the road we came upon the scene of the road block which had been broken earlier that morning by the tanks of the regiment [7th Hussars]. It was a scene of indescribable carnage: burnt-out lorries piled together with the dead crews hanging grotesquely out of the driving cabs.

A mortar shell hit the lorry blowing Metcalfe into a ditch. He escaped unhurt, but Padre Funnell was later ambushed and butchered in cold blood near Prome. Brigadier Anstice ordered 7th Hussars to proceed north to a rubber plantation near Taukkyon.

Winston Churchill had sent General Harold Alexander to take supreme command of all forces actually in Burma, although the abrasive and difficult American general, Joseph Stilwell ('Vinegar Joe'), commanding the Vth and VIth Chinese Armies already in eastern Burma, disputed the command situation. Soon after his arrival on 5 March Alexander realised that Rangoon was doomed. He ordered all surviving forces to cut their way northward through many roadblocks to reach Prome 200 miles north of Rangoon. Alexander also gave orders for the destruction of the great oil refineries at Rangoon.

Twenty-four miles north of the city at Taukkyon the Japanese 33rd Division, moving swiftly from east to west in its drive to capture Rangoon, had erected a formidable road block across the main road. With two 75mm guns and several machine-guns firing from the flanks it was a tough nut to crack. Waiting to get through the road block (it could not be bypassed) were most of 17th Indian Division, all of 7th Armoured Brigade and General Alexander and his entire Army HQ. Lieutenant-Colonel Fosdick, CO 7th Hussars, sent Lieutenant Basil Young's troop of 'B' Squadron with infantry support to clear the block. The Stuart tank was hit by a 75mm shell and the infantry took heavy casualties. The Essex Yeomanry guns then supported Major Bonham-Carter's 'D' Squadron, 2 RTR, with 1st Gloucesters – they failed too. General Alexander even suggested to Lieutenant-General Hutton that the British troops might disperse and try to fight their way north *through the jungle*. A third attack was planned for dawn with 'A' Squadron 7th Hussars, 1/10 Gurkhas, 1/11 Sikhs under RAF bombing and all artillery available in support. At first light on 8 March Major Bonham-Carter, 2 RTR, discovered that the enemy had gone. This was one of the classic military blunders of the war. General Iida's master plan was for Rangoon to be captured from the west. He was sure the British/Indian forces would stay and fight for Rangoon, as he would have done in similar circumstances. So after General Sakurai, GOC, the Japanese 33rd Infantry Division, had very efficiently blocked the main road, and *after* passing his whole formation across it at Taukkyan, he 'obeyed' his rigid orders and abandoned their roadblocks. General Sakurai was astonished to find Rangoon undefended and the city empty. The huge column of British and Indian formations retreating from Rangoon were equally astonished at being given a head start. Most of 2 RTR were still in the Hlegu area south of Taukkyan. When 'B' Squadron's attack on the roadblock failed, a possible escape route *on foot* to Bassein, in the hope of finding boats or a ferry there, was planned, but fortunately not needed. Captain James Lunt, Burma Rifles, met a 2 RTR trooper and asked him how the fighting in Burma compared with his experiences in North Africa. 'Much the same amount of shit flying around, but the trouble with these Japanese bastards is that they don't run away like the Italians.'

2 RTR tankcrew in Burmese jungle, April 1942. *Tank Museum*

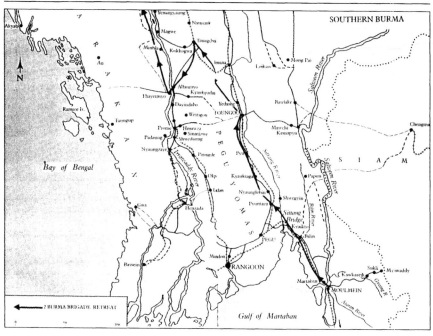

The 2nd Burma Brigade retreat.

Churchill wrote:

> The Japanese did not press our northward retreat, after the severe fighting and heavy
> casualties and long marches they had made. The Burma division fought a steady delaying
> action back to Toungoo [100 miles north of Pegu] while the 17th Division and the
> Armoured Brigade moved by easy stages to Prome [70 miles west of Toungoo on the River
> Irrawaddy].

The main rearguard were 2 RTR. During the next week the withdrawal
continued via Gyobingauk, Paundge and Wettigan. On 13 March
Lieutenant-General Bill Slim, appointed by Wavell as the new Corps
Commander, arrived at Prome for his first conference with Major-General
Bruce Scott, GOC, 1st Burma Division, and Major-General 'Punch'
Cowan, GOC, 17th Indian Division. All three had served together in the 6th
Gurkhas and knew each other well. General Alexander then gave his orders
to Slim's 1st Burma Corps. Five days later 7th Armoured Brigade and 17th
Division halted in the Nattalin area (20 miles south-east of Prome) to cover
the concentration of 1st Burmese Division at Prome. Meanwhile only one
division of the Chinese V Army had reached Toungoo in the River Sittang
valley, the rest of the V and VI Army slowly following behind them. Captain
James Lunt described the Chinese

> as unreliable. They had no logistics worth the name and time meant nothing to them. They
> travelled the country like the Tartar hordes looting, stealing and burning. No Chinese general

felt bound to carry out an order with which he disagreed. Their discipline was rough and ready. Very few Chinese spoke English, none of us spoke Chinese. They demolished bridges and constructed road blocks through which the British and Indian formations would travel. Along the road to Prome the 40-mile long convoy of 1,400 British and Indian vehicles were held up from time to time by roadblocks made up of tar barrels, felled trees and overturned captured lorries defended by field guns on both sides. Only determined 'hook' attacks around the flanks were likely to succeed.

Lieutenant-General Bill Slim visited all the troops under his command:

Brigadier Anstice's 7th Armoured Brigade was also under Cowan's command and I was delighted to see it and note its condition. Its two regiments of light tanks, American Stuarts or Honeys mounting as they did only a two-pounder [37mm] gun and having very thin armour which any anti-tank weapon would pierce, were by no means ideal for the sort of close fighting the terrain required. Any weakness in the tanks however was made up by the crews. The 7th Hussars and 2nd Royal Tank Regiment were as good British troops as I had seen anywhere. They had had plenty of fighting in the Western Desert before coming to Burma and they looked what they were – confident, experienced, tough soldiers. Their supporting units, 414 Battery RHA, 'A' Battery 95 Anti-tank Regt and 1st Bn West Yorkshire Regt were up to their standard.

General Slim made a careful assessment of the situation, including 'our first intimation of a Japanese move was usually the stream of red tracer bullets and the animal yells that announced their arrival on our flank or rear', and 'the Japanese were obviously able to move for several days at a time through jungle that we had regarded as impenetrable. They had developed the art of the road block to perfection. We seemed to have no answer to it'.

Slim now tried to concentrate his two divisions, Cowan's 17th near and around Prome with 7th Armoured Brigade with the reserve infantry brigade in the rear at Nattalin. In Taungdwingyi were 75,000 gallons of high-octane fuel for the Stuarts. Slim thought that the country immediately south of Prome would be suitable tank country. On 20 March the Chinese Army launched an attack to prevent the Burma Road being cut, but four days later their 200th Division of V Army in Toungoo was suddenly cut off by the Japanese 55th Division. On the 28th Alexander asked Slim to take the offensive to relieve pressure on the Chinese. Cowan then sent Brigadier Anstice with 7th Hussars, two troops of Essex Yeomanry, three infantry battalions, including the Gloucesters, to re-occupy Paungde and advance on Okpo, both on the main road and railway line 25 and 50 miles south of Prome. Two thousand Japanese held Paungde, and after initial success the British/Indian brigade was driven out after inflicting heavy casualties. However, worse was to come. A strong Japanese force had appeared in Shwedaung only 10 miles south of Prome, thus cutting off Brigadier Anstice's withdrawal. Cowan sent two Indian battalions to clear Shwedaung from the north. Just after 1800 hrs Anstice's advance guard launched an attack – which failed – and two more attacks were also repulsed. During the morning of the 30th the 7th Hussars and infantry burst through the Japanese road blocks in Shwedaung. The town was burning furiously, many trucks were set on fire and Japanese aircraft machine-gunned and bombed

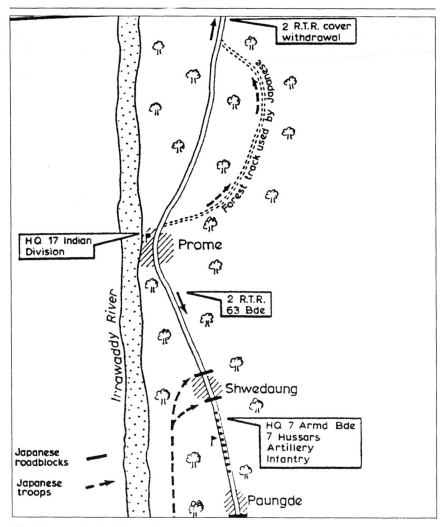

The disastrous Battle of Shewedaung.

the allied convoys. Several hundred Japanese and rebel Burmese were caught and killed, but the 7th Hussars lost 10 Stuarts, the Essex Yeomanry 2 guns the column over 300 vehicles and the infantry lost over 350 killed or wounded. The Dukes [Duke of Wellington's] suffered the worst, losing 5 officers and 117 other ranks. Of the 7th Hussars 'C' Squadron, under Major Congreve, smashed through a road block and Lieutenant Palmer managed to get through to Div HQ in Prome. Lieutenant Pattison MC was taken from his knocked-out Stuart, was beaten and flogged with sticks and was tied to a road block. The first 25-pound shell to hit the roadblock by good fortune actually enabled Pattison to escape in the darkness. Two tanks, driven by Sergeant V. Cowley MM and Sergeant Hipsey, charged over a

2 RTR in the Burmese jungle, April 1942. *Tank Museum*

road bridge and crashed over the embankment. By 1400 hrs the battle was over and the remains of the column, assisted by 'A' and 'B' squadrons of 2 RTR, managed to break out. On 28 March 'C' Squadron, 2 RTR, were sent on a wild-goose chase to help a column of 1st Burmese Division. Meanwhile the Chinese 200 Division in Toungoo were still surrounded and had to fight their way to safety suffering 3,000 casualties and losing all their guns and vehicles. A general Chinese withdrawal took place towards Pyinmana. The Japanese now had total command of the skies. The remaining British-flown Hurricanes and American P40s put up a gallant defence. Slim estimated that 233 Japanese planes had been destroyed in the air and 58 on the ground. The main airfields at Magwe and Akyab were put out of action by 150 Japanese bombers.

It was now essential to deny the oil fields at Yenangyaung to the Japanese some 100 miles north of Prome. Slim's lines of defence were planned to be from Minhia (west back of the river Irrawaddy) east to Taungdwingyi, and Pyinmana (an important rail junction 50 miles north of Toungoo) to Vith Loikaw. The Chinese Vth Army would defend Pyinmana and Vith Loikaw. By now 'Vinegar Joe' Stilwell had poisoned relations between himself and the British. Both sides thought that the other would collapse in front of the Japanese advance.

On 1 April Slim was visited by Generals Wavell and Alexander at Allanmyo, Corps HQ, 35 miles north of Prome. Meanwhile, on the same day, the 17th Indian Division around Prome was eventually driven out. The

A cannibalised plane in Burma. *Major Norman Plough*

7th Armoured Brigade were in action on the 2nd as part of the rearguard and the 2 RTR Stuarts ferried 2,500 infantry over 15 miles in 8 hours. Often the tanks had to tow each other out of dried river beds on their way to Dayindabo. It was the hottest season of the year with midday temperatures between 110 and 120 degrees Fahrenheit. The Japanese now had a foul reputation for atrocities. Twelve British soldiers and marines captured in Padang village, all wounded, were tied to trees and bayoneted. A tank crew of 7th Hussars on outpost duty were offered eggs and chickens by Burmese villagers. Drawing out their dahs they promptly cut down three troopers. The historian of 7th Hussars wrote: 'At a lower level the troops soon found that now the great British Raj was apparently crumbling, the Burmese villagers had few scruples about changing allegiance.'

By now 7th Hussars's tank strength was down to thirty-eight and many B vehicles had been lost to enemy action and bombing. Lieutenant-Colonel Yule was now CO of 2 RTR, acting as rearguard. On the evening of 7 April near Myaungbintha, Major Bonham-Carter's 'B' Squadron fought an action against three enemy vehicles, which may have been captured Stuarts, and hit them all. On the 11th, 7th Hussars' patrol sighted a captured Stuart flying a Japanese flag, but unfortunately out of range.

For over a week General Slim awaited the arrival of a Chinese regiment to garrison Taungdwingyi, but in vain, despite Stilwell's promise; 48 Brigade and 7th Armoured Brigade were at Kokkogwa 10 miles west of Taungdwingyi. So Slim moved his Corps HQ to Magwe on 8 April.

A Stuart Honey tank in Burma. *Major Norman Plough*

The battle for the vital oil fields started on the 11th and continued for a week. One of the desperate actions was against 48 Brigade at Kokkogwa. The enemy attacked fanatically and in strength. It was a pitch-dark night lit by violent thunderstorms. At dawn on the 12th 'B' and 'C' Squadrons, 2 RTR, were in action and the tanks, according to General Slim, 'moved out to a good killing'. Unfortunately, some of the 7th Hussars' tanks captured in the Shwedaung battle had been repaired and went into action with Japanese crews. 2 RTR were again in action near Magwe and had brisk actions at Thadodan and Alebo.

From 13 to 17 April 2 RTR were kept busy day and night. They ferried the KOYLI up the main road to Milestones 310, then 336 and killed 50 enemy in the village of Tokson. Second-Lieutenant Timmis, 'C' Squadron, and his crew were killed when his tank was hit six times at very close range by a 75mm gun. On several occasions a dangerous alternating sandwich situation occurred as Japanese roadblocks split in three pieces elements of the Burma Frontier Force, 1st Burma Division, 7th Armoured Brigade HQ and of course 2 RTR. At one stage the situation was so critical that General Alexander 'asked' Lieutenant-General Joe Stilwell to move the Chinese 38 Division 'at once' into the Yenaungyaung area.

The Japanese frequently dressed in the uniform of the Burma Rifles or as civilians and it was difficult to tell friend from foe. The 1st Burma Brigade in particular suffered heavily. General Alexander wanted to keep the dilatory Chinese 'on side' and insisted that Slim keep the 17th Division in and

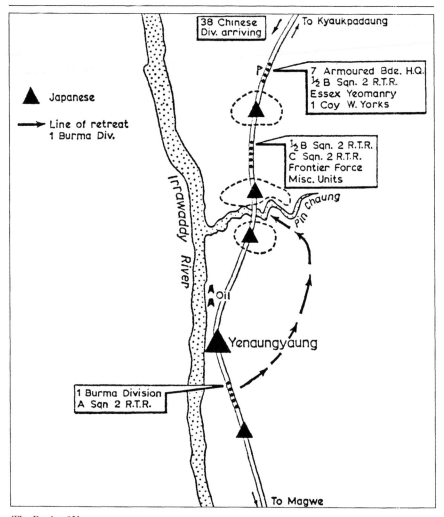

The Battle of Yenaungyuang.

around Taungdwingyi. Slim wrote: 'For the next two days the 1st Burma Division pulled back devotedly covered by tanks of 7th Armoured Brigade, to the Yin Chaung watercourse.' Three Chaungs – Pin, Kadaung and Yin – all flowed from east to west to join the Irrawaddy. The battle of Yenangyaung turned out to be a disaster fought in an area of about 20 square miles. The northern limit was the Pin Chaung and the southern in Yin Chaung. Japanese forces (33 Division) had cut the Magwe road between Slim's two divisions, who were about 50 miles apart. 1st Burma Division retreated northwards bombed and machine-gunned by the Japanese airforce. Slim wrote '7th Armoured Brigade again covered the withdrawal; what we should have done without that brigade I do not know.'

At 1300 hrs on 15 April General Slim gave the fateful orders for the demolition of the vital oil fields and refinery. The oil wells were stopped with cement, although the Japanese later were able to tap supplies by redrilling the wells. Slim watched 'a million gallons of crude oil burning with flames rising five hundred feet . . . over all hung a vast, sinister canopy of dense black smoke. It was a fantastic and horrible sight'. The Stuart tanks of 7th Armoured Brigade had long since exceeded the track mileage laid down for workshop attention. Nevertheless on 16 April Captain James Lunt, Burma Rifles, reported:

> The 2 RTR did sterling work ferrying back the exhausted infantry picking up the wounded and constantly counter-attacking to delay the advancing enemy. Moreover theirs was the only reliable communication available to General Bruce Scott and his harassed brigade commanders. Two tanks were lost but it is virtually certain that without the brilliant work of 2nd Royal Tanks 1st Burma Division would never have got clear of Magwe. That evening Slim ordered most of his precious 7th Armoured Brigade to withdraw through Yenangyaung to beyond the Pin Chaung.

Now the arrival of the Chinese Lieutenant-General Sun Li Jen, commanding the 38th Infantry Division at Slim's HQ, was much welcomed. He had no artillery or tanks of his own and Slim decided to offer the maximum (which wasn't very much) artillery and tanks to support Sun's attack. Slim wrote 'Long-suffering Brigadier [J.H.] Anstice commanding 7th Armoured Brigade threw me the look of a wounded sambur when he heard me give this out, but as always he rose to the occasion and he and Sun got

A detachment of 2 RTR Stuarts takes advantage of a brief lull in the fighting as they successfully covered the British withdrawal to the Chindwin. *Major Norman Plough*

2 RTR Stuarts north of Rangoon. *Tank Museum*

on famously together.' Slim had privately told Sun, inexperienced with tanks, always to consult with Anstice *before* employing them. General Slim's only link with Bruce Scott (GOC 1st Burma Division) was by radio from 7th Armoured Brigade HQ, the command tank of 'A' Squadron 2 RTR. Captain Norman Plough recalls:

> 'C' Squadron RTR were part of a small mixed brigade supporting the Chinese infantry division in the area of the Magwe oil fields. The Chinese had marched several hundred miles from Mongolia down the Burma road. . . . We discussed tactics and agreed that our tanks carry 10–15 soldiers on each tank, penetrate as far into the jungle as possible, drop them off and cover their attack with all tank weapons and RHA 25-pounder guns. The Japanese mortars were causing us the most damage. . . . Every evening after returning to the Chinese HQ we discussed the day's operations and Chinese casualties. Our medical unit concentrated on helping wounded soldiers. The General was most grateful for this help (bandages and some iodine). He personally interviewed each soldier who returned and rewarded anyone who had killed a Japanese.

Plough noticed that most of the Japanese prisoners, hands and necks noosed, strangled themselves. Major Mark Rudkin MC, Captain Plough and four other officers and NCOs of 2 RTR were subsequently awarded the Chinese Medal of Honour.

For the next three days the Chinese 38th Division, with 'B' and 'C' Squadrons, 2 RTR, attacked southwards and 1st Burmese Division with 'A' Squadron 2 RTR attacked northwards. On 19 April the two divisions met near the Pin Chaung river after heavy casualties on both sides. 'A' Squadron put up a magnificent fight and probably saved the division from being overrun.

Their squadron leader, Major N. Bourne, was subsequently awarded the DSO. 'C' Squadron and a troop of Essex Yeomanry 25 pounders remained with 38th Chinese Division for a week. Major M.F.S. Rudkin wrote: 'It seemed most unlikely that the counter-attack could start on time. I asked the British LO [Liaison Officer] with the Chinese what was happening. They had put their watches back one hour from 0630 as they were late and did not want to lose face by being seen to be late.' The 2 RTR tanks carried many of the wounded infantry in their Stuarts. Led by their GOC, Major General Bruce Scott, they formed up the Burma Division column, guns in front, wounded in ambulances, trucks next, with a spearhead of Stuart tanks and infantry until the track turned to sand, and with abandoned transport his division fought their way to and across the Pin Chaung. The survivors concentrated around Gwegyo. On the 19th the Chinese 38th Division, thrilled with tank and artillery support, took Twingon, a key suburb of Yenangyaung, rescuing 200 Inniskilling Fusiliers, prisoners and wounded. The next day with 2 RTR they put in such an attack on the rest of Yenangyaung and Pinchaung that the Japanese suffered heavy casualties. But the Allied forces were too weak to hold the oil fields and were obliged to retreat. 1st Burma Division was withdrawn 40 miles north to the Mount Popa region to reorganise, having lost most of its equipment. General Slim wrote 'As usual 7th Armoured Brigade covered 1st Burma Division as it lay gasping but not dying.'

At a meeting with General Alexander, Stilwell and General Slim on 19 April it was decided that *inter alia* '7th Armoured Brigade and one brigade group of 17th Division [would go] to Lashio with Chinese Vth Army *for China*.' But the Japanese onslaught on the 20th and 21st practically destroyed the Chinese VI Army, which simply vanished, and the bulk of Vth Chinese Army was involved in scattered, confused fighting.

On 23 April revised plans were drawn up. 17th Indian Division and the remnants of 1st Burma Division were to stand astride the Chindwin River to cover Kalewa and 7th Armoured Brigade, with 38th Chinese Division to hold from the Mu River to the Irrawaddy River. However, Slim noted that if the evacuation of Burma became necessary some British forces, including 7th Armoured Brigade, would accompany the Chinese forces back into China. It is probable that none of the Desert Rats in Burma were aware of this possibility. Slim then immediately ordered 7th Armoured Brigade with all speed to Meiktila, 70 miles north-east of Yenangyaung, and on the 25th, east of Meikfa, they surprised an enemy armoured and mechanised column and shot it up with considerable loss to the Japanese.

Major Rudkin's 'C' Squadron, 2 RTR, stayed with the Chinese 38th Division until the 26th, acting as their rearguard. On their last day about eighty-five members were each presented with one rupee by the grateful (and impoverished) Chinese unit. Major Bonham-Carter, OC 'B' Squadron, set off for Pyawbee with two scout cars to meet the Chinese. A mile from the town he suddenly encountered three Japanese tanks 75

Left to right: Captains Bill Low (RAMC), Vyvyan John, Major Ralph Younger and Lieutenant-Colonel 'Rhino' Fosdick, 7th Hussars. *Author*

yards away, but their fire was much too wild. Captain Ray Nickel's troop of 7th Hussars ambushed a column of enemy transport on the Toungoo road and wrecked most of them. In Kadang 'A' Squadron helped the West Yorkshires occupy the village during a hard-fought day. On the 27th both 7th Hussars and 2 RTR withdrew into leaguer north of Wundwin. However, the next morning 'B' Squadron, 2 RTR, passing through Ngathet quickly lost two Stuarts to a group of four enemy anti-tank guns. By mid-morning four enemy tanks were seen moving north by Captain Chaplin, FOO Essex Yeomanry, and several were hit. Throughout the day enemy infantry with armour support were infiltrating around Ngathet and Shanbin nearby. Brigadier Anstice instructed Lieutenant-Colonel Yule to keep in action while 7th Hussars and 'C' Squadron, 2 RTR, lifted on their tanks to safety most of the 63 Brigade troops. Captain Dumas was second in command 'D' Squadron, 2 RTR (Major Bonham-Carter was recovering from a severe snakebite), and was in action most of the day. Throughout the night of the 27th the ferrying operation on tanks and Essex Yeomanry gun limbers continued. The next morning SSM Ainley's 'C' Squadron troop, 7th Hussars, encountered another enemy transport company and destroyed half of them. But a Jap dive bomber destroyed a Stuart in Lieutenant Allen's troop.

At Kyaukse 7th Hussars and 48th Brigade were in a good defensive position, with mountains on one side, the Sittang Marshes on the other, and with a Gurkha battalion spent the 28th to the 30th in action every day. Two tanks were lost, 10 men killed but 150 Japanese were accounted for and 12 lorries captured. Cowan's 63rd Brigade around Wundwin were bombed heavily, but the Desert Rat Stuart tanks held back strong enemy infantry and artillery groups, including some light Japanese tanks, which when engaged scuttled back to shelter. Slim wrote 'The action at Kyaukse was a really brilliant example of rearguard work.'

The decision had now been taken officially for a withdrawal back into India across the Irrawaddy River, not only of General Slim's Corps but Sun's 38th Chinese Division. On 28 April the Corps orders stressed that 17th Division would cross the Irrawaddy River by ferry and boat and 238th Chinese Division and 7th Armoured Brigade would hold the east bank of the river from Sagaing to Ondaw. The great Ava Bridge had been allotted to 7th Armoured Brigade (and Vth Chinese Army). On 28 April they started to cross over and, as the last tank of 7th Hussars crossed, the bridge was blown up to cut the main road. General Slim watched the General Stuart tanks cross the Ava Bridge. A notice said that the maximum weight was six tons. A Stuart weighed thirteen tons. Slim was told the name of the British engineering firm who had built the bridge and reckoned they had built in a safety factor of 100 per cent. He ordered the Stuarts across one by one. The centre bridge spans were blown at midnight on 30 April. Burma had been lost.

The glamorous city of Mandalay had been devastated by Japanese bombers. It was full of deserted dumps, stores and camps of every kind including a dump (supposedly guarded) of high octane fuel for the Stuart tanks. A 'supposed' Burma Army Colonel had ordered it to be destroyed – and it was.

So the next dreary retreat started. The advent of the heavy monsoon rains due on about 20 May was a key factor. Slim's route northwards would run through Ye-u to Kaduma, 20 miles north-west and then into the jungle for 120 miles until the Chindwin River was reached at Shwegyin. Then a 6-mile river journey up-stream to Kalewa, along the Kabaw valley through jungle to Tamu to reach a road that might link Imphal to Assam. Slim wrote that 'It would be an impossible march if the monsoon came before his Corps had completed it.'

Monywa was a vital river port on the Chindwin River 50 miles west of Mandalay. Vital because if captured by the Japanese they could use the river to outflank the British, Indian and Chinese Allied forces. A reasonable road and railway went through the town on the east bank of the river. Slim's HQ was 16 miles north. On 30 April a sudden attack by 33rd Japanese Infantry Division from the west bank of the river, marching north after their capture of Yenangyaung, established a bridgehead on 1 May. HQ of 1st Burma Division was overrun and Slim ordered all available units to counter-attack. 7th Armoured Brigade supporting the 38th Chinese Division on the Irrawaddy line were sent post-haste to the rescue, travelling at night via Ettaw for a 140-mile march.

'C' Squadron, 7th Hussars, separately came up from the south with 63rd Indian Brigade to help and lost two tanks in the process. The 215th Japanese Infantry regiment war diary states: 'Our division tank company was composed of six enemy tanks captured at Shweddaung. The tank company led the column. . . . Our tanks bumped into enemy tanks, destroying two enemy tanks and forcing the others to retreat. This was a fight between British-made tanks and we won.' 2 RTR then acted as rearguard during the slow withdrawal to Ye-u where Generals Alexander and Stilwell were quartered. Slim sent in a counter-attack on 2 May to recapture Monywa by the 1st Burma Division, which was thwarted by vigorous Japanese defence in the town and from motor launches in the Chindwin River. Unfortunately a radio message, apparently from a senior officer of Brigadier Anstice's staff to 13 Brigade who passed it on to 1st Burmese Div HQ, ordered the whole division to pull out and withdraw to Alon – which they did.

Lieutenant G.S.B. Palmer, 7th Hussars, gives an account of 2 May:

> I soon met Pat Howard-Dobson's troop [south-east of Monywa] who diverted me to Sqn HQ. John Congreve was very pleased to see us as he was under the impression they were completely cut off. I was taken to the Brigade Commander [Anstice]. I briefed him on my orders and explained that I had worked my way round without seeing any Japanese. He was very worried about getting his wounded away. I called up my regiment and they organised a bullock-cart convoy which was brought down to us under escort by Basil Young. At 1700 the Brigade started to pull out. 'C' Sqn who only had a few tanks left Shorty White to stay with me. Our two troops then carried out a series of leap-frogs to cover the withdrawal and we had only slight trouble from some mortaring and a few rounds of anti-tank fire. We rejoined the squadron at Ye-u, and soon snipers started up from the river area. During the night Ray Nickel whose troop had been missing came in. He had been wounded and his troop sergeant killed. Basil Young who had covered our withdrawal had had a bad time and had destroyed one of his tanks which had broken down.

Three members of 'A' Squadron were stabbed to death by Burmese dacoits, but the squadron and West Yorkshires returned to take a terrible revenge. 'The roads were a horrible sight crowded with civilian refugees many of whom had been killed by dacoits,' wrote Lieutenant Palmer. 'The Burmese had been quick to take their revenge on Indian shopkeepers and moneylenders.'

On the same day, 2 May, 2 RTR were widely dispersed over a 50-mile triangle, now concentrated at Budalin. Major M.F.S. Rudkin described the 2 RTR rearguard action. 'The regiment withdrew at very slow speed up the road [from Monywa] for the next four hours. The speed was governed by the marching infantry in front who had animal transport with them.' One Stuart tank shed a track in heavy going and Rudkin left another to guard it while the crew effected repairs. At 0400 hrs tanks were heard moving towards the RTR leaguer. The NCO commanding the guard tanks in the leaguer assumed they were the stragglers returning. He heard excited Japanese voices inside one tank (a captured Stuart) that shot and set on fire a genuine RTR tank and burned and killed the crew. According to Major Rudkin:

The road to Kalewa was only about 12 feet wide, through thick and hilly country. In many places there were ravines on one side and the surface being soft many vehicles were lost over the side. Broken down vehicles were also pushed over the side to keep the road clear. There were many sharp corners and many soft river beds. The many inexperienced drivers in the column added to the hold-ups and breakdowns. Eventually after 24 hours in which we covered 54 miles, the regiment formed a leaguer about eleven miles from the ferry on the Chindwin. Three tanks had engine seizures beyond hope of repair and were abandoned after being destroyed [6 May]. Little time had been spent on maintenance for eleven weeks during which many tanks had covered 2,400 miles.

2 RTR lost two more tanks, one falling into a chaung in the dark, another on 4 May by enemy action around Budalin. The Japanese claimed that in the retreat from Monywa the Burmese Division had suffered 1,200 casualties, 2 tanks and 158 vehicles.

Captain James Lunt, Burmese Rifles, described the coming monsoon period. 'Jungle tracks would disintegrate into muddy bogs, impassable to all vehicles including bullock-carts. There would be malaria, blackwater fever, jaundice, typhus and the dreaded cholera. The jungle would become a sodden, dripping mess, shrouded in a dark and penetrating mist making it impossible to stay dry.' There were 2,300 wounded Allied soldiers not yet evacuated from Shwebo, 50 miles north-east of Monywa.

The rearguard continued their retreat through the huge teakwood forests towards Kalewa ferry on the Chindwin River, averaging 12 to 15 miles a day.

Burnt out vehicles, Burma. *Major Norman Plough*

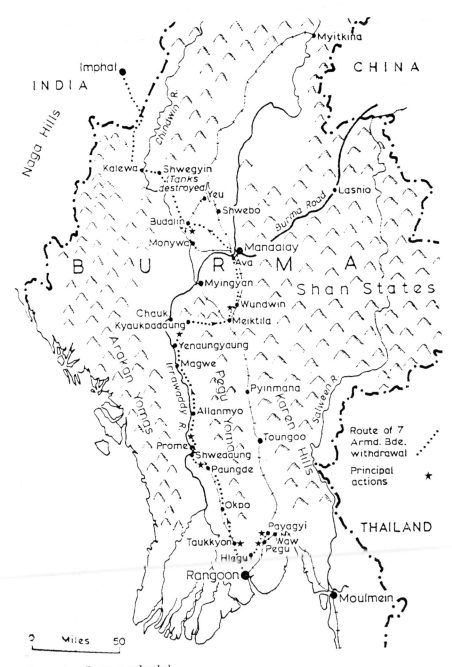

Retreat from Rangoon to Imphal.

Again after Ye-u the remaining Stuarts and 7th Armoured Brigade transport ferried troops. The whole Corps reached Shwegyin, a so-called river port, without a direct crossing over the Chindwin. River steamers had to sail four miles upstream to Kalewa, unload and return, a journey of several hours.

The Japanese General Sakurai, GOC 33rd Infantry Division, had embarked a flotilla of forty launches from Monywa towards Shwegyin upstream and arrived on 10 May. Slim had got all of 1st Burma Division across the river, with the help of booms and vigorous defence of the 'basin', a horseshoe-shaped flat space surrounded by sheer 200-foot escarpment around the loading pier. Despite heavy Japanese bombing, Gurkha battalions held off determined enemy attacks. The British 25-pounders were brought down to the water's edge and kept firing to the last moment before they were ferried upstream. After a huge last barrage the remaining guns and tanks were destroyed. General Slim wrote 'We had saved one third of the guns (28) some of the best (80) mechanical transport and 4-wheel lorries but the loss of the [70] tanks was a terrible blow. True they were worn out, obsolete, hard to replace in India but they held such a sentimental place in our esteem for what we owed them and their crews that it was like abandoning old and trusted friends to leave them behind.' They had smashed through twenty roadblocks and lost forty in the process. The 7th Hussars had lost thirty-three officers and men killed in action and a similar number wounded. 2 RTR have seventeen killed in action buried in St George's Church, Mingaladon.

It was a bitter moment for both tank battalions. They had lost forty-five tanks in the eleven-week campaign, about half to enemy action and half to accidents (toppling into deep chaungs) or mechanical failure. Major Rudkin, 2 RTR, noted that

> the Japanese weapon which did most damage was their 50mm mortar. They used this with extreme accuracy and they penetrated the top of the tanks where the armour was thinnest. One tank of 'B' Sqn stopped for a few moments in an open bit of ground and within one minute received six direct hits. The Japanese 75mm gun used over open sights was fairly effective and stopped a tank but this did not penetrate the front, it often penetrated the side or rear and would only damage the front. About a quarter of the tanks hit by 75mm guns were knocked out.

Major Llewellen Palmer, 7th Hussars, persuaded a ferry-boat captain to tow a Stuart tank, bizarrely named *The Curse of Scotland*, across the river on a raft. The ferry-boat crews threatened to strike if ordered to tow another. Later, stripped of its turret, this tank became the command vehicle of the Indian 7th Light Cavalry. The remaining seventy tanks were destroyed with sledgehammers; engine sump and radiator drain plugs were removed. The engines were run at high revs until, with oil and water drained, they seized up. Optical equipment, radios and wiring were smashed, ammunition was taken away and buried. A week had been allowed for the Chindwin crossing but Shwegyin was a deadly bottleneck once the Japanese had fought their way up to the escarpment overlooking the basin. The six river steamers could carry 500 or 600 men packed tight, but not more than one lorry, two or three guns and a jeep or two, but no tanks. The 7th Hussars officers wore their distinctive crossbelts and Padre Metcalfe took sufficient prayer books for a full-scale service to be held on arrival in India. The monsoon started on 12 May bursting with torrential rain. Soon Slim's survivors were marching on foot, the Armoured Brigade organised as infantry rifle battalions for the 90-mile slog from Kalewa through the Kabaw Valley to Tamu on the Indian border. On half rations, marching in the morning and evening to avoid the heat of the day, they reached India on 15 May. Fever was rampant, food and drink short and climbing the hills on foot on tracks inches deep in slippery mud and soaked to the skin was an ordeal. Low clouds kept the Japanese airforce away. South of Tamu Indian-driven lorries drove south to meet the columns. The drivers were so frightened they took their lorries into the jungle and hid. General Slim wrote, 'This difficulty was overcome by putting beside each driver a man from 7th Armoured Brigade who saw to it that they (the Indian drivers) went where they were told – a last service of this magnificent formation.'

Captain Norman Plough, 2 RTR:

> After we destroyed our tanks near Kalewa we reorganised as infantry. All ranks carried their rifles and revolvers and some had tommy guns. Rations had been issued to all ranks. We started the march to Imphal in an organised column with a few of our own vehicles. The going was rough through the foot hills of the mountain range with many small rivers to cross. This kept us clean after the humid and hot days of the march. We mostly moved at night. It was chilly and often very wet.

Plough rather liked the tinned sausages, but still lost weight, as did the survivors. Lieutenant-Colonel George Yule, Major Peter Stratton and Norman Plough, promoted to Major, after Dinapur, Dhond, Poona and Bombay, eventually went on leave in the Nilgris hills near Coonor and played golf most days.

The Brigade stayed for a week, alternately marched or were ferried by lorries, on a barren hillside at Milestone 108, called 'Dysentery Hill'. Lorries arrived to ferry the Desert Rat 'infantrymen' to Imphal and on 25th by lorry to Manipur, thence by cattle truck/train and bus to Ranchi to be met by Lieutenant-General Sir Charles Broad. In his dispatches General Alexander wrote 'The 7th Armoured Brigade showed the value of disciplined, experienced troops. They retained their fighting qualities and cheerful outlook throughout.' A few individuals stayed on as instructors at the Indian Armoured Corps Depot at Ahmednagger, but both regiments returned to the Middle East via Persia and eventually fought in the Italian campaign.

General Wavell visited the brigade before they left India. He had known them in North Africa and commented that the formation was the finest in any command he had held.

CHAPTER TEN

The Battle of Gazala, the Cauldron, Operation Aberdeen

Rommel abandoned Derna, Barce and Benghazi, and the garrisons cut off at Bardia, Sollum and Halfaya surrendered in January 1942. British wounded in Derna hospital were rescued and when General Gott and Brigadier Jock Campbell visited the hospital in Benghazi, they found it full of wounded British prisoners who were carefully flown back to safety in the Delta.

It all seemed too good to be true. However, when Alan Moorehead talked to Generals Auchinleck, Willoughby Norrie and 'Strafer' Gott early in the New Year he found that none of them was particularly confident about the future. On 1 January Auchinleck wrote to General Ritchie, 'I have a most uncomfortable feeling that the Germans outwit and outmanoeuvre us as well as outshooting us.' But to Churchill the 'Auk' put on a braver face, 'I do not think it can be said that the bulk of the enemy divisions have evaded us. [Rommel's] divisions are divisions only in name . . . these are much disorganised, short of senior officers, short of material and due to our continuous pressure are tired and certainly not as strong as their total strength of 35,000 might indicate. . . . I am convinced that we should press forward.' By mid-January General Godwin-Austen's XIII Corps were occupying Cyrenaica. Two brigades of 4th Indian Division occupied Benghazi and Barce, the 2nd Armoured Brigade were training around Antelat, the Guards Brigade were at Mersa el Brega, with 7th Armoured Division Support Group near Wadi Faregh. Major General Frank Messervy (an infantryman) was the new GOC of 7th Armoured Division.

On the other side of the fence the Afrika Korps had successfully carried out a well disciplined withdrawal, without losing huge quantities of stores, without any panic (no Gazala gallop) and their morale was high. They did not regard themselves as a defeated army. The Royal Navy had suffered losses in the Mediterranean and supplies and convoys were getting through – including 55 brand new Panzer tanks, 20 armoured cars and a large consignment of fuel. Rommel now had, in the rechristened Panzer-Armee Afrika, a force of 110 tanks.

At the same time the British high command were expressing doubts about their tanks' inferior gun performance, the mechanical unreliability of their cruisers and their tactical leadership in the field. In his telegram to the Prime Minister of 31 January 1942, General Auchinleck stated:

> I am reluctantly compelled to conclude that to meet German armoured forces with any reasonable hope of decisive success our armoured forces as at present equipped, organised and led must have at least two to one superiority. Even then they must rely for success on working in very closest co-operation with infantry and artillery which except for their weakness in anti-tank guns are fully competent to take on their German opposite numbers . . . some personnel of Royal Armoured Corps are losing confidence in their equipment.

But a new 'Super' American tank and a new British 6-pounder anti-tank gun – in small numbers – might become a key factor in the next inevitable large-scale battle.

Rommel struck on 21 January a couple of weeks after his rearguard had retreated to El Agheila. It must rank as one of the quickest (and most successful) turn-abouts in military history. The old foes – 15th, 21st Panzers and 90th Light – fell on the 2nd Armoured Brigade Valentines near Adjedabya and the bases south of Benghazi fell – Saunu, Antelat, Soluch and Ghemines. Soon the vital Msus fell where the main supply depots were based. And Benghazi was doomed despite stout defence by an Indian brigade. The Support Group lost 16 of their 25-pounders, much transport and 100 prisoners. Oberleutnant Heinz Schmidt, Rommel's ADC, wrote in his book *With Rommel in the Desert,*

> We had now developed a new method of attack. With our twelve anti-tank guns we leap-frogged from one vantage-point to another, while our Panzers, stationary and hull-down, if possible, provided protective fire. Then we would establish ourselves to give them protective fire while they swept on again. The tactics worked well and, despite the liveliness of his fire, the enemy's tanks were not able to hold up our advance. He steadily sustained losses and had to give ground constantly. We could not help feeling that we were not then up against the tough and experienced opponents who had harried us so hard on the Trigh Capuzzo. . . .
>
> We were not entirely happy about our petrol position. Yet one young officer who said to Rommel, 'Herr General, we need more fuel', received the brisk answer: 'Well, go and get it from the British'.

Major F.W. von Mellenthin, Rommel's intelligence chief, wrote:

> On the right flank 21st Panzer met little opposition but six miles NW of Saunu, 15th Panzer ran into very superior tank forces. These were overwhelmed by Panzer Regiment 8, closely supported by anti-tank guns and artillery. It soon became apparent that the British tank units had no battle experience and they were completely demoralised by the onslaught of 15th Panzer. At times the pursuit attained a speed of 15mph and the British columns fled madly over the desert in one of the most extraordinary routs of the war. After covering 50 miles in under 4 hours, 15th Panzer reached Msus airfield overwhelming numerous supply columns.

Unbelievably, 96 tanks, 38 guns and 190 lorries were captured or destroyed. The unfortunate 2nd Armoured Brigade had lost seventy tanks in the first two days of Rommel's assault and within four days had been destroyed by the Afrika Korps.

By 4 February the Axis forces had, in two combat groups, pushed the bewildered British and Indian forces back behind the so-called Gazala Line. This was a series of defensive boxes, surrounded by wire and minefields, each containing a brigade. For every 10 miles they stretched from Bir Hacheim in the south (defended by the French Foreign Legion), El Adem, Tobruk and Knightsbridge to the sea. Roving armoured groups patrolled the gaps. Alan Moorehead wrote:

> The underlying idea was this, the Nazi tanks were at liberty to bypass or surround these sealed up boxes and seize all the rest of the Gazala area if they so desired – it was just empty desert anyway. But they could not proceed far lest the British should sally out of their boxes and take them in the exposed rear or flank. Moreover the British tanks were kept fluid outside these boxes and were in a position not only to attack the enemy in the open whenever they wanted but also to go to the assistance of any box that was hard pressed.

For almost four months both armies built up their strength with minor operations 'Fullsize', 'Sinbad' and Buckshot' by the 8th Army.
Winston Churchill wrote:

> Rommel had again proved himself a master of desert tactics and outwitting our commanders regained the greater part of Cyrenaica. . . . This retreat of nearly 300 miles ruined our hopes and lost us Benghazi and all the stores General Auchinleck had been gathering for his hoped-for offensive in the middle of February. Rommel must have been astounded by the overwhelming success of three small columns with which he started the attack. He supported them with whatever troops he could muster.

Churchill realised from Ultra messages that the immense Luftwaffe attacks on Malta and consequent loss of air control allowed Rommel's supplies and convoys to increase dramatically. Operation Aida had been agreed by the Führer and Duce at Berchtesgaden on 1 May – a counter-attack by the Axis armies to forestall the British offensive and the defeat of the 8th Army in the Gazala line and the capture of Tobruk. Operation Venezia was the codename for Rommel's great attack on the night of 26 May with a huge force of 332 Panzer tanks plus 228 Italian M–13s and 14s. The Axis troops included the three professional Afrika Korps formations plus eight Italian (Sabrata, Brescia, Pavia, Trieste, Bologna, Trento, Littorio and Ariete – the last two being armoured). Each side had about 10 divisions, about 130,000 men, and their artillery and airforces were fairly evenly matched in quantity. The Desert Army had 850 tanks (XIII Corps under 'Strafer' Gott, 276 Matildas and Valentines and XXX Corps under Norrie, 167 Grants, 149 Stuarts and 257 Crusaders).

On 23 February young Lieutenant Roy Farran, 3rd Hussars, was driving Major-General 'Jock' Campbell towards Matruh from Halfaya Pass. The staff car overturned on a battered wet road surface and Campbell was killed. He had just been awarded the Victoria Cross, which had been pinned to his blouse by General Auchinleck, and had taken command of 7th Armoured Division. His loss was very bad for morale. In the battle of Sidi Rezegh he seemed to be immortal, risking his life on a score of occasions.

Major-General Frank Messervy, an infantry divisional commander, succeeded as Divisional Commander. His main strike force was 4th Armoured Brigade, commanded by Brigadier G.W. Richards, with 8th Hussars, 3rd and 5th RTR and supported by 1 RHA (with new A/Tk 6 pounders) and 1 KRRC. The original 7th Armoured Brigade were now on their way to the Far East and were replaced by 7th Motor Brigade with 4 RHA, 9 KRRC, 1 and 9 Rifle Brigade Battalions. The Divisional Support troops were the King's Dragoon Guards who had taken over from the Cherry Pickers, 102nd RHA (Anti-tank) 15 LAA Regt, plus Signals, Engineers, RASC, RAOC and RAMC. Sergeant Jake Wardrop, 5th RTR, approved of

the new [American Grants] tanks. [They] were arriving now and they were super, the finest things we had ever seen. They had a nine-cylinder radial engine, were quite fast [up to 26mph] and had a crew of six, commander, gunner and operator in the top turret, and driver, gunner and loader down below. The gun was a .37mm and the bottom one a 75mm.

In fact the Grant suffered one handicap, having its 75mm gun mounted in a sponson on the right-hand front of the hull, so it had a very limited traverse and could not be used in a fully hull-down position. Importantly, this gun could fire HE as well as AP, and had, at 1,000 yards, a penetration better than the German long 50mm gun and much better than their short 50mm. The 8th Army now had 167 of these new American tanks.

Lieutenant-Colonel 'Pip' Roberts was the new CO of 3rd RTR:

At this time we were re-equipping and training near the Pyramids and at the end of March were moved up to the desert to an area some 15 miles west of Capuzzo. The Hun had recently done one of his 'come-backs', but this time had been halted on the Gazala-Bir Hacheim line. Most of April was spent in this general area: training was continued and certain operational Recce's were carried out. [3 RTR] was organised with two Squadrons of Grants [twelve in each] and one squadron of Honeys [sixteen] and RHQ had two Grants and two Honeys.

Winston Churchill was well aware that General Auchinleck was determined to build up his defensive basis before any offensive could be mounted and declined an 'invitation to visit London in March 1942'. So the Prime Minister wrote to him on 15 March:

The delay you have in mind will endanger Malta. Moreover there is no certainty that the enemy cannot reinforce faster than you, , , , Your losses have been far less than the enemy's who nevertheless keeps fighting. For instance the 7th Armoured Division was withdrawn to the Delta to rest, although its losses were far less than those of the 15th and 21st German Armoured Divisions, who came back at you with so much vigour.

Behind the scenes there was a malaise among the British Generals. Messervy, an infantryman, commanded an armoured division. 'Strafer' Gott, an artillery and armoured professional, now commanded XIII Corps with its infantry divisions. Major-General Lumsden, GOC 1st Armoured Division, cordially disliked Major-General Messervy and was reluctant to cooperate in any way. Gott and Major-General Dan Pienaar, GOC 1st

South African Division, disliked each other intensely. Lieutenant-General Neil Ritchie, GOC 8th Army, responsible in the field to Auchinleck, although in everyone's book 'an awfully nice chap', was over-promoted and his decisions were reached by committee and conference. (He was relieved of his command on 25 June.)

The malaise went even deeper into the heart of the 8th Army. Rommel led from in front of his Panzer-Armee (with its minuses as well as its pluses), but as a result was a very popular commander, whose fame and charisma had spread through the ranks of the Commonwealth troops. In their turn the Desert Army lacked confidence in their own commanders. Sergeant Jake Wardrop, 5 RTR, wrote, 'We had a silly old man from the Indian Army [Messervy], who had never seen a tank and he was so slow that he was captured the first morning of the campaign – imagine a General being captured. . . .' Later, 'we never seemed to get going. Of course a poor General makes a lot of difference. We had one ourselves until he got his bowler hat and I've a shrewd suspicion he wasn't the only one.' Peter Roach, 1 RTR, wrote of his life out of battle:

> Life was elemental, ordered, simple and mentally numbing. We rose shortly before the sun, rolled our bedding, strapped it on the back of the tank, warmed the engine, tuned the radio, out with the fire tin, in with the petrol, brew tin filled with water. . . . We stood around gulping scalding hot tea. Breakfast was porridge made from crushed biscuits, sweetened somehow, bacon and beans, hard biscuit and gooey sweet jam or marmalade, liquid margarine. A *cordon bleu* lunch of hard biscuits, processed cheese dusted with a fine sprinkling of sand. After sundown supply trucks arrived with food, water, stores – perhaps mail. Supper was hot bully beef stew and one last brew of tea.

The Battle of Gazala lasted for about four weeks and ended as a disaster for the 8th Army. The following account mainly concerns the Desert Rats 'strike' formation of 4th Armoured Brigade (3 and 5 RTR and 8th Hussars) backed by 7th Motor Brigade of motorised infantry and artillery. They had returned to the desert around Sidi Azeiz in April, commanded by Brigadier G.W. (Ricky) Richards DSO, MC, who had been GSO1 of 7th Armoured Division throughout Crusader. The 22nd Armoured Brigade had joined 1st Armoured Division. Barrie Pitt's superb book *Year of Alamein 1942* gives a very detailed description of the long and complicated battle ebbing and flowing around the defensive boxes. Rommel's main line of attack was towards the south-west of the Gazala line defences with the Free French in Bir Hacheim as their target. Lieutenant-Colonel 'Pip' Roberts, now commanding 3 RTR, wrote, 'Enemy movement is reported towards [Bir] Hacheim; the brigade [4th Armoured] will take up position 'Skylark' (south-east of Hacheim) the brigade will RV and form up at point [about 3 miles away] 3 RTR leading, 8th Hussars left, 5 RTR right, RHA batteries moved with armoured regiments, 1 KRRC in reserve, be in position at RV at 0815hrs.' The light squadron with 20 Stuarts led with the Grant squadrons either side of RHQ following behind. The famous 'Chestnut' troop RHA was catching up. Brigade reported that

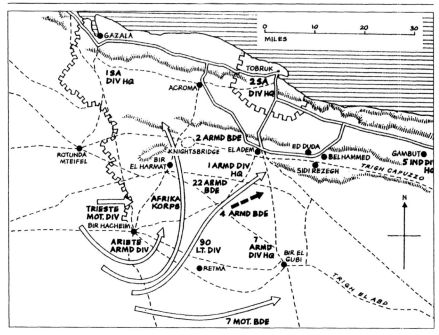

The Battle of Gazala.

the Indian Motor Brigade east of Hacheim had been over-run [by the Ariete division]. Ahead of 3 RTR Roberts exclaimed 'Gosh! There they are – there are more than 100! Yes, twenty in the first line and there are six, no eight lines, and more behind that in the distance. A whole ruddy Panzer division is quite obviously in front of us.'

Major J.W. (Shan) Hackett, was OC 'C' Squadron, 8th Hussars. His Light Squadron of Honeys was ordered to meet the Germans at a prepared position called 'Blenheim'. 'I took my squadron up a slight rise and reached the top and saw what looked like the whole bloody German army coming up the slope below. I radio'd back "am engaging now" and put up the black battle flag – well any tank will shoot at anything resembling a command tank, so everyone fired at me. In minutes my tank was on fire and I was burned quite badly.' The indomitable Hackett went back to 'B' echelon and got another tank. The 8th Hussars got badly knocked about during Cauldron, 'we had no CO, no Adjutant, no QM, just fifteen tanks [out of 68] and some 'B' echelon – we formed up with 3 RTR into a composite regiment.' In front of 4th Armoured Brigade was the whole of Rommel's Afrika Korps sweeping between Bir Hacheim and Retma.

5 RTR was now commanded by Lieutenant-Colonel R.D.W. Uniacke and Sergeant Wardrop described their first two days:

At about ten o'clock [on the 26th] we moved to a position already decided on to wait for the bad men when they arrived. We gave them a good warning with the big 75 [Grant main gun]. It quite shook them and they turned and ran for it. [Later,] the order came to get up to El Adem aerodrome and cut off a column heading for Tobruk. The day ended with a scrap at night, a lot of fires all over the place, lorries and tanks blazing.

Lt Colonel 'Pip' Roberts, CO 3 RTR, wrote:

The tank versus tank battle was in progress. The leading enemy tanks had halted about 1,300 yards away. All our tanks were firing, there was no scarcity of targets – certainly two of our tanks were knocked out but the enemy had also had losses. I could see one tank burning and another slewed round and the crew baling out. Good show.

Roberts asked his adjutant Peter Burr to tell Brigade HQ that

We are holding our own but I do not anticipate being able to stay here for ever, suggest 5th Tanks should come up on our right. They would then prevent us being outflanked and might get a good flank shoot at the enemy. . . . The 8th Hussars were fighting a battle near their original leaguer area against a large number of enemy tanks and had not had time even to get into battle formation.

By the end of the day's fighting 3 RTR were down to seven Grant tanks and eleven Honeys. The next morning, the 28th, Major Shan Hackett, with six 8th Hussar Honeys, linked up with 3 RTR, 5 RTR still at full strength, and the brigade were ordered to attack two MET columns. Major Charles Armitage brought his RHA battery into the attack, and under a smokescreen, a screen of deadly 88mm anti-tank guns were attacked and two knocked out. Roberts noted, 'The next few days seemed to consist of orders, counter-orders and at times disorders.' The GOC 7th Armoured Division, Major General Messervy and his staff officers including GSO1 Lieutenant-Col H.E. Pyman, were captured at Bir Beuid, but later managed to escape. 90th Light Division had caused mayhem with 7th Motor Brigade, and rushed through and past them to El Adem and onto Belhamed. Rommel wrote afterwards.

There was also a British surprise awaiting us here, one which was not to our advantage – the new Grant tank which was used in this battle for the first time on African soil. Tank after tank, German and British, was shattered in the fire of the tank-guns. Finally we succeeded in throwing the British back to the Trigh el Abd although at the cost of heavy casualties.

The 22nd Armoured Brigade caught facing the wrong way by the Ariete Armoured Division (which had over-run 3rd Indian Motor Brigade and passed between the Desert Rats and Bir Hacheim) had suffered badly at the hands of 21st Panzer Division. The 7th Motor Brigade (including 1st KRRC – the old Support Group) were forced back on the 27th to the Retma box and then to El Duda. The 9th KRRC, a newcomer to 7th Armoured Division, were overrun by the Panzers at Retina and 4th Armoured Brigade's 'B' Echelon were also overwhelmed with most of the ammunition and petrol lost.

Trooper John Ireland, a tank gunner with 5 RTR, noted:

The regiment fell right into a trap; unknown to our command the Germans took advantage of the sandstorm and withdrew their tanks leaving behind a screen of well dug-in 88mm anti-tank guns. The regiment pushed on in pursuit of the tanks but were met with a hail of fire and lost almost an entire regiment. . . . Lots of tank crews were killed, wounded or taken prisoner. . . . This set-back in the regiment seemed to have a demoralising affect on the men and I, in particular, began to doubt the effectiveness of our tanks. . . . We had lots of grub and the rum issue made life brighter, although the strain of long hours in battle, days on end, made one wilt a little. From first light around 5 a.m. until 10 p.m. was a very long day especially hearing over the intercom the fate of some other crews.

The 7th Armoured Division, nursing their heavy losses (3 RTR and 8th Hussars), were not involved in a massive tank battle on 29 May when 2nd Armoured and 22 Armoured Brigades were smashed up near the Knightsbridge box (defended by 201st Guards Brigade). Rommel again:

The sacrifice of the 7th Armoured south of Bir Harmat (south of Knightsbridge) served no tactical purpose whatsoever since it was all the same to the British if they met me there or on the Trigh Capuzzo where the remainder of their armour entered the battle . . . their aim should have been to bring *all* their armoured forces into battle at the *same* time.

Meanwhile in the south General Koenig's Free French defended the Bir Hacheim box magnificently against land and Luftwaffe onslaughts (until on the night of 19 June the survivors were withdrawn).

Rommel's battles in what became known as 'The Cauldron' went on from 28 May to 4 June. On the 31st the gallant British 150th Infantry Brigade's box was finally overwhelmed and 3,000 survivors, out of ammunition, surrendered. The British 1st Army Tank Brigade was almost destroyed in the same battle. On 1 June Major R.E. Ward, 5 RTR, took 'A' Squadron with six Stuarts through a gap in the minefield south of Bir Hacheim, and turning north lay up in ambush. They caught an MET convoy, drove off the armoured-car escort, captured 60 vehicles and brought most of them back to 5 RTR, although shelled in the process by the Free French.

On 2 June 5 RTR put up a strong defence against the 170 tanks of 21st Panzer Division. Although 7 Stuarts and 11 Grants were lost they managed to knock out 20 Panzer MkIII and IV tanks. Their CO, Lieutenant-Colonel Robie Uniacke, was killed in that action. There were 15 casualties and 45 taken prisoner. At the end 5 RTR were down to 9 tanks. Major Cootle assumed command, and when 12 new Grants came up on 3 June the regiment moved the next day to relieve 3 RTR near Bir El Taaleb. For the next three days the joint 3/5 RTR formation helped the French bastion at Bir Hakeim. Sergeant Jake Wardrop commented 'We'd lost about ten tanks and Wag Fry, Topper and a lot more were gone. Stan and I had been together, so we went to look for George' (who had baled out, was wounded, but was safe).

Lieutenant-Colonel 'Pip' Roberts, CO 3 RTR and Captain Peter Burr, his adjutant, were both badly burned in the Cauldron battle, so temporarily

5 RTR tankcrew in the desert. *Author*

Captain Granton commanded the regiment. Major Michael Carver, GSO2 at XXX Corps, wrote: 'By now all armoured brigades were much depleted and disorganised. 1st Armoured Brigade brought up to Capuzzo was split up and distributed among the other brigades. Regiments were amalgamated and reformed every day. Brigades changed regiments and divisions changed brigades. Sometimes more than once a day.' Sergeant Fred Dale, 'A' Squadron 3 RTR, noted 'We still had 10 Honeys left in one squadron. The other squadrons only had eight heavy Grants left. What tanks the 8 Hussars had left came to the 3rd Tanks. . . . We now have two regiments left in the brigade, 3rd and 5th.' On 3 June the 22nd Armoured Brigade was again attached to the remnants of 7th Armoured Division.

General Ritchie, perhaps optimistically, launched Operation Aberdeen on the night of 4/5 June, a frontal attack on Rommel's positions in the Cauldron between Sidra and Aslagh ridges. Attacks by 22nd Armoured Brigade (2nd Royal Gloucester Hussars suffered badly) and the 10th Indian Brigade were wiped out by enemy counter-attacks. 32nd Tank Brigade ran into a minefield protected by German anti-tank guns, losing fifty of its seventy Matilda tanks. Rommel launched 21st Panzer into a series of attacks on the French defenders of Bir Hacheim.

Major F.W. von Mellenthin, Rommel's Chief of Intelligence, wrote 'From the tactical point of view this was one of the most ridiculous attacks [Aberdeen] of the campaign.'

Playfair's *Official History, Mediterranean and Middle East* simply states

> The unpleasant turn taken by the battle was soon realised at the Tactical HQ of 7th Armoured and the 5th Indian Divisions, but each was occupied by its own problems and there was nobody in sole command to concert their actions. . . . No help reached the doomed units in the Cauldron, for although the 2nd and 4th Armoured Brigades had been placed under General Messervy who was now in sole command, he was unable in the prevailing confusion to bring them to action.

Operation Aberdeen was a disaster, and Rommel now concentrated on the capture of the French-held Bir Hacheim. Sixty Luftwaffe Stukas dive-bombed, and General-Leutnant Ulrich Kleeman, GOC 90th Light Division, and elements of 15th Panzer battered with tanks and infantry. A few tanks, some 2nd KRRC and Rifle Brigade infantry, a RHA battery of 7th Armoured joined the fray. On the night of 10/11 June orders reached General Koenig for the box to be evacuated. No. 550 Company, RASC, a Desert Rat formation, brought in their lorries and ambulances, guarded on one flank by 2nd Rifle Brigade and by the KRRC (60th Rifles) on the other. What was left of 5 RTR were also involved, as Sergeant Jake Wardrop recounted: 'The French at Bir Hacheim were having a pretty thin time and one night we were told we were going to give them a hand. They had beaten off repeated attacks and the Bosch were giving them a going-over with Stukas and big artillery.' On the way Wardrop's tank was disabled. 'There was a lot of shelling and messing around . . . that night infantry of ours fought their way in with the bayonet and they evacuated the place. So ended Bir Hacheim the desert stronghold – it was a pity.' Von Mellenthin commented, 'In the whole course of the desert war we never encountered a more heroic and well sustained defence.' Eventually some 2,700 French and Foreign Legion troops were evacuated, although 900 were taken prisoner. It was a small triumph for 7th Motor Brigade.

All the British armour had been so badly mauled in the battle of the Cauldron that on 11 June the remnants of the 1st, 2nd, 4th and 22nd Armoured Brigades were amalgamated under command of the 4th and concentrated between the Knightsbridge and El Adem box. The two armoured divisional commanders (Lumsden 1st Armoured and Messervy 7th Armoured) cordially disliked each other and cooperation was limited. When the Corps Commander, Lieutenant-General Norrie, tried to co-ordinate their activities, he had scant success. Messervy was nearly captured – for the second time – and was out of action for a day hiding in a disused well.

During the night of 13/14 June Knightsbridge box was evacuated and the Guards Brigade retired to Acroma. General Ritchie ordered Gott's XIII Corps, followed by the remains of Lumsden's 2nd and 22nd Armoured Brigades back to the Egyptian frontier. A week later Tobruk with its garrison of 33,000 men – South Africans, Indians, a Guards Brigade (many of whom fought their way out) and 4th and 7th Royal Tank regiments – surrendered.

Churchill, the Desert Army and the Home Front in Britain were absolutely horrified.

Churchill had hoped for a relieving force. Lieutenant-Colonel Michael Carver, then a XXX Corps staff officer, wrote a history of the 4th Armoured Brigade and recounted the last week of the Battle of Gazala. 'The 7th Armoured Division was reforming in the desert to the south and on [the] 20th received orders to despatch a force in aid – but Rommel was too quick for them. Before it had even started all was over.' Carver continued:

During the 12th the enemy moved in groups eastwards from the minefield near Bir Harmat to the Wadi running south-west for El Adem, near Hagfet Sciaaban. By the end of the day he had concentrated all his armoured strength in this area behind us and directly threatening El Adem, Belhamed and the gateway to Tobruk. During the night he dug in his anti-tank guns on the lip of the Wadi. On the morning of 13th June we were ordered to advance south from our battle position, around the withered fig tree of Naduret el Ghesceuasc, to engage the enemy concentration. Using hardly any of his tanks, but almost entirely with his anti-tank guns, the enemy reduced the brigade to a handful of tanks. Up till then his losses in tanks had generally been in the same proportion to his total strength as our own. By the end of the 13th we had lost almost all we had left and he none at all. The die was cast: the initiative was now his, with Tobruk and Belhamed crammed with unnecessary stores and L of C troops, put there for the projected offensive, with 50 Div and the South Africans still strung out well to the west of Tobruk. It was a grim prospect. That night the gallant Guards Brigade, who had clung so grimly to Knightsbridge, were withdrawn, 2nd Armoured Brigade taking command of all tanks west of El Adem, while we took over all the tanks east of it, which included the daily flow of motley tanks and crews formed from stragglers and recovered and repaired tanks. While Tobruk was defended and lost and the whole army withdrew eastwards, the brigade daily fought delaying actions against Rommel's 15th and 21st Panzer Divisions, who strove in vain to cut off the columns retreating along the coast. Daily our strength fell: sleep was as precious as it was rare. When we reached the Matruh-Siwa road, we were relieved by 1st Armoured Division and handed over to them the mixed collection of regiments and tanks we still had left.

CHAPTER ELEVEN

Operation Gamebirds – the Battle of Alam Halfa

By 1 July 1942 the remnants of the 7th Armoured Division were back behind a line based on Alamein railway station – southwards and tankless. Their surviving tanks had been handed over to Lumsden's 1st Armoured Division on the Matruh-Siwa road. Rommel's forces were equally tired but not dispirited, since they had won an astounding victory. Although they only had forty-four battleworthy tanks they had complete control of the battlefields and their tank-recovery teams were highly professional. Soon their tank strength was restored. Major von Mellenthin, Rommel's Chief Intelligence Officer, wrote: 'The booty [at Tobruk] was gigantic. It consisted of supplies for 30,000 men for three months, more than 10,000 cubic metres of petrol. Without this booty, adequate rations and clothing for the armoured divisions [15, 21 Panzer and the Ariete] would not have been possible in the coming months.' Moreover the tank-repair workshops in Tobruk were of a high quality.

Rommel was now promoted to be Field Marshal and determined to destroy the small British forces left on the frontier and invade Egypt. Adolf Hitler was delighted: 'Destiny has offered us a chance which will never occur twice in the same theatre of war. . . . The English 8th Army has been practically destroyed. In Tobruk the port installations are almost intact. . . .' This was part of a letter to Mussolini, who became equally enthusiastic. Only Marshal Kesselring disliked the invasion plan and threatened to withdraw his Luftwaffe forces from their North African bases back to Sicily. Mussolini flew to Derna on 29 June 1942, with a white charger for a triumphant entry into Cairo.

Rommel launched his DAK from Bardia on a 100-mile swing west of Fort Capuzzo, Sidi Omar, then south, then north-east, and by 25 June had advanced towards the rapidly cobbled together forces – British, South African, Indian and New Zealand – with ninety-nine assorted tanks. 4th and 22nd Armoured Brigade were temporarily under 1st Armoured Division command, while 7th Motor Brigade was deployed west of the Siwa track. General Ritchie had been relieved of command on 25 June by Auchinleck, who himself took control in the field. A new X Army Corps, under Lieutenant-General W.G. Holmes, was entrusted with the defence of Mersa

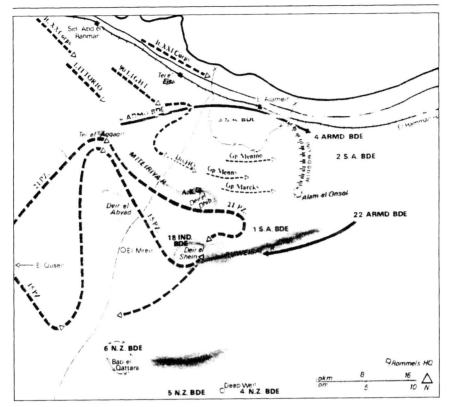

First Battle of El Alamein, 1 July 1942.

Matruh on the coast. By mistake XIII Corps were ordered to withdraw from the south-west flank towards the north-east. By the 29th Rommel had won the battle of Mersa Matruh (the first battle of El Alamein). In very confused fighting the remains of the 8th Army had withdrawn to the Alamein area, which runs 35 miles south to the impassable Qattara Depression. Alexandria was only 40 miles away, so lines of communication and supply were adequate. Ultra reported that on 4 July Rommel had reported to his masters that he was suspending his attacks and going over to the defensive and regrouping his forces. Nevertheless, there was great panic in Cairo and on 2 July GHQ burned many confidential papers and files.

The 7th Armoured Division was now commanded by Major-General J.M.L. Renton (a Greenjacket who had done so well at Beda Fomm), and during July regrouped with 4th Armoured Brigade (that became 4th Light Armoured Brigade) and 7th Motor Brigade. The Cherry Pickers returned from Iraq and with the KRRC and Rifle Brigade were in frequent action.

During 2 and 3 July Lieutenant-Colonel Consett, CO 1st Bn Rifle Brigade, and 1st RHA, played key roles on the eastern edge of the Ruweisat Ridge.

The historian of the Greenjackets in *Swift and Bold* wrote:

Next day, 3rd July, was the turning point of the battle for the El Alamein line. Some will believe it was the turning point of the war. It was plainly Rommel's intention to smash the remnants of our armour, break through our defences and sweep on to the prizes of the Delta. He had every right to expect success. Before him he had the remains of an army which was desperately tired after a withdrawal of 350 miles. It had been reinforced in infantry but not in tanks, and here the enemy was definitely superior. But if we were tired, the enemy, as it turned out, were slightly more so, and not even the rich delights of Cairo and Alexandria could lure them on to a supreme final effort.

They tried, however, very hard indeed. About 0900 hrs on 3rd July they launched a heavy attack on the 4th and 22nd Armoured Brigades. 'A' Company (Captain P.A. Stockil) and 'B' Battery, 1st Royal Horse Artillery, were deeply involved, and the company suffered a grievous loss in the death from a shell splinter of Sergeant Roe, the anti-tank platoon commander. But the main onslaught was on the 22nd Armoured Brigade, who fell back on our right. The 4th Armoured brigade conformed. All British armour concentrated on some high ground known as Baoshaza. It was possible that the next determined attack by the enemy would overwhelm the two Brigades. Then the way to the Delta would be opened.

At this point the Commanding Officer, 1st Royal Horse Artillery, made a decision. He announced his resolve to fight to the last with his Regiment. Lieutenant-Colonel C d'A.P. Consett concurred on behalf of the Battalion. 'D' Company accordingly took up a position in front of 'E' Battery; 'A' Company dug in a few hundred yards in advance of 'B' Battery, whose right flank was covered by 'B' Company.

During the evening the enemy put in another attack with twenty tanks and infantry. It was easily driven off by 'E' Battery and 'D' Company. The Germans were too weary to make the final effort that day. But they evidently had plans for the following morning as they leaguered only about 1,000 yards away from our forward troops.

At first light the artillery observation posts discovered this leaguer still in close formation. Immediately a tremendous barrage was put down on the sleeping Huns by the 1st Royal Horse Artillery and other batteries and did tremendous damage.

The first Battle of Ruweisat Ridge took place on 14/15 July and then heavy fighting took place at Tel el Eisa. The second Battle of Ruweisat Ridge took place on 22nd and then Operation Splendour, in which 23rd Armoured Brigade lost 93 out of 104 tanks in a XIII Corps operation. A XXX Corps attack, Operation Manhood, occurred on 26 July. About 7,000 Axis prisoners were taken, but Commonwealth losses were greater.

In July 1942 the Medical Research Section at GHQ, MEF, wrote a detailed report on the daily stress and strain endured by the 8th Army tank crews:

Fatigue in tank crews has been one of the major problems of the present campaign in Libya. This is attributed to the longer hours of daylight than in previous campaigns, and to the more intense and prolonged fighting.

The following is a brief outline of the average tank crew's day. The men are awakened at about 0500 hours: ie before daylight, and get into their tanks which they drive out of leaguer to battle or patrol positions, which they reach by first light.

Battles commonly occur in the early morning or in the late afternoon or evening. In the middle of the day the heat haze is usually so great as to make accurate fire difficult. It is unusual for actual fighting to occupy more than three of the daylight hours. The rest of the time is spent in alert watchfulness or patrolling, and in waiting for or preparing an attack. It is universally agreed that these hours of expectancy are much more trying than the actual battle periods. The Commanders have a particularly fatiguing time, because in order to get immediate all-round vision they keep their heads above the turrets. This necessitates their standing because tank seats as at present constructed cannot be adjusted at a height which will allow them to sit.

Intrepid 'tankie' General Bernard Mongomery, August 1942. *Author*

Occasionally it may be possible for one or two of the crew to get out and stretch their legs or to 'brew up', but it is not at all uncommon for the crew to remain in the tank for the whole of the daylight hours. Engine noise and fumes, gun fumes and the wearing of headphones all day add to fatigue.

It is usually 2100 hours or later, at this time of the year, before the opposing tanks gradually draw apart and finally seek their respective leaguers. This often necessitates two or three hours of night driving on the part of the tank crews in order to reach some suitable point for the next day's battle. On reaching leaguer, they must first refuel, load and stow away ammunition – a process which requires one and a half to two hours – and must then carry out minor repairs and general maintenance of the tank, and distribute rations. It is rarely earlier than 0030–0100 hours when the men are at last able to get into their blankets. Nor is the day's work done yet, for each man in turn must stand an hour's guard. It is evident that three hours is the maximum sleep that can be obtained.

In the earlier days of the campaign, when the moon was full, frequent attacks were made by the enemy at night on our leaguers, both from the air and by tanks from the ground. These attacks will further reduce the hours of rest, and a number of officers have stated that they have gone 48 and 72 hours without being able to get to sleep.

It is a generally accepted opinion among the senior regimental officers interviewed that, under the conditions outlined above, it is impossible for men to go on fighting with any degree of efficiency for more than a week, and many would make the period even shorter. It has, however, been the policy in the present campaign to use troops until casualties prevented them from functioning as a unit, at which juncture they were amalgamated with similarly depleted units. Some of these units have seen almost continuous fighting for 18–20 days. The opinion was expressed that experienced troops, though exhausted, were better than troops without battle experience.

It appears that some form of alternation of tank crews must be devised, in order to ensure a necessary minimum of rest and recuperation, especially for prolonged campaigns. It has been suggested that a fifty per cent increase in the personnel of tank crews . . . would enable units to alternate those crews which needed it most.

Each tank crew, besides fighting and performing numerous duties must prepare its own meals. Crews can cook only when they can leave their tanks and this they can usually do only when in leaguer: But, they leave and return to leaguer during the hours of darkness when a strictly maintained blackout prevents the lighting of fires. The only opportunity for a hot drink is during a lull in the fighting in the daytime and this is often impossible.

Nights in the desert, even at midsummer, are cold enough to make it necessary to wear an overcoat: inability to get a hot drink before retiring to sleep or at breakfast in the morning is a great hardship.

Some units tried sending up hot foot in hayboxes by night with the 'B' Echelon. The food having been cooked 12–15 hours before was often cold and unpalatable on arrival. 'B' Echelon often arrived after the men had retired when they would rather sleep than eat. Sometimes 'B' Echelon failed to appear for a day or two at a time. German armoured units have a travelling field kitchen which is kept well forward and supplies tank crews with a hot meal at night and a hot drink in the morning.

Winston Churchill flew to Egypt on 4 August, and met General Auchinleck and Field Marshal Smuts. General Wavell arrived from India, and the recently appointed CIGS, General Alan Brooke, RAF Marshal Tedder and Admiral Harwood also came. The next day the Prime Minister visited the Alamein positions and met the South African and newly arrived Australian 9th Division. 'The troops were very cheerful and all seem confident and proud of themselves, but bewildered at having been baulked of victory on repeated occasions.' General Auchinleck was now relieved of his command and two totally non-desert-trained officers arrived on the scene. General Harold Alexander became Commander-in-Chief Middle East and Lieutenant-General Bernard Montgomery took command of the 8th Army. 'Monty' acted vigorously. He put up a silver First World War tank badge on a black RTR beret, despite his Royal Warwickshire infantry background, to encourage the battered but considerable armour under his control. He imported two more 'fresh' generals from the UK; Lieutenant-General Oliver Leese took command of XXX Corps and Lieutenant-General Brian Horrocks Command of XIII Corps. Both proved to be first-class Corps Commanders in the desert warfare ahead of them. On 19 August the Prime Minister again visited the Desert Front, and Alexander drove him out 130 miles to meet Monty in his command caravan at Burg-el-Arab, 'drawn up amid the sand-dunes by the sparkling waves'. Incredibly, Monty – in a week – had visited all his fighting units and their commanders, and had decided on his plans. He needed six weeks to reform all his divisions into integral tactical units. Three hundred brand new Sherman tanks would go to the 'new' 1st and 8th Armoured Divisions.

Many of the leading armoured commanders had been killed or wounded in the long-drawn out battle of Gazala. Major-General Lumsden and Brigadier Alec Gatehouse had been wounded, General 'Strafer' Gott killed on 7 August. 'Pip' Roberts, recovered from his wounds, was promoted to command 22nd Armoured Brigade situated just south of the Ruweisat Ridge, 'it was stinking, dusty and full of flies – a most unhealthy spot in every respect'. All the remaining Grant tanks in the 8th Army were to be grouped in 22nd Armoured Brigade, now part of the Desert Rats, and due to remain with them until Berlin was reached. Roberts wrote, 'We would have a motley collection of combined units, to wit 1st/6 RTR, 5 RTR, Royal

Gloucestershire Hussars, 3/4th County of London Yeomanry and a complete regiment, the Royal Scots Greys. Then in addition we had the 1 RHA and 1st Rifle Brigade. We were to be positioned out of centre, or a little south of Alam Halfa. South of us would be the 4th Light Armoured Brigade consisting of one regiment of Honeys (4/8th Hussars), two regiments (inc the Cherry Pickers) of armoured cars and one artillery regiment.' Brigadier Mark Roddick replaced Brigadier Carr posted back to the UK, and 4th Light Armoured Brigade were now part of the Desert Rats.

Churchill sent a telegram back to the War Cabinet on 21 August 'Have just spent two days in the Western Desert visiting HQ. Eighth Army. [Alan] Brooke, Alexander, Montgomery and I went round together seeing the [new] 44th Division, 7th Armoured Division and 22nd Armoured Brigade.' He met 'young Brigadier Roberts who at that time commanded the whole of our armoured force in this vital position'. Monty, by talking to the majority of his troops and telling them of his general plans, improved morale almost overnight.

Sergeant Jake Wardrop, 5 RTR, wrote: 'General Montgomery had arrived and he said that we'd start now. There was tons of stuff coming to the country, the Highland Division had arrived and the plans were being made for the big push.' Monty visited 1 RTR on the 16th in their battle position code 'Pheasant', and four days later Churchill and his entourage reviewed the two Grant squadrons of 1 RTR in hull-down positions. But Major-General Callum Renton, GOC of the Desert Rats, made the mistake of

Churchill accompanied by Lieutenant-General Sir Brian Horrocks, then commanding XIII Corps, just leaving 5 RTR after visiting the regiment before El Alamein, August 1942. Lieutenant-Colonel Jim Hutton is on the right of the three saluting figures, and in the centre is Brigadier Pip Roberts then commanding 22 Armoured Brigade. *Author*

Before Alamein, Monty shares a brew with his tank crew. John Poston, 11th Hussars, who was GOC-in-C's ADC, looks on. *Author*

arguing with Monty about the best employment of armour during the forthcoming battle. He was relieved of the command a few weeks later. Monty had ensured that the brand new, more effective Sherman tanks were all allocated to the so-called 'Corps de Chasse', Lieutenant-General Gatehouse's X Corps, with mainly new, fresh Yeomanry tank regiments. They might be considered to have more dash than the desert-experienced and perhaps desert-cautious Desert Rats.

Brigadier Francis de Guingand, Monty's Chief-of-Staff, advised that Rommel would probably make his main effort on the south or inland flank and the DAK would make a right hook to get in behind the 8th Army. The northern flank must be strengthened on the front of XXX Corps with minefields and wire. Monty spent a day examining the southern flank and the two important dominating ridges of Ruweisat and Alam Halfa in particular. Monty and de Guingand got to the heart of the matter.

Monty wrote, 'I had pondered deeply over what I had heard about armoured battles in the desert. Rommel liked to get our armour to attack him. He then disposed of his own armour *behind* a screen of anti-tank guns knocked out our tanks and finally he had the field to himself.' Monty decided that the British tanks would not rush out at the DAK, but stand firm in the Alamein position, hold the Ruweisat and Alam Halfa ridges *securely* and let him beat up against them. 'We would fight a static battle and my forces would not move. His tanks would come up against our tanks dug in hull down positions at the western end of the Alam Halfa Ridge.' And that was the way Operation Gamebirds – the battle of Alam Halfa from 31 August to 7 September – turned out to be. Monty stationed XIII Corps in the vital south-west sector, 22nd Armoured Brigade between the 2nd New Zealand Division and Alam Halfa, 7th Motor Brigade patrolling from the New Zealand position down to Heimeimat and the light tanks and armoured cars of 4th Light Armoured Brigade around Heimeimat itself. Rommel and many of his men were ill (jaundice, desert sores, dysentery were commonplace), the RAF bombing raids were intense, his Italian allies were being difficult and, importantly, his oil and petrol supplies were very limited. But he still had over 200 Panzer tanks (out of 500 in total) and 850 anti-tank guns, although the 8th Army had a 2:1 superiority in numbers of troops, tanks and artillery.

Brigadier 'Pip' Roberts's armoured regiments had two squadrons each of twelve Grant tanks and a light squadron of either Crusader or Stuart tanks. But 4 CLY only had one squadron of fifteen Grant tanks, plus a light squadron. Six American tank crews were dispersed throughout 22nd Armoured Brigade who had come to the desert for battle experience. Roberts 'walked the course' and placed the 6-pounder anti-tank guns of 1st Rifle Brigade and a battery of RHA in an area of flat and unbroken area, put the Grant tanks into the broken foothills and if necessary bull-dozed hull-down positions. He placed the Royal Scots Greys with the newest Grant

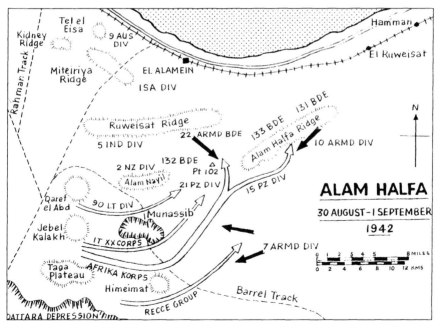

The Battle of Alam Halfa, Operation Gamebirds, 30 August–1 September 1942.

tanks on the eastern slopes as a mobile reserve. A careful artillery programme covered SOS tasks on areas when the enemy was close to the main defensive positions. One nasty surprise was soon revealed when the Axis forces attacked on the night of 30 August. They had twenty-six of the new Panzer Mark IV tanks with the long 75mm guns that were more formidable than any of the Grant squadron's guns.

The codeword for the move up by 22nd Armoured Brigade was 'Gamebirds Twelve Bore', and on the 31st 'Pepsodent' which meant 'Stand to' for immediate action.

Second Lieutenant Richard Tryon, 'A' Squadron 4 CLY, was in the thick of the ensuing battle:

> At 6pm – the Germans seem to love an evening scrap . . . there are German tanks emerging from the low ground ahead. Their commanders are well out of the turrets . . . they appear to be forming up at 2,000 yards to attack – four rows deep with some big chaps with nasty looking guns in the front. There are 60 facing our squadron and a lot more to the right. . . . Before we start firing we lose a tank. 'Heyday 1' is on fire and he is bailing out. He has a dead man in his tank and one or two wounded.

A furious tank battle ensued and all of 'A' Squadron's 12 Grants were knocked out. Tryon continued:

> The Germans are falling back now. They have failed to get through and they are leaving some 20 dead tanks behind them. They have had a nasty knock and though we've lost many men and all our 12 tanks, they've lost a lot more. Maybe, who knows? This little action near El Alamein may mean the turning point in the Battle of Egypt.

Stuka dive-bombers caused more casualties on the 25-pounder support and 'A' Echelon vehicles.

1 RTR observed 200 tanks in front of them, but were not in action, but 5 RTR lost one and the Scots Greys four tanks. Sergeant Jake Wardrop, 5 RTR:

> One night we beat off an attack by tanks. What a party! There were about 30 of them coming down the valley but we shook them. Fearless [Lieutenant-Colonel Jim Hutton, from 3 RTR, CO 5 RTR was nicknamed 'Fearless Jim'] was talking on the air. 'Here they come. Five, hold your fire a bit longer. Now let them have it. That's the stuff.' We certainly shook them up, we knocked out fifteen.

At about 1700 hrs the head of a large column of tanks was sighted by the 1st RTR moving north-eastward across its front. According to Captain B.C. Forster:

> They were about 2,000 yards from our tanks and not a shot was fired from the Brigade position. The wind deadened the noise of their engines and they came on in silence. Our tanks, where possible, were turret down with the commanders standing on the turrets. At 1730 the column was still moving up though its head had stopped in suspicion . . . one tank, elbowed out of the mass and more northerly than the others, approached the exact position behind which was Major Pink's tank. He had no alternative but to advance to a hull down position or be caught behind his bank. But before he could get on to his prepared platform the other tank had seen him and stopped. The two tanks were at too steep an angle for their

guns to bear and both the commanders looked at each other at a range of under 30 yards. After what seemed a very long time the German tank reversed and rejoined the stream.

At 1800 hrs the whole column was halted with about fifty tanks directly opposite the Regiment at range of 1,500 yards, and an intense fire was brought to bear on the squadron of 4 CLY, who were positioned between the Regiment and 5 RTR Tks on the left. At 1810 hrs Brigade ordered fire to be opened and all tanks adopted hull down positions and started firing. The clouds of dust resulting from the muzzle blast made observation extremely difficult. At 1930 hrs the enemy broke off the engagement leaving thirteen tanks behind, opposite the Regimental position. Our casualties had been nil as the enemy's fire had been mostly AP with very little HE landing on the position.

It had been a long, nerve-wracking day. One felt that at any time the Regiment's position could have been overrun by sheer weight of numbers. . . . This was most probably not so though. Each tank was in a well reccied position and had every opportunity of bringing accurate fire to bear . . . as it turned out no massed assault had to be dealt with and we were enabled to have tanks all along the line moving up at odd intervals to fire a few rounds and then reverse back whilst another tank left or took up the fight.

Brigadier Roberts called up his reserves. 'Come on the Greys. Get out your whips. They charge down the hill they are quite clear of the hole they have to plug and they go straight in.' The 15th Panzer had seen a gap where 'A' Squadron 4 CLY had been destroyed and were 300 yards from the Rifle Brigade anti-tank screen. Despite losses the Panzers overran the forward platoons, but when they saw the Scots Greys, retreated for the protection of *their* 88mm anti-tank screen, fully confident that the rash British tanks would follow in hot pursuit. They didn't.

On the morning of 1 September only 15th Panzer Division had sufficient petrol to mount an attack against the western end of Alam Halfa Ridge. They knocked out 7 Grants and lost 2 of their own Mark IIIs; 4th Light Armoured Brigade had a terrific time on the enemy's southern flank, discovered a MET supply convoy of 300 lorries and destroyed 57 of them. The Desert Rats played a small but key role in Gamebirds. Overall, British losses were 1,750 and the Axis forces almost 3,000. Only 38 Panzers and 11 Italian tanks had been destroyed, and despite Monty's caution 67 British tanks had been written off. But, nevertheless, over the five days Monty's battle had gone to plan – a defensive victory, helped greatly by the RAF Desert Air Force.

CHAPTER TWELVE

Operations Lightfoot and Supercharge – the Second Battle of Alamein

After the defensive success of Gamebirds, several major changes were made to 7th Armoured Division. Still part of Lieutenant-General Brian Horrocks' XIII Corps, the new GOC was Major-General John Harding. Brigadier Pip Roberts wrote of him, 'He was full of humour, always enthusiastic, always approachable, tremendously alert and quick on the uptake and of great energy. We understood one another well.' He had previously been Deputy Chief-of-Staff at the Cairo HQ. He gave the newly arrived General Montgomery a first-class briefing on the state of the Desert Army after the disastrous battle of Gazala. In addition to 4th Light Armoured Brigade, and 22nd Armoured Brigade, the new-comers (joining 25 October) were the 131st Queens Infantry Brigade, consisting of 1/5, 1/6 and 1/7 battalions of the Queens Royal Regiment. The brigade had arrived from England in the liner *Windsor Castle* along with 15,000 troops in a convoy of reinforcements. Initially part of 44 Division they had lost many casualties at Munassib in fierce fighting and 1/5th suffered 300 casualties in one day.

Pip Roberts's 22nd Armoured Brigade now consisted of 1 and 5 RTR, 4 CLY and two field gunner regiments, 4th and 97th (Kent Yeomanry). The Brigade 2 i/c Lieutenant-Colonel Mark Roddick was promoted to command 4th Light Armoured Brigade (still with the Desert Rats) consisting of 4/8 Hussars, Royal Scots Greys, 2nd Derbyshire Yeomanry, 12th Bn KRRC and 3 RHA.

Monty placed XXX Corps in the north of the Alamein line and XIII Corps in the south with X Corps (de Chasse) initially in reserve. The initial objective of XIII Corps (7th Armoured, 44th Division, 50th (Tyne-Tees) Division and brigades of Greeks and Free French) was to pin down by a feint attack some of Rommel's armour, including 21st Panzer Division (150 tanks) in the south, while the main attack went in on the northern flank. The 7th Armoured Division, with its high-mileage Grants, was told at Corps level 'not to press too hard or receive exceptionally high casualties as Monty wished to keep his forces balanced'. Some of the Mark III Crusader Cruiser tanks with the *new* 6-pounder gun were very popular. Training with tanks and infantry took place, and rehearsals for negotiating long and narrow minefield gaps – at night – sand-table exercises and many VIP visits occupied the Desert Army. Monty visited most front-line units, and Major-General Harding visited all the Desert Rat formations. The American politician Wendell Willkie visited Pip Roberts and in particular 4 CLY, as American tank sergeants had fought in Major Sandy Cameron's 'A' Squadron at Alam Halfa and had their tanks knocked out – but none received a scratch.

The plan for 7th Armoured Division in Operation Lightfoot (the defeat and destruction of the Axis forces) was for a night approach to break through two minefields, called 'January' and 'February', south of the Munassib Depression (held by the Italian Folgore Division) and form a bridgehead into which would follow the Stuarts, Grants and armoured cars of 4th Light Armoured Brigade and the infantry of 44th Division. General Koenig's Free French Brigade would swing south of the Heimeimat crests to capture the ground to the west. With the bridgehead firmly held the Desert Rats and Free French would attempt to exploit as far as Jebel Kalakh and the Taqa Plateau. The chief objective was to engage 21st Panzer Division and the Ariete, known to be in reserve, and prevent them intervening in the main attack in the north. Initially two British minefields, 'Nuts' and 'May', had to be circumnavigated. Six miles west was 'January' and two miles further on 'February'. Lieutenant-Colonel Corbett-Winder commanded the 'minefield task force'. Six Scorpion mine-clearance tanks (Matildas with iron-mounted flails), backed by 4th Field Squadron Royal Engineers, were tasked with the minefield clearance. They would be guarded by a squadron of Royal Scots Greys, two companies of 1 KRRC and all the carrier platoons of 44th Division. It was planned to make four gaps in January and February through which 5 RTR would follow on the right, 1 RTR on the left.

The German Engineer CO, Colonel Hecker, had sown half a million mines: 'devil's eggs' they were called. Many of them had been captured from Gazala and Tobruk *British* minefields; 95 per cent were anti-tank, many were booby-trapped, many were interlinked. Apart from buried aircraft and heavy-calibre shells (captured at Tobruk) the remainder were 'S' anti-personnel mines. The long, deep minefields were so placed to channel any force breaking through the outer belt into enclosed 'killing grounds' where artillery SOS targets and anti-tank guns nests were sited. Although 500 new electronic mine-detectors were available, and some elderly Scorpions, the main method of clearance was by prodding each square foot of sand with a bayonet until metal was struck (gently) and careful checks underneath for trip-wires or booby traps.

The CRE (Commanding Officer Royal Engineers) of the 7th Armoured Division had produced written advice and instructions for minefield recognition signals:

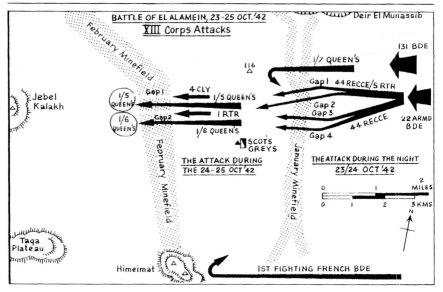

XIII Corps attacks during the Battle of El Alamein, 23–5 October 1942.

In minefields always keep to lanes BETWEEN lamps. OWN minefields have lanes marked on each side by *same* coloured *hurricane* lamps as the Axis (yellow or red). Enemy fields lanes marked on each side by ELECTRIC lamps (amber or green). At entrance to and exit from each minefield there are *TWIN* lights at each side of each gap. Lamps in minefields are spaced at 50 yards interval on each side of lane.

General Montgomery held conferences for the senior officers and told them he wanted

methodical progress: destroy enemy part by part, slowly and surely. Shoot their tanks and shoot the Germans. We must therefore keep at it hard; no unit commander must relax the pressure; organise ahead for a 'dog-fight' of a week. Whole affair about ten days. Don't expect spectacular results too soon.

Peter Roach, 1 RTR, wrote:

Mood had now changed from chagrined defeat and humiliation to a hard confidence tinged with wonder. Then miracle of miracles we paraded and were told the outlines of the battle to come. This was genius. Our primary task was to simulate an attack in the south drawing the Italian divisions without transport further into the desert – the main breakthrough in the north. General Montgomery's orders were read out – his stilted cricketing metaphors accepted by this highly irreverent bunch of military pirates.

Monty brought many fresh ideas to this great battle. Whole brigades of dummy trucks and tanks, a dummy railhead, fake dumps, bogus wireless traffic, appeared to fool the Luftwaffe reconnaissance planes and spies in Cairo. The little general planned a major assault at night, sometimes practised by the DAK but never by the Commonwealth forces. The full moon in October shone on the night of the 24th, which was chosen and agreed for the assault. Monty had massed and coordinated the artillery support of 882 guns into concentrated barrages (plus 1,200 anti-tank and 883 A/Ack guns). Monty sent a personal message to all commanding officers. 'This battle for which we are preparing will be a real rough house and will involve a very great deal of hard fighting. There must be no weak links in our mental [and *physical*] fitness.'

He foretold that the battle would be in three phases: a 'break' into and through the key minefields on the opening night of 23/24 October; a 'crumbling', or freely translated, a war of 'attrition' lasting several days, even weeks, while the key enemy forces were badly weakened; and a final 'breakthrough' called Operation Supercharge. Initially the main attack would be in the northern sector with XXX Corps's four divisions, and then through two minefield corridors; X Corps's de Chasse would be unleashed on the Tel el Aqqaqir ridge. In the south XIII Corps would stage two attacks: past the Heimeimat peaks and on to the Taqa Plateau (7th Armoured and 44 Infantry Divisions) and the second into the area of Jebel Kalakh (Free French). Monty was anxious that action against the enemy armour would *only* be undertaken when the infantry battle had been fought and won. In the skies the RAF, SAAF, RAAF and USAAF Mitchells and Liberators had almost complete control over the battlefield arena.

Rommel was again ill and had departed on sick leave, replaced temporarily by General Stumme, a panzer divisional commander from the Russian Front. Rommel was greeted as a hero when he visited the Führer's 'Wolf's Lair' in Berchtesgaden. Before he left the Alamein line he insisted that German and Italian divisions should be thoroughly intermingled, so that 'control' of the Duce's forces would be firm but not too obtrusive. In every way the 8th Army had a 2:1 superiority in numbers – men, artillery, tanks. In fact there were only 50,000 German troops in position plus 62,000 Italians (many of whom fought efficiently and bravely). Under the barrage of 882 medium and field guns, which opened up at 'H' hour (2140 hrs), Brigadier Roberts wrote:

> It took a little time to locate the eastern edge of 'January' minefield and by the time the actual 'gapping' started the enemy brought down quite heavy fire from artillery, mortars and machine guns. The Scorpions were continually breaking down through over-heating and when the mines were cleared, sometimes by hand, vehicles got stuck and could not get forward. The two southern gaps proved the most difficult because of soft sand. At about 0145 hrs number two gap was through thanks to some excellent work by 1 RB in knocking out the enemy anti-tank gun and its supporting troops. The most menacing fire was coming from the left flank towards the towering Heimeimat. I urged 5 RTR to get through number two gap, then prepare to move south and help at the extrication of those in gaps three and four. Part of the [Royal Scots] Greys were already through and moving south.

Sergeant Jake Wardrop, 5 RTR, with Stanley Skeels and George Stimpson were the crew of Major Paddy Doyle's tank:

> We had a bottle of Gilbey's Spey Royal that night to keep out the cold. None of us slept, we were all a bit excited. About four in the morning we pushed off and got through three

minefields with little trouble. There was some shooting back and a couple of tanks were on fire but we had to carry on until the open ground was reached.

Lieutenant-Colonel Corbett-Winder reported at 0300 hrs to Brigadier Roberts that due to heavy casualties he only had sufficient men to make two gaps in February minefield. He started his force off again at 0530 hrs with artillery support, but they never reached February. 'On the left,' wrote Roberts, 'they got there but came under heavy fire. In the meantime 1 RB supported by 5 RTR made some progress southward.'

When dawn broke it was obvious that the breaching of February by one brigade *in daylight* was impossible. As the Free French had failed to capture the Heimeimat heights, the Axis forces could dominate the gap between the two minefields. Roberts went up at dawn through No. 2 gap between January and February and found 'complete chaos, vehicles, tanks and carriers facing in different directions some still burning, some at curious angles and enemy shells arriving fairly steadily.' Roberts was encouraged, 'the leading troops were within 3,000 yards of Heimeimat, these were 1 RB and 1 RTR who had by then got through No. 3 gap, and 5 RTR were on the northern side of the area.' Peter Roach, 1 RTR, described their approach march up to their FUP (Forming up Point):

We moved off in the dark, a long winding snake of vehicles each wrapped in its own cloud of dust, each towing empty petrol cans to accentuate the noise and dust and size of the approaching threat. I listened to the voices on the radio and recognised the boredom, the fear, the exasperation, the excitement. This was my world, hot in the extreme, full of fine blowing dust, noisy, cramped and blind. Should we fight my job was loading the [Sherman] guns. It grew dark and we moved again to the external chaos of an advance. The leading tanks ran into trouble in the minefield gaps. The Colonel was desperately trying to elicit the facts from scared and harried tank commanders, who in turn were trying to elicit the facts from harried and scared engineers [trying to clear the minefields], who were trying to elicit the facts from the crew of a tank immobilised and shocked by the explosion of a mine.

Peter Roach's crew drank cold coffee and rum.

The GOC, Major-General John Harding, noted that 'It would have proved extremely costly to continue the effort in daylight. We would renew the attack on the night of 24/25th. 131 (Queens) Infantry brigade of 44 division was placed under my command.' Harding called an 'O' group at the western end of Gap No. 2 under constant shellfire. Roberts noted that

The plan was not difficult, each of the two gaps was to be cleared by the Sappers (no Scorpions this time) protected by a battalion of 131st in each case making a 'bridgehead' and then the armour would go through – 4 CLY on the right and 1 RTR on the left. 1/5 Queens and 1/6 Queens were to meet the gapping parties at 1800 hrs. We departed from this 'O' group with relief.

In the event, the two Queens battalions had to march several miles and zero hour had to be delayed twice. Derrick Watson, a young subaltern with 1/5 Queens, initially led their enormous convoy 'along an unmarked track, with only a scribbled sketch map and a useless reference'. Led by their CO, Lieutenant-Colonel Lance East, they crossed the 1,000-yard-wide February minefield:

> We suffered casualties from booby traps attached to the barbed wire. Private Mansell was blown to pieces by one of them. Ted Sarginson's platoon on my right had a number of casualties owing to one gun [from the supporting barrage] firing short. Major Cooper leading the way on a compass bearing outdistanced [everyone] until he was hit by machine gun fire. We had reached our objective having cleared the minefield and were in close contact with the enemy. There was a period of confusion in the darkness while we vainly attempted to regroup and advance further. [later,] we occupied our slit trench sangar for the next seventeen hours and the battalion suffered heavy casualties particularly from mortar fire.

The 4 CLY on the right gap lost twenty-six tanks trying to get through February, some from mines but most from anti-tank fire. Harry Ramsbottom (Middlesex Yeomanry Signals attached to 4 CLY) remembered how

> The enemy anti-tank defences opened fire on a fixed line. Within seconds it seemed as though the whole war was revolving round the Regiment with bursting shells and tracer illuminating the scene. There were many nasty moments. It was difficult to tell when the tank was clear of the minefield in this inferno. It was a helpless position with gunners trying to machinegun the unseen foe, but unable to bring accurate fire to bear. Lt Colonel PMR Scott, the CO, had his tank knocked out; Major David Silvertop the 2 i/c did wonders, Lt Neville Gillman was wounded and lost a leg, Neville Burrell and RS Torlot killed, Tony Tulloh captured.

The 1 RTR War Diary recorded:

> 25/10 0100 moved up to pass through January 0300 held up between 'J' and 'F' by concentration of friendly vehicles ahead. 0400 'A' Sqn move through RE gap. 0410 leading tank up on a mine; enemy shelling from both flanks; 3 more Stuarts up on mines, 1 KO'd by A/tank fire: 1 RTR area 880255: 0600 enemy artillery fire 2 ORs killed in action, 1 wounded. 1,000 moved east back through January minefield.

Major-General John Harding reported to the Corps Commander, Lieutenant-General Horrocks, who then consulted Monty who decreed that 7th Armoured Division was 'to be kept in being'. As a result, further operations were called off, CLY withdrew to reorganise themselves and 1 RTR and 5 RTR supported the two Queens battalions pinned down in the stony ground on the west side of February.

Major-General John Harding was informed that '4/8 Hussars covering the right flank of the Desert Rats ran into heavy enemy anti-tank fire and minefields and began to lose tanks faster than I could afford, so the movement was stopped.' Harding's ADC, Harry Cosgrave, was killed as he and the GOC drove through a minefield, and the CRA (Commander Royal Artillery), Roy Mews, was wounded at TAC HQ. On the 28th most of the division went into reserve, close to the east side of the January minefield. The Desert Rats' first part of Operation Lightfoot was over. They had lost considerable casualties including sappers, infantry and tanks, and held in check the enemy armour in the southern part of the Alamein line for forty-eight hours.

★ ★ ★

General Montgomery had the equivalent of seven infantry and three armoured divisions, so the Desert Rats only played a minor role in the main 'crumbling' or attritional period. The German commander, Stumme, died of a heart attack on 24 October, and Rommel, at Hitler's request, left hospital in Germany and flew back to resume command late on the 25th. Fierce fighting continued by 9th Australian and 51st Highland Divisions in the northern sector. Rommel urged on his two faithfuls, 15th and 21st Panzer Divisions in the Kidney Ridge area on the 27th and 28th. But Commonwealth anti-tank guns, tanks and the air forces blunted the Axis attacks. By the 26th XXX Corps had 4,643 casualties, X Corps 455 and XIII Corps 1,037.

On the night of the 29th/30th the division was involved in the staging of a dummy attack, and the next day moved north behind the main battle area (with 131st Queens Brigade). Operation 'Supercharge' started at 0100 hrs on 2 November, the breakout stage of the whole battle. In the initial stages in the tank battle of Tel el Aqqaqir the Yeomanry of 9th Armoured Brigade were virtually destroyed. Bryan Perrett in *Iron Fist* describes the battle vividly. On the morning of 4 November the Desert Rats, led once again by 11th Hussars, followed by 22nd Armoured Brigade in three armoured regimental columns with the Queens battalions bringing up the rear, set off for Tel El Aqqaqir, then moved west into the open desert bound for El Daba. The division passed through the 5th Indian Brigade and 51st Highland Division and saw the remains of the Yeomanry-Panzer three-day duel. Brigadier Roberts wrote:

I was pressed by John Harding to get on. We altered direction due west and got two regimental groups 'up' on a frontage of 2,000 yards. About mid-day we encountered a large Italian armoured force on our left flank, most of what was left of the Italian Ariete Armoured Division; there were guns, anti-tanks, at least 30 tanks – M13s – no match for our Grants and hardly equal to the Crusaders or Stuarts. It was very good battle practice for the brigade! We wheeled left to face south, the Italians were moving northwest. The CLY turned immediately left and 5 RTR swung a bit wider to head them off. Meanwhile the gunners were getting into action close behind. The Italians must have felt all hell had been let loose. We outgunned them so we stood back and picked them off. There was no object in closing in and getting casualties.

Harry Ramsbottom, CLY:

It was 'goodbye Alamein', already the air seemed to be cleaner and sweeter as we left the massive minefield area far behind, to manoeuvre in open spaces. Late in the morning we caught up with a force of Italian M-13 and anti-tank guns just short of El Daba. A lively battle ensued in which a few German tanks also joined. Our old enemy the 88mm was once again in evidence. The duel continued throughout the afternoon. The number of burning M-13s bore witness to the terrific punishment the enemy was taking. Our losses were negligible – it was the anti-tank guns that were the menace rather than the inferior burning M-13s. By nightfall the battle was over. The Regiment leaguered a few hundred yards from the 25 burning Italian tanks. This was the first time the Regiment had used its 6 pounder Cruisers in a tank *v.* tank action.

The Rifle Brigade rounded up about 500 POWs. 1 RTR War Diary noted:

4/11 approaching Deir el Mura, 15 enemy tanks seen. 'C' Sqn engage. 'B' Sqn take on two 88mm. 'A' Sqn KO 1 x 88mm, other KOs. Sergeant Horsfield killed at T37921. 1000 hrs 'C' Sqn + 2 Troops 'B' Sqn engage, 1 tank on fire, other crews bailing out. 1730 until last light engage four 88mms and MET.

Peter Roach, 1 RTR, wrote:

At first grey light, the ground was beaten and pounded by shellfire. The sun came up and we moved on. Now the light squadrons out in front were in contact with the enemy. The voices on the radio told their own tale. Calm and easy, taut and strained, querulous and demanding. The heat increased and the day wore on and on. At a halt, I saw from the driver hatch a column of the German 90th Light division come rocketing through. All our tanks were firing. I saw the turret of a German armoured car go flying with a direct hit. Italian prisoners were brought in with their suitcases and white flags. Through the heat and dust we moved and fought and moved until the bliss of night and the bliss of oblivion.

Sergeant Jake Wardrop, 5 RTR, noted in his diary:

The Highlanders took a licking, they were lying all over the place. We got to the scrap as quickly as possible. This other crowd of ours, the 9th Brigade took a severe hiding, the Boches had taken one too. There were Mark IIIs and IVs all over the place. . . . The line had been broken well and truly and we were behind it on the blue with plenty of room to dash about in as we had done before. There was a line of guns and tanks further to the west but we were off at first light [4 November] and tore straight through them and off. The bugle had blown and we couldn't stop. There were thousands and thousands of prisoners. If we happened to stop beside any we nipped out, pinched their watches, binoculars, or anything they had and carried on.

The next day, the 5th, Brigadier 'Pip' Roberts's birthday, his brigade moved some 20 miles, were held up by a dummy minefield, but then advanced another 10 miles. On the next day moving north-west at first light directed on Qasaba shortage of petrol halted the advance. The Echelon vehicles with petrol had got mixed up in the night with a German convoy. By 1600 hrs 'we came up against a strong enemy rearguard consisting of tanks and anti-tank guns'. Then two things happened, Lieutenant-Colonel Lushington, RA, put down a two-regimental stonk that landed on Roberts's TAC HQ and the skies opened to heavy and heavier rain. 1 RTR War Diary. '6/11 actions all day. 50 MET, half of them tanks, heavy rain but Grant Squadrons KO five tanks, two 88mms, five lorries, losing two 'B' Squadrons Grants with seven casualties. More rain.'

5 RTR encountered a strong fast column with British trucks and Honey tanks. 'They had a lot of our stuff, 25 pounders and Ford lorries,' remarked Sergeant Wardrop, 'but were they British? Old Fearless [the CO, Lt Colonel Hutton] must have thought it was a bit fishy, so he gave the order to halt and open fire. The range was 3,000, visibility was poor with the rain and they were moving fast.' 5 RTR were sure it was Rommel's HQ heading west of Fuka.

5 RTR claimed to have KO'd five enemy tanks (in their War Diary) at Bir el Himaiyima twenty miles west of Fuka. But Rommel sped west as Operation Supercharge was successfully concluded.

The newly arrived 131 Queens Brigade had suffered heavily during Operation Lightfoot. In the gapping of the January minefield by 1/7 Queens their CO, Lieutenant-Colonel R.M. Burton, the 2 i/c, Major E.W.D. Stilwell, were among eleven officers killed or wounded with 179 other ranks killed in action, wounded or missing. The Italian Folgore Division and Ramcke's 22nd Parachute Brigade had produced a ferocious defence. 1/6 Queens had ten officers and 187 other rank casualties and 1/5 Queens lost eight officers and 110 other rank casualties during the Battle of Alamein. During Operation Braganza (the attack on Deir El Munassib 30 September to 1 October before the Queens joined 7th Armoured) 1/5 Queens suffered 272 casualties and 1/6 Queens 56 casualties.

General Alexander sent a telegram to Churchill on 9 November.

> This great battle can be divided into four stages. The grouping and concentration of our forces for battle and deception methods employed which gained for us surprise, that battle winning factor. The break – in attack – the great concentration of force of all arms which punched a hole deep into his defences and by its disruption created artificial flanks which gave us further opportunities for exploitation. The thrust now here, now there, which drew off his forces and made him use up his reserves in stopping holes and in repeated counter-attacks. The final thrust which disrupted his last remaining line of defence and broke a way through – through which poured our armoured and mobile formations.

Churchill then noted, 'We lost more than 13,500 men at Alamein in twelve days.'

CHAPTER THIRTEEN

Hot Pursuit to Tripoli – Churchill's Victory Parade

As might be expected, Rommel's Axis troops fought a whole series of defiant rearguard actions. With not more than twenty tanks, twenty anti-tank guns, fifty field guns and very little petrol, they had a secret weapon.

Generalleutnant Karl Buelow was chief engineer to the much reduced Panzer-Armee. He was an expert on demolitions and booby traps and set to work at once. Generalmajor Hermann Ramcke, with his 600 ex-Luftwaffe Fallschirmjäger, turned up unexpectedly, having escaped from the Alamein battles. Despite huge congested traffic jams (one of 25 miles along the coast road to Halfaya and Sollum), the various desert air forces failed to halt the orderly retreat, even though Kittihawks and Spitfires were in action daily and Wellingtons and Halifaxes at night. On the night of 10/11 November 1942 Stuarts of 4th Light Armoured Brigade helped New Zealand infantry storm Halfaya Pass, taking many prisoners of the Pistoia Division. On the 15th, 4th Light Armoured Brigade, with two composite squadrons of Scots Greys, 4th and 8th Hussars, backed by 3 RHA and 1 KRRC, set off in hot pursuit by the coast road towards Benghazi. Another 7th Armoured 'task' force of 11th Hussars, some RHA and 1 KRRC, followed by HQ of 7th Armoured, headed south-west towards Msus. 90th Light Division was nearly trapped on the 15th, but were saved by a Mediterranean storm coming in from the sea.

Major-General John Harding wrote, 'On 13th November I was ordered to establish the [7th Armoured] division west of Tobruk to cover the opening up of that port and to push forward reconnaissance elements to report on the Derna-Martuba airfields.' Tobruk was found unoccupied, and by the 14th 4th Light Armoured Brigade was patrolling into the Jebel, 22nd Armoured Brigade in the El Adem area and the Queens Brigade in Tobruk.

From 14 November for a week the Queens Brigade occupied Tobruk, guarded dumps of captured enemy materials and the Bermondsey 1/6 Queens appropriately worked the docks and unloaded stores from incoming shipping. Lieutenant-Colonel Lance East, CO 1/5 Queens, worked out a tactical plan for 507th Coy RASC who provided the 3-tonner troop carrying vehicles (TCVs). Each TCV carried half a platoon. A Queens battalion moved across the desert in a square with a lorried company at each

1/6 Queens Infantry march into Tobruk. *Imperial War Museum*

corner and battalion HQ in the centre. Their 6-pounder anti-tank guns formed the front and flank faces and 53rd Field Regiment the rear face. Vehicles by day moved 200 yards apart, but night leaguer closed up to five yards between vehicles.

Petrol supplies were now very short (for both sides). Major-General Harding then organised the armoured car columns – the Cherry Pickers leading one, the Royal Dragoons another towards Antelat and Agedabia plus the 1 RTR column (of 22nd Armoured Brigade).

Alan Moorehead described

a cruel business, mining – a stab in the back and the stabber ran no risks himself. The German developed this mining to a science along the road to Tripoli. Everything likely or unlikely was mined or booby trapped. When the retreating German sappers got to work on a bridge first the bridge would be blown up. Then the fallen rubble would be S-mined [projected three prongs above the ground which when stepped on exploded a metal ball crammed with small shot at waist height wounding or killing soldiers on foot]. Then the approaches to the crater on either side would be mined with [round metal tin anti-tank] Teller mines.

Some of the Tellers were placed one on top of another and then booby-trapped. If a tank crew jumped out of their Teller-mined tank they might land on S-mines. Wooden-cased mines, not vulnerable to metal detectors, were also being introduced into General Buelow's devilish repertoire.

Meanwhile Brigadier 'Pip' Roberts, 22nd Armoured Brigade, settled down to re-equip at Mrassas between Tobruk and Bardia. Bets were now taken as to which formation would get to Tripoli first with evens on the Desert Rats and the 'Highway Decorators' (51st Highland, so known for their prolific signposting). Battledress was issued for the North African winter which can be unusually cold.

Lieutenant Charles Pearce, Troop Leader No. 4 Troop 'C' Squadron 4 CLY, kept a diary for the remainder of the North African campaign. Their CO was Lieutenant-Colonel HB Scott DSO, known either as 'Harry' or 'Black Harry', a great disciplinarian. 'He never worried how all ranks were dressed so long as the guns worked.' He had replaced Lieutenant-Colonel Frank Arkwright DSO who was killed in action in July 1942 in the long withdrawal from the Gazala line to Alamein. One of the many supply problems with the 8th Army was the wide range of tank spare or replacement equipment. The Panzer-Armee had standardised on their Mark II, III and IV, but 4 CLY had two 'heavy' squadrons mainly of Shermans but also Grants, while 'C' Squadron was equipped with 6-pounder Crusaders. 1 RTR, now commanded by Lieutenant-Colonel David Belchem, and 5 RTR, under Lieutenant-Colonel Jim Hutton, had the same sort of mix.

Brigadier 'Pip' Roberts got a warning order to equip one armoured regiment and 'acquired' new Sherman tanks from the very reluctant 10th Hussars. By the evening of the 18th the lucky 1 RTR formed part of a Desert Rat task force with a squadron of Shermans, another of Stuarts, 1st Bn Rifle Brigade and 4th Field Regiment RA. The tanks were on transporters, and starting on the 19th reached Agedabia – a distance of 230 miles – on the evening of the 21st. Roberts wrote:

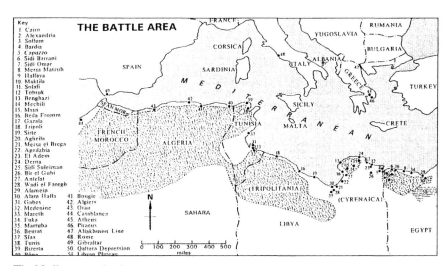

The Mediterranean battle area.

This had been good going and I think General John Harding was quite pleased with us. Monty visited me on the 18th before we left El Adem and said 'Now you are not to get a very bloody nose – you must keep your armoured regiments in good shape,' [ie push on, win your battles but don't suffer casualties to men or tanks.]

Two more Desert Rat columns were formed to drive on El Adem, through Tengeder, capture the landing ground at Msus and probe towards Antelat. Sergeant Jake Wardrop, 5 RTR: 'We milled around for a bit then swooped on El Adem aerodrome and captured twenty-five ME 109s and all the Luftwaffe personnel who were having dinner.' 5 RTR put some 75mm shells among the Luftwaffe. 'We piled into the Mess and ate their dinner so it didn't go to waste. You should have seen all the dirty "Desert Rats" sitting round a table with a white cloth on, shouting "Hoch" to each other – it was one of the high spots of the war.' Lieutenant-Colonel 'Fearless Jim' Hutton, their CO, gave 5 RTR a lecture on the war situation, and an hour later tank transporters with fifty brand new Sherman tanks arrived, and an hour after that a composite squadron was on the move into 'the blue'.

By 18 November 90th Light Division were in Benghazi with a rearguard at Benina, 21st Panzer at Ghemines, and 15th Panzer at El Magrun. By the night of 23/24 all the Axis troops were back in the Mersa Brega positions from where they had set out with such élan ten months earlier. The Cherry Pickers and the Desert Rat Stuart tanks approached these hastily erected defences with understandable caution. In six days the famous Panzer-Armee – its remnants – had been harried and pursued hotly for 250 miles.

Lieutenant-Colonel Teddy Mitford, known as a famous and skilled desert traveller (ex 1 RDG), commanded a Desert Rat task force. Major Maunsell had a 5 RTR Sherman squadron, two squadrons of 1 RTR, plus companies of Rifle Brigade and a RHA battery. They set off for Msus aerodrome, Fort Antelat, cut the road to the west then to Agedabia and Mersa Brega. On 6 December the new tanks were handed over to the Scots Greys.

Peter Roach, 1 RTR, noted

At the El Adem airfield we were re-equipped, the two heavy squadrons with Sherman tanks – for the first time we had parity with the panzer units so long dominant. A stupendous boost to our morale. We set off on tank transporters in high spirits towards El Agheila.

The 4/8 Hussars also handed over their tanks to the Scots Greys, and 4th Light Brigade continued their pursuit through the Jebel. Brigadier Roddick was wounded on a mine and Brigadier Roscoe Harvey, a determined and skilful steeplechaser, took command. It was probably a dead heat 'First into Benghazi' on 20 November; the Cherry Pickers from the south, or 4th Light Armoured from the north. The 1/7 Queens and 131st Brigade HQ reached Benghazi on 23 November via Barce and the Tocra pass – a distance of 310 miles. 'A' Company was sent to the docks and 'C' Company guarded the new HQ of XXX Corps under Lieutenant-General Oliver Leese. The Italian barracks in the town became the Queens base when 1/5 and 1/6

Queens, via Sidi Magrun airfield, arrived – again to use their expertise in the docks. Brigadier L.G. 'Bolo' Whistler was the new brigade commander. Lieutenant-Colonel R.J.A. Kaulback was CO 1/6 Queens and Lieutenant-Colonel R.H. Senior, DSO, became CO 1/7 Queens. The brigade stayed in Benghazi until 12 December.

Major N.G. Crouch, OC 'C' Squadron 1 RTR, gave this account of a typical day in action – 22 November – at El Agedabia:

'C' Squadron moved forward on left of RHQ to high ground overlooking Agedabia and came under fire from A/tank guns from the north. Sgt Place T23604 lost a track but in the afternoon fitters repaired it. Sgt McConnachie MM T144986 received a direct hit from a HE shell which blew off his AA gun and cupola fracturing his jaw. His tank had to withdraw. No. 5 Troop Lt J Mears at 1030 proceeded S to report movements of 6 six-wheeled armoured cars and 3 MkIII tanks in the low ground to the SW. Engaged at 2,000 yards, they withdrew but Lt Mears troop registered hits and destroyed one. At 1330 hrs an 88mm A/Tk gun hampered replenishment. Mears was ordered SE on a recce as the rest of 'C' Sqn came under mortar and A/Tk fire from SE of Agedabia. My tank (Major Crouch) received several hits. The attached Motor Coy with 6 pdrs, and No. 5 Tp drove off at 1600 hrs four more [enemy] armoured cars. I reported 12 enemy tanks to the left front hull down in battle line. These were engaged and driven off. 'C' Sqn followed up but the enemy withdrew out of range. Up to last light transport and gun positions were engaged with effect.

By the end of November 1942 Montgomery had made plans for the next operation – pushing the Axis rearguard out of the 40-mile-long Mersa Brega line by General Oliver Leese with the 'new' XXX Corps Division (7th Armoured, 51st Highland and the New Zealanders). D-Day was set for the night of 16/17 December. Rommel, in the meantime, had flown to see his Führer at Rastenburg. The 'Desert Fox' now recommended a 'strategic' withdrawal to Tunis in order to defeat the Anglo-American armies probing from Morocco, into Algeria and towards Tunisia. His views caused a predicable storm. A compromise was reached with Mussolini in Rome (since Italian forces were in a majority now) and a discreet withdrawal back to the Buerat line (halfway between Agheila and Tripoli) was agreed. The Giovani Fasciti, the Pistoia and the Ariete divisions moved out at night and the Via Balbia was crowded with Panzers and guns driving westwards. Every conceivable form of mine had been laid and the Cherry Pickers lost men and cars, but still managed to reach 'Marble Arch' (Mussolini's triumphant edifice) on 16 December. 4th Light Armoured Brigade supported the New Zealanders, and the next day near Nofilia had a day-long battle against the 15th Panzer rearguard. The Scots Greys encountered 30 Panzers and gave a good account of themselves taking 200 prisoners. On the 21st the 4th Light Armoured Brigade (less the Greys) rejoined 7th Armoured Division.

Christmas Day was celebrated in reasonable style. General Oliver Leese had organised that XXX Corps should be well fed. The whole of 7th Armoured Division had an issue of *fresh* pork, rum and extra cigarettes. Sergeant Jake Wardrop, 5 RTR, had two Christmas dinners, one in mid-December and another on Christmas Day with three bottles of beer and a scrounged bottle of Cyprus wine. General Montgomery decided that the 8th Army should do no fighting on Christmas Day. They didn't, but the luckless Cherry Pickers provided a screen working in shifts. Monty and General Leese visited the Desert Rats when they saw the Queens Brigade at Wadi Matratin. Monty remarked that they were 'a good, tough body of men.' Brigade HQ of 22nd Armoured Brigade, out of sheer bravado, bathed in the particularly uninviting sea. By the end of 1942 all of Rommel's forces were back in the Buerat defences 230 miles east of Tripoli.

On 9 January 1943 General Alexander informed Winston Churchill and the CIGS of his plans.

> The advance will start night January 14–15th with XXX Corps. 7th Armoured Division and 2nd New Zealand Division will advance to Sedada. There will probably be opposition from the Gheddahia area. After this has been dealt with direction of advance will be Beni-Ulid-Tarhuna, 7th Armoured Division leading. 51st [Highland] Division will follow the line of the main coastal road. 22nd Armoured Brigade is with Army Command, X Corps is not being brought up. XXX Corps will have approximately 500 miles of petrol and ten days rations and water for the whole force.

On 19 January 1/6 Queens, under Lieutenant-Colonel Bill Kaulback, occupied the small town of Tarhuna in front of the main enemy positions. Two days later 1/5th and 1/6th put in a successful night attack through the hills along goat tracks. There were no mules to carry heavy loads, so spare drivers and cooks carried the wireless sets, mortars and ammunition. When Lieutenant-Colonel Kaulback reached the FUP to wait for the artillery barrage the Arabs in a nearby cave presented him with cheeses, but no military information.

Captain C.A. Howard won a posthumous MC when 1/5 Queens were clearing wadis in the Tarhuna hills. Private Jack York described the action:

> At last after a long weary struggle we neared the top of the highground, feeling exhausted and dizzy from the heat and lack of food. . . . Suddenly mortar bombs started to explode across the valley with an echoing crash, sending waves of compressed air, flying stones and shrapnel over a wide area.

Captain Howard identified the target and within ten minutes an artillery barrage was laid on. Private York was the radio operator and saw and heard 'the vicious sound of enemy Spandaus mingling with the explosions ahead'. Blood was seen pouring from a wound in Howard's arm:

> The ridge ahead was wreathed in smoke. The Captain with another officer and about 20 men moved forward and lobbed grenades round the enemy positions. As the smoke cleared I could see him revolver in hand and black huddled shapes crouching behind a machine gun. Suddenly there was a yellow flash and an indescribable mêlée as more men rushed up. A fearful agitation and twisting of bodies as the smoke cleared. . . . In one or two trenches lay upturned machine guns resting on dead and mutilated bodies. The men just lay gasping on the ground after their ordeal and orgy of killing . . . the brave Captain dead beside a weapon pit . . . two trenches had received direct hits from our artillery. The occupants were just dark, grotesque shadows, motionless in the pale sunlight.

22nd Armoured Brigade with 1 RTR, 5 RTR and 4 CLY were usually the main strike force of 7th Armoured Division. But when Major-General Harding was wounded late on 19 January, Brigadier 'Pip' Roberts was appointed by the Corps Commander Oliver Leese to command the Desert Rats (with Lieutenant-Colonel Mike Carver as GSO1). This he did for five days until the [Brigadier General Staff] Bobby Erskine took over command of the Desert Rats, which for a time consisted of 4th, 8th (Red Fox's Mask) and the Queens brigades under Brigadier 'Bolo' Whistler. Major-General Harding wrote: 'That was the end of the hunt for me and the most bitter disappointment. For over two years my target had been Tripoli and it was with great joy that I heard later on that 7th Armoured Division was the first in that port.' 'Pip' Roberts acting GOC with two turretless Honey tanks had closely followed 11th Hussars at 0500 hrs into the town (Sergeant H.P. Lyon in Car No. 118775 was first in) just ninety minutes ahead of the

Churchill inspects the Desert Rats in Tripoli. *Imperial War Museum*

Gordons of 51st Highland Division. Harding continued, 'In command of 7th Armoured Division, the finest body of desert warriors, the most devoted comrades-in-arms from Alamein to Tarhuna, nearly 1,400 miles as the crow flies, in less than three months – what greater honour, what more exhilarating or inspiring experience can any soldier have ever had?'

Winston Churchill flew from Cairo to Tripoli where he was met by General Montgomery:

I spent two days in Tripoli and witnessed the magnificent entry of the Eighth Army through its stately streets . . . in the afternoon [4th February] I inspected [in the Corso Italo Balbo] the massed parades of two divisions. I stayed in Montgomery's caravan . . . and addressed about two thousand officers and men of his headquarters.

(The full speech is shown as Appendix A.) Perhaps the key phrase was 'When a man is asked (after the war) what he did, it will be quite sufficient for him to say "I marched and fought with the Desert Army".'

Alan Moorehead noted:

In the swaying battle of the desert, Tripoli had for two and a half years appeared as a mirage that grew strong and now faded away again and was for ever just beyond the Eighth Army's reach. So many had died or been withdrawn through wounds at a time when the struggle looked futile and endless.

Moorehead wrote of the sense of anti-climax – so much achieved, so much more to be achieved before the Axis armies were to be hounded out of Africa.

Sergeant Jake Wardrop enjoyed 5 RTR's stay outside Tripoli:

We did quite well for sugar, tins of butter . . . there was wine and brandy too and we did a little drinking. [On 5 February,] the Prime Minister arrived about eleven with a great escort of motorcyclists and 11th Hussars in armoured cars. Well done the 'Cherry Pickers' they would have to be in front. There were three car-loads of big shots, Monty, Alexander, General Leese, Randolph Churchill, Air Marshal Tedder and a lot more. They drove round the streets past all the lads then came back to the saluting base.

Wardrop noted that Churchill had a good long chat with his CO, 'Fearless' Jim Hutton. Each tank regiment supplied two officers and sixty men for the victory parade. Peter Roach, 1 RTR:

Outside Tripoli we stopped, no petrol, no ammo waited in limbo for a victory parade. We merely lined the route with our tanks while the crews stood smartly in front. Mr Churchill drove past us in high spirits and waved cheerily to the locals. We were proud and pleased.

1 RTR under Lieutenant-Colonel David Belchem, with their 21 Crusaders, 27 assorted Grants and Shermans, plus 6 scout cars, had a fighting strength of tank crews – 25 officers and 231 ORs, and 'dismounted' of 5 officers and 232 ORs. For a week out of action they had lectures – the new German MkVI Tiger tank was shown. Sappers gave lectures on anti-tank and anti-personnel mines; smoke demonstrations were made by the

Churchill, Alexander, Montgomery, Alan Brooke and Freyburg at the Victory Parade, Tripoli, 1943.

Close Support (CS) Crusader tanks, and on 9 February Monty addressed all available XXX Corps officers. The new 1 RTR Dingo troop was formed and trained, and on the 11th patrols crossed into Tunisia. Monty's stirring talk ended with 'Forward to Tunis! Drive the enemy into the sea.'

The Queens Brigade had a three-day rest at Suani Ben Adem bivouacked on large farms or in the woods with ample water, fresh vegetables and wine. They also received two large armoured control vehicles (ACK1 for the Brigade Major, ACK2 for the 'Q' staff at Rear HQ). They were fitted with brand new wireless sets that sent the signallers into raptures. There was excellent reception of the Afrika Korps' song 'Lili Marlene'. More 6-pounder anti-tank guns, towed by portees, arrived soon to be put to good use. On 26 January Queens Brigade advanced to Zavia, Sabratha, Mellita to Zuara – slow progress due to enemy rearguards, mines and demolitions. There were daily casualties to booby traps and 3rd (Cheshire) Field Squadron RE arrived to help with this problem. By 12 February the Queens Brigade had assembled at El Assa – an area of flat salt marshes passable when dry, but terrible after rain.

CHAPTER FOURTEEN

Forward to Tunis

Brigadier 'Loony' Hinde was now commanding 22nd Armoured Brigade, and Brigadier 'Pip' Roberts took over 26th Armoured Brigade in 6th Armoured Division within the 1st Army still struggling eastwards. On 14 February 1943 American forces were overwhelmed at the Kasserine Pass. Some of the best Axis divisions had reinforced Rommel's troops in Tunisia – the Hermann Goering, the 10th Panzer, the Young Fascists and the 9th Division.

The 22nd Armoured Brigade on tank transporters moved west 70 miles on 10 February to Zuara, then the next day 36 miles to El Votia, and in the next few days a further 80 miles to Tegalmit. On the 14th 1 RTR moved into Tunisia and helped the Free French forces at Fort Sidi Toui. 5 RTR led the Brigade in heavy dawn mist into the Tadjera Hills. Their CO, 'Fearless' Hutton, was an expert in desert navigation, and led in his armoured car. Fire was brought down on the enemy using the road below. 'The Boche were a bit jittery,' wrote Jake Wardrop. 'We threw in a right flank with a few tanks. We took quite a lot of stuff here, mortars, guns and a good number of prisoners. It was a very stout performance and it was well thought of by Monty. The ridge is now known as "5th Tanks Ridge".'

The Queens Brigade secured Medenine on the 19th, and the Desert Rats, 51st Highland and 2nd New Zealand Divisions with almost 500 anti-tank guns now faced Rommel's rearguards. By the 28th the Scotsmen were holding the north of the line near the sea, the Desert Rats astride the Medenine-Mareth-Gabes road with the Queens Brigade in front and the armour behind. Rommel decided to launch a major attack in the Medenine area. On 6 March the 15th, 21st and 10th Panzer divisions came down from the hills like wolves on the fold, backed by 1,500 infantry. It was a brave but unusual tactic for the Panzers to go hell for leather into the most powerful anti-tank gun screen the 8th Army had yet assembled. Much of the force of the frontal attacks of the day fell on the Queens Brigade. Major R.B. Johnson's book *The Queens in the Middle East and North Africa* had an excellent account of the battle of Medenine. By the end of the 6th the Axis forces withdrew, leaving fifty-two tanks destroyed by gunfire. Forty-five of these were knocked out by 7th Armoured Division (mainly by the Queens 6-pounder anti-tank guns).

The Queens Brigade were defending a 2-mile front west of the main Medenine road. 1/5th in the north-west sector fended off enemy infantry,

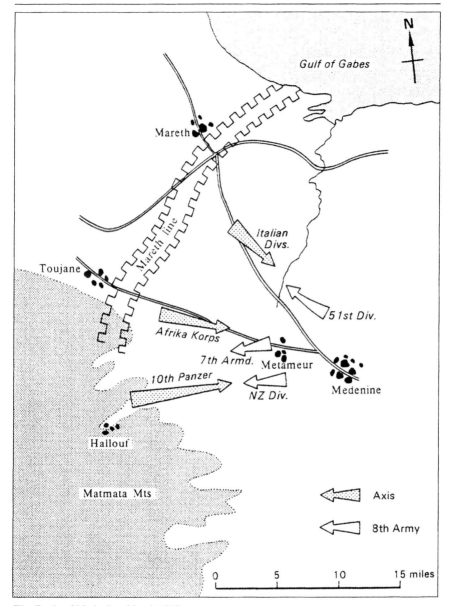

The Battle of Medenine, March 1943.

1/7th in the centre were defending two danger points, a narrow pass and a long wadi on their southern border with 1/6th. When the early morning mist dispersed a column of about twenty-two enemy tanks were spotted by the No. 5 6-pounder gun crew of 1/7th anti-tank platoon under Sergeant Andrews. He deliberately allowed four to proceed along the track through the pass, opened fire and knocked out the next two. He successfully engaged

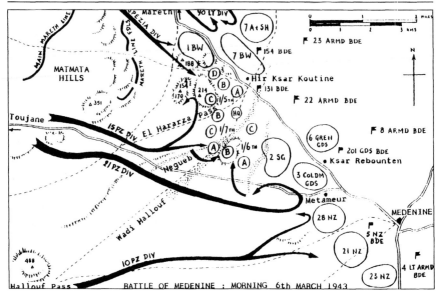

The Battle of Medenine on the morning of 6 March 1943.

the next four while the remaining dozen swung into hull-down positions. In the battle that followed No. 5 gun parapet was smashed and Sergeant Andrews himself continued to load and fire. Two more enemy tanks were knocked out and the remainder prevented from entering the vital wadi. They did get into a smaller Wadi Hallouf running to the east and were engaged by Sergeant Crangles's No. 7 gun and No. 8 under Sergeant Vincent. Eventually both Queens anti-tank guns were put out of action and three surviving enemy tanks overran No. 10 Platoon, 'B' Coy 1/6 Queens and also captured Sergeant Crangles and his brave crew. In all No. 7 gun claimed fourteen tanks and the Queens over twenty-seven in the morning's battle. Andrews and Crangles were awarded the DCM for their bravery. Major R.C.G. Foster noted that 'Within a few hundred yards of the Queens Brigade's positions the ground was littered with disabled and abandoned tanks and vehicles, twenty-seven tanks on the 1/7th Battalion's front alone.'

Sergeant Jake Wardrop, 5 RTR, was watching the battle:

> The 131st Brigade had towed their six pounders from Alamein and never used them, but they had a party that day. The 17-pounder too was beginning to arrive; in fact the Guards [201st Brigade] had some this day . . . everybody was dug in. Just the Scotsmen and the Englishmen lying in a little hole smoking Vs [cigarettes] and waiting. It was a great scrap.

Montgomery had backed his defences with massed field artillery support from the three divisions. The Guards MGs also did great damage. No British tanks were lost and casualties were but 130. Churchill wrote 'Nothing like this example of the power of massed anti-tank artillery had yet been seen against armour. This was probably Rommel's sharpest rebuff in all his African exploits.' Shortly after, Rommel – a sick man with jaundice – was invalided back to Germany; he flew out on 9 March. He was succeeded by General von Arnim. General Montgomery watched the battle from Major Hill-Wood's tank of 'B' Squadron 4 CLY . Both 'A' and 'C' Squadrons, 1 RTR, were in action fending off two enemy thrusts against the Queens Brigade. In front of them were ten destroyed tanks, two ammunition lorries, two half tracks, a staff car and a captured 50mm PAK anti-tank gun. When 1 RTR followed up in the renewed chase it was through the FDLs where sprawled the little blue bodies of the Italian Folgore Division.

The French had constructed a sophisticated 20-mile-long defence system in case the Duce should ever invade Tunisia. It ran inland from the Gulf of Gabes, including the formidable natural anti-tank ditch, the Wadi Zigzaou through Mareth into the Matmata hills. Concrete pill-boxes, wire and minefields made for a 'Maginot' line. Field-Marshal Rommel, before he left for Germany, had installed six divisions, two of them German, with 15th Panzer Division in reserve. A possible outflanking movement had been reconnoitred by the Long Range Desert Group, which involved a long detour of 150 miles south, then west, then north to the narrow defiles of Djebels Tebaga and Melab. The Axis forces had fortified the 'Tebaga gap' and it was guarded by a German Panzer group and Italian infantry.

For Operation Pugilist, Montgomery based his main attack with XXX Corps tackling the strong Mareth line defence a few miles from the Gulf of Gabes. 7th Armoured Division was in support of 50th Tyne Tees and 51st Highland Divisions. On 20 March the gallant Tyne Tees struggled all day to get across the Wadi Zigzaou, but were eventually driven back on the 23rd by counter-attacks to where they started. For three days the regiments of 22nd Armoured Brigade waited under shellfire. 'C' Squadron, 4 CLY, had tanks hit but without casualties. 5 RTR were bombarded by the six-barrelled mortar, 'Moaning Minnies', and had a tank set on fire.

The X Corps left flanking attack was an outstanding success, and 8th Armoured Brigade (Red Fox's Mask) combined brilliantly with 2nd New Zealand Division, and with much close support from the RAF and USAAF forced the Tebaga gap. By the night of 26/27 March 1st Armoured Division in the north had broken through, and despite threats from German Tiger tanks nearly reached El Hamma. General von Arnim had to withdraw his strong forces still guarding the Mareth line before they were cut off. No fewer than 7,000 Axis prisoners were taken.

In fine weather 22nd Armoured Brigade advanced slowly and cautiously northwards through the Mareth line along tracks, unmade roads with mines and booby traps everywhere. The Italian General Messe withdrew his forces to the Wadi Akarit, 10 miles north of Gabes. It ran inland due west from the sea for 10 miles to join the Sholt el Fedjadj, an impassable salt lake 4 miles wide and over 20 miles from east to west. Besides

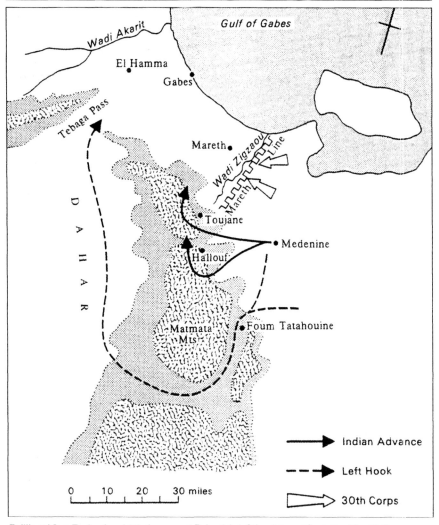

Brilliant New Zealand and 8th Armoured Brigade's left hook to outflank the Mareth line.

minefields and wire there was a 15-ft-deep anti-tank ditch along the whole of the defence line. General Messe had three Italian divisions holding the 10-mile line with the three indomitable Germans in reserve – 15 and 21 Panzer and 90th Light. General Montgomery sent a telegram to Winston Churchill on 6 April:

> I delivered a heavy attack against enemy in Akarit position early this morning. I did two things not done by me before in that I attacked the *centre* of enemy positon and in the dark with *no* moon. Attack delivered by about three infantry divisions [51st Highland, 50th Tyne Tees, 4th Indian] supported by 450 guns and enemy was surprised and overwhelmed and all objectives were captured. . . . My troops are in tremendous form and have fought splendidly. Will press on northwards when I have finished here.

After the battle of Medenine Lieutenant-Colonel R.D. Thicknesse took command of 1/6 Queens when Lieutenant-Colonel Kaulback was wounded. Lieutenant-Colonel N.D. Leslie took command of 1/5 Queens from Lieutenant-Colonel Lance East (who had just won the DSO) and the popular Brigade Major, D.S. Gordon, became CO of 1/7 Queens. Monty visited the Queens Brigade to congratulate them on their splendid defensive action at Medenine.

The 4 CLY were lent for the battle of Wadi Akerit, Major Cameron's 'A' Squadron to 50th Tyne Tees Division and a composite 'B' and 'C' Squadron to 51st Highland Division. Lieutenant John Philip-Smith's troop on the left of the Djebel el Roumana feature lost two tanks blown up on mines, but 'A' Squadron suffered heavy casualties from enemy artillery, well concealed tanks (including a Tiger), anti-tank guns and machine-guns. Major Cameron added a DSO to his two MCs. The 6th Green Howards were very grateful for the CLY support. Lieutenant C.W. Pearce, 'C' Squadron, described their support of the Argylls, Gordons and Seaforths of 154 Brigade. Their attack was planned to cross Wadi Akerit and moved towards the dominating hills of the Roumana Ridge on which the Germans had excellent OPs. 'The wadi looked almost sinister, not a movement or a shell burst anywhere, these enormous hills overlooking everything.' 4 CLY moved up in the dark, the barrage started at 0400 hrs. Scorpion flail tanks led, followed by REs to clear the minefields and blow up the anti-tank ditch.

At first light in mist and clouds of dust we waited at the edge of the wadi. The shelling was getting very heavy and several tanks were hit but not put out of action. Every five minutes, four 88mm airbursts would crack right over us – very demoralising. Thousands of prisoners were pouring in and the Germans kept shelling them leaving a trail of dead. Many of these Ities were in pyjamas. They had enormously deep slit trenches in the front line making them impossible to defend. There seemed to be hundreds of wounded or dead Highlanders everywhere. . . . The Highland brigadier wanted more tanks across the wadi. Major Peter Scott agreed to send two Sherman troops plus the two Grants with Tony Jarvis to control. Our chaps got through the minefield and pushed out a bit the other side. Shelling was heavy all the time especially on the minefield gap. The Brigadier wanted more tank support. Peter Scott led, then my troop, followed by the others. The Shermans went forward, I went right and Mike Ritchie left. Suddenly all six Shermans blew up, direct hits – a few people got out but they were mostly killed. The order came to pull back but too late.

Pearce's Sherman was hit four times, a track shot away, in the engine 'with a hell of a crash', by the starter-motor and by the wireless operator 'it then began to catch fire.' The 4 CLY survivors got back to the anti-tank ditch (the wadi). 'There was an absolute shambles, Italians and Highlanders all together. Firing was coming from all directions including from behind!' The 90th Light Division had infiltrated the Highlanders' right flank. 'Six Messerschmitt 109s came down this wadi and really let us have it.' 'C' Squadron started with eighteen tanks and ended with seven. Captain Peter Scott added a bar to his MC and Lieutenant-Colonel Harry Scott a bar to his DSO.

Alan Moorehead wrote:

> Montgomery went crashing in for his last great battle in the south at Wadi Akarit. This time he charged head-on with his Highland Division, the Indians and the Fiftieth. The Eighth Army was a wonderful machine when it was geared up to fight. It went forward with a terrible momentum and in a wonderfully adjusted rhythm – first the bombers, then the guns, then the infantry, then the tanks. Six gaps were blasted in the enemy line along the Wadi Akarit.

Although the enemy made determined counter-attacks, by nightfall the battle was won.

The hot pursuit continued, through the Gabes gap. The Cherry Pickers captured a Tiger tank. (It had broken down, its crew dismounted and the Hussars caught them from the rear.) On 9 April 1 RTR had a brisk action with a mixed force of all arms east of Agareb. The surprised enemy convoy retreated at high speed, but 1 RTR set five lorries in the middle of the column on fire; some were trapped in a wadi. When eight enemy tanks appeared to try to rescue the convoy with infantry support, three were hit. In three days of pursuit 1 RTR destroyed five tanks, sixteen guns and fifty-eight vehicles. Sfax was captured the next day by the Cherry Pickers. Sergeant Wardrop, 5 RTR, noted:

> racing for Sfax. It was a good trip but there was quite a lot of stuff to hold us up, guns and in places, mines. The country was nice, groves of peaches and olives. In Sfax we were cheered and feted by the [French] civilians. It was quite a day.

Sousse, 70 miles to the north, fell on 12 April and Montgomery held a victory parade. Sergeant Wardrop, 5 RTR, again:

> The Boches were nicely boxed in up in that north-eastern corner with a line running from Bizerta round through Medjez-el-Bab to the coast to Enfidaville. We drove through the Holy City of Kairouan. The Arabs made pilgrimage there yearly just like Mecca.

The 4th Light Armoured Brigade were wearing the black Jerboa Rat emblem. Lieutenant-Colonel Carver wrote of them at the time of the Alamein battle. 'Although officially now an independent brigade we continued to serve under command of 7th Armoured division and to carry their sign.' In nine months they had five brigade commanders, Brigadiers Carr, Roddick, Roscoe Harvey, Newton King and finally John Currie. Sometimes they acted as a 'Monty Marauder' sent off to hold the line, act as flank protection or participate in a pitched battle supporting the New Zealanders, or 7th Armoured Division. Their final role in the Mareth battle was the taking of the steep hills astride the main road to Toujane, brilliantly carried out by 2nd KRRC and 1st Rifle Brigade resulting in the capture of a large part of the Italian Pistoia Division. The Royal Scots Greys accompanied the sturdy New Zealanders for most of the hot pursuit campaign after Alamein.

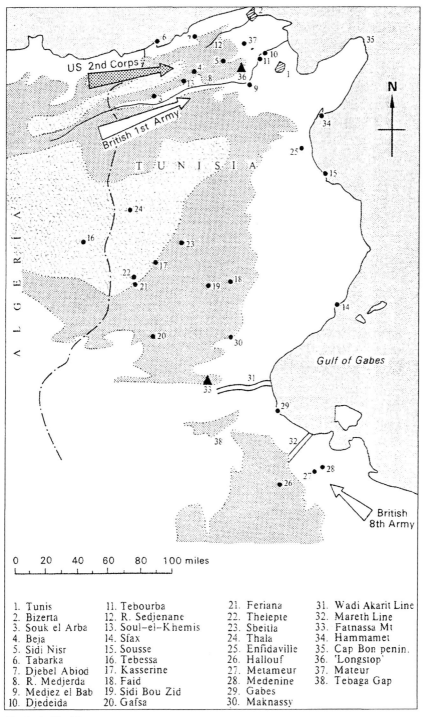

1. Tunis
2. Bizerta
3. Souk el Arba
4. Beja
5. Sidi Nisr
6. Tabarka
7. Djebel Abiod
8. R. Medjerda
9. Medjez el Bab
10. Djedeida
11. Tebourba
12. R. Sedjenane
13. Soul-el-Khemis
14. Sfax
15. Sousse
16. Tebessa
17. Kasserine
18. Faid
19. Sidi Bou Zid
20. Gafsa
21. Feriana
22. Thelepte
23. Sbeitla
24. Thala
25. Enfidaville
26. Hallouf
27. Metameur
28. Medenine
29. Gabes
30. Maknassy
31. Wadi Akarit Line
32. Mareth Line
33. Fatnassa Mt
34. Hammamet
35. Cap Bon penin.
36. 'Longstop'
37. Mateur
38. Tebaga Gap

Battles in Tunisia.

In Kairouan troops of the First Army met the veteran desert troops of the 8th Army. The latter naturally, but regrettably, rather looked down on the 'newcomers'. Some of the Desert Rats had survived over three years of constant campaigning. They had their own extraordinary, often bizarre clothing and their equally strange language of Egyptian Arabic terms, 'sayeeda' (Go with God), 'shufti' (have a look), 'may-ah' (water) and many more. About 30 miles north of Sousse (a battered little town and partly destroyed by the RAF and USAF bombers) lies the village of Enfidaville. Here the mountains come down to the sea, an obvious place for General Messe's rearguards to make another forlorn stand. The main role of 22nd Armoured Brigade was to protect the left flank from possible enemy armour attacking from the north-west. It was rugged country; olive trees, fruit and vegetables grew everywhere, but hills and step wadis made it difficult tank country. Alan Moorehead was astonished by 'the fantasy of colour, a rich deep Persian carpet woven of bluebells and poppies, of sweet peas and tulips of daisies and lilies, growing so thickly that for miles you could not see the ground or the grass, only flowers.'

Lieutenant-Colonel W.R. Elrington, CO 1/5th Queens, had appointed Lieutenant Derrick Watson on his return to the unit with thirty reinforcements to be 'Battle Patrol Officer' and his platoon called the 'Battle Patrol'. Around Enfidaville he and Sergeant George Cole went out on recce patrols, and 'Foxy' Pavitt, the company barber, emptied his Sten gun into the only German they encountered – who was fast asleep. Watson was then made Battalion IO (Intelligence Officer). This was on about 14 April 1943.

Generals von Arnim and Messe, with their quarter of a million Axis troops, were now compressed into the north-east corner of Tunisia. They still controlled the vital passes: Longstop Hill in the Medjerba section, the Bald and Green Hills in the Sedjemane section and in the south Pont du Fahs and the hills north of Enfidaville. 1 RTR supported Gurkhas, Indians, New Zealanders and the Guards trying to infiltrate the Enfidaville heights. The days of bitter fighting brought many casualties. Churchill wrote to Stalin explaining the difficulties:

> Since we entered Tunisia we have taken some 40,000 prisoners and killed or wounded some 35,000 German or Italian troops. 1st Army have lost about 23,000 men, 8th Army about 10,000. Two thirds of these casualties have been British. The terrain is mountainous with flat plains surrounded by rugged peaks, every one a fortress.

A final attack on the Enfidaville hills on 24 April failed. The 1st Army had five days of hard fighting on the western flanks with heavy losses on both sides. On 30 April Montgomery and Alexander switched 7th Armoured Division, 4th Indian and 201st Guards Brigade over to the 1st Army sector, to join IX Corps commanded by Lieutenant-General Brian Horrocks.

Along the defence perimeter of 130 miles the remainder of the 8th Army aggressively contained the Axis forces in the Enfidaville Hills, while the French forces tackled Pont du Fahs, and the Americans advanced towards Mateur. But General Alexander's main decisive thrust would be along the Medjerda Valley. Operation 'Strike' was the codename for the capture of Tunis.

On 6 May the final decisive attack was launched with IX Corps making the principal assault on a narrow front on either side of the Medjez-Tunis road. The leading infantry 4th British and 4th Indian Divisions were closely followed by the 6th and 7th Armoured Divisions. The Allied Air Forces carried out 2,500 sorties bombing everything in sight (including 1 RTR and 4 CLY). A new draft of sixty men came to 11th Hussars fresh from England. The war had now been on for three and a half years, and the seasoned troops were not at first impressed by the new entry. 'They seemed good fellows,' says the War Diary, 'but were young and short of training. One looked about 14 years old, but we did not look at his teeth. Several NCOs were sent back to instruct them in MT, Gunnery, Elementary Wireless and 11th Hussar ideas.'

The Desert Rats tanks had been painted dark green and the desert rat sign covered up with grease. It took five days to cover the 300 miles from Enfidaville back to Kairouan, south then west and north to within 30 miles of Medjez. Sergeant Wardrop, 5 RTR, wrote:

it was a great trip. We sat on top of the tanks and whistled to the mademoiselles in the villages. Le Kef was a garrison town of the French Foreign Legion and on view were Spahis, Algerian irregulars, Indo-Chinese as well as the Legionnaires who were reputed to have excellent German sergeants and warrant officers.

Wardrop met Sergeant Jock McLeod, alias 'Red Haggis', his troop sergeant in 'C' Company, 5 RTC, now with the 1st Army. 'They all rallied round to shake his hands, Stanley, George, Henry, Cliff, Woody, Middy, Len, Posty, George Carter, 'Snake Bite' and 'Mad Coutts' from the other squadrons.' Lieutenant-Colonel 'Fearless' Jim Hutton told 5 RTR 'Well gentlemen, we are going into Tunis tomorrow.'

Lieutenant-Colonel Harry Scott briefed 4 CLY on the forthcoming battle. The plan was for 7th Armoured and 4th Indian Divisions to attack in parallel with 4th British and 6th Armoured – so definitely a strong element of competition to be first into Tunis. The Indians would take their objectives in front of Medjez by first light and dig in, and 22nd Armoured Brigade would pass through towards a sector 12 miles north-east of Medjez. 4 CLY were on the left flank with the River Medjerba on its left, 5 RTR were in the centre and 1 RTR on the right flank. The Queens Brigade were to follow up closely behind the three armoured regiments. Field Marshal Lord Michael Carver (then CO 1 RTR) has written an excellent blow-by-blow account of the four-day battle to seize Tunis in his published campaign articles.

From Medjez-el-Bab, Forna, Massicault, St Cyprien, Point 112, Manouba into the centre of Tunis was about 30 miles. Alan Moorehead followed close behind 7th Armoured Division through the triangle of villages around Sidi Salem, Sidi Abdallah and Peters Corner on a 3,000-

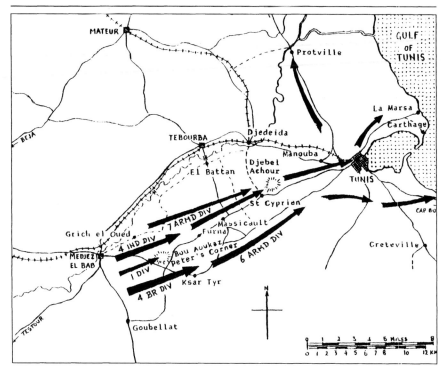

Operation Strike: the Capture of Tunis, 6–8 May 1943.

yard front. Once the Indians had penetrated the German lines of outposts and MG nests, Horrocks unleashed the armour. Alan Moorehead wrote:

> The tanks charged ahead. They went straight at the gap, the infantry had made for them passing through practically unscathed like releasing the floodgates of a dam. In scores, in hundreds this vast procession of steel lizards went grumbling and lurching and swaying up the Tunis road . . . the line was pierced . . . they roared on.

5 RTR reached St Cyprien, 10 miles from Tunis, where, according to Alan Moorehead, they encountered

> A mosque and group of white farmhouses . . . standing there were the men and the guns of the [5th] Royal Horse Artillery – the Desert Rats, the *original Desert Rats*. The guns that had fired from the beginning of the African war for Wavell and Strafer Gott, for Jock Campbell and Alec Gatehouse. . . . They had come all the way from Alamein and they had been through everything: young Cockneys and Lancaster boys in shorts and shirts and burnt by the sun, men of the Seventh Armoured Division who had fired the first shots in the African war, some of the finest gunners in the world.

'C' Squadron 4 CLY had been strafed by USAAF fighters despite seven-foot squares painted with RAF roundels tied over the tank engine compartments. Later nine RAF Bostons dropped their bombs on the regiment. At Saida 2 miles from Djedieda 'A' Squadron received hits from a 88mm gun which caused casualties. 4 CLY then stayed three days at Djedieda. 5 RTR in the centre of the advance, despite throwing yellow smoke bombs, were also bombed causing casualties. Sergeant Wardrop:

> The first day [6th] we made very good time and did more than half of the distance. We shot up guns and lorries and took thousands of prisoners. The RBs were rounding them up and just shoving them back to march on their own. There was some fair shooting, too, Cliff knocked two lorries off the road in two shots and Big Bill Beady is credited with a hat-trick for six shots from the MG at 500 yards, just one burst . . . the next morning we cracked on again. About mid-day [7th] we were sitting on a ridge overlooking the town and shooting up some guns. There were a lot of fires burning. The Brigadier ['Loony' Hinde] came up here in a Dingo and he and Fearless [Hutton the CO] had a chat.

5 RTR then entered the outskirts of Tunis firing 75mm HE shell into any buildings that had defenders showing resistance. The Bey's Palace caused trouble and two troops of tanks were soon in action. Captain Chave and Sergeant Wardrop went in the front gate. 'We loosed off a few 75s at various windows and the firing stopped. In every one of the buildings there were Boches and we had to root out some of them with the Tommy gun.' The Rifle Brigade were indispensable as ever rounding up prisoners. Both RB and 5 RTR also rounded up Lugers (pistols probably for sale to Americans), cameras, watches and rings. Sergeant Wardrop helped himself to a pair of binoculars. Many American and British First Army prisoners were also released. The civilians brought out wine and invited their liberators into their houses for a wash. Most of 5 RTR slept that night ('after a nice little session of red wine and brandy') on the pavements. 'The war was going fine; the Boches had all been killed or captured.' The floor of the turret in most of the RTR tanks was soon covered with bottles of rum, brandy and wine. The War Diary of 1 RTR recounts:

> May 7th helped infantry final objective Jebel Achour ridge, north of Massicault. 1 RTR crossed Wadi Chaffrou and deep irrigation ditch beyond encountered A/Tk guns, tanks inc a Tiger. Held up until artillery support forthcoming. More enemy tanks encountered on a ridge near Bahrane. Bn ordered to wheel northwards cut main Medjez–Tunis road west of La Mornaghia. Found a concealed route to the west, though delayed by a deep wadi. Bn worked its way losing only one tank, KO-ing A/Tk guns on way. Party of 12 enemy tanks refuelling east of the ridge surprised, driven off without loss. Further advance to road junction south of Bardo, outskirts of Tunis, little resistance, many POWs collected. But 5 RTR captured 2,000 POWs on May 8th. Last day. 1 RTR held up on ridge covering bridge over river Medjerba at Protville, blown up by enemy. Rest of day exchanging gunfire across the river. End three years continuous campaigning. 5 RTR pushed through Tunis to secure high ground north of Ariana and Aouina aerodrome, captured 5,000 POWs, several hundred lorries, two aerodromes at Aouina and Sidi Aoud with 100 damaged aircraft and 5 intact.

'From Enfidaville onwards it was all go for weeks,' noted Lieutenant Derrick Watson, 1/5 Queens. 'Constantly being shelled by the retreating enemy until we embarked on a route of 140 miles to join the 1st Army. We finally motored into Tunis on 6th May. Flowers, vino and a total of 170,000 prisoners. The Queens had charge of 7,000 of them,' including many

Germans from 334th Infantry, the 999th Leichte and Hermann Goering Divisions. The Queens Brigade, advanced along two axes with 1/7 Queens acting as vanguards on each route. 1/6 Queens followed up on the northern Grich el Oued road, 1/5 Queens on the southern route. The day was fine and hot and Panzergrenadier Regiment 115 defending the sector put up surprisingly feeble resistance. During the day Queens Brigade advanced 15 miles.

By chance Alan Moorhead met his friend, the journalist Alexander Clifford; between them, they had covered all the African campaigns. Lieutenant-General Brian Horrocks had told them that the 11th Hussars were given their objective as Tunis Central railway station. But the Derbyshire Yeomanry leading 6th Armoured were neck and neck. In the Avenue de Bardo 'I saw I was again among the Desert Rats. The Red Jerboa in the red circle was painted on the battered mudguards, the most famous symbol in the whole Desert War. And the men in the vehicles were the Eleventh Hussars, the reconnaissance unit that had led the 8th Army across the desert since Wavell's time.' But the mailed fist symbol of 6th Armoured Division was – more or less – there at the same time. Street fighting went on until dark on 7 May, but all resistance in Tunis ended the next morning.

The Queens, according to their historian, found

the entry into the city bizarre and unforgettable. Despite the pouring rain, dense crowds of almost hysterical French men and women thronged the streets, threw flowers, clambered on

The 4 County of London Yeomanry in Tunis. *Imperial War Museum*

to the vehicles and offered wine to the troops, all this amidst the smoke and flames of burning vehicles and buildings with the noise of rifle and machine guns from the enemy posts that were still holding out.

For troublesome snipers the 6-pounder anti-tank guns were used to good effect. 'B', 'C' and 'D' Companies of 1/7 Queens were the first allied infantry to enter Tunis. Stuart Playfair's 'B' in the city centre found it difficult to control with dense crowds of revellers, many snipers and enthusiastic ladies embracing the riflemen. Lieutenant R.A. Burton in 'C' Company occupied a large fort crammed with arms and ammunition. The important bridge leading to Cap Bon on the south side of the city was seized despite a close-quarter battle with grenades and machine-gun fire freely exchanged by both sides. Finally 'B' Company advanced to the north-west and cut the main escape road from Tebourba. 1/7 Queens played a major role in the capture of Tunis. 1/5 and 1/6 Queens reached Protville 12 miles north-west of Tunis on 9 May. Half the brigade had a day's leave in Tunis on 11 May, the other half on 13 May. Major-General Bobby Erskine inspected the Queens on the 15th and presented medals to those already gazetted, and so to Homs on the 19th.

The Cherry Pickers were in at the finish. On 9 May Captain Churton and 'C' Squadron were probing into the pockets still held by 15th Panzer Division in the Cap Bon Peninsula. His armoured cars were held up by poor terrain so Churton went down to the beach on foot, armed only with a revolver and with no escort except an English-speaking captain of the 15th Panzers. By himself he 'captured' 9,000 prisoners whom he proudly handed over to the first American troops to arrive. Major Van Burdon's 'C' Squadron forded a river in a native mule cart in order to arrange another surrender. The local Arabs charged 50 francs a head for their horse and mule ferrying operation; several handsome enemy staff cars found their way on to the 11th Hussar vehicle strength.

The Desert Rat advance continued as they wheeled northwards and pursued the remnants of 15th Panzer Division up the coast as far as Porto Farina, outside Bizerta. On 13 May General Alexander signalled to the prime minister, 'We are masters of the North African shores.'

CHAPTER FIFTEEN

Homs – Desert Rats Beside the Sea

After the capture of Tunis and Bizerta and the end of hostilities in North Africa, the Desert Rats had a few days of considerable relaxation. Corporal Peter Roach, 1 RTR, recalled:

> We parked on the edge of Tunis to enjoy the fruits of our victory. Rather like children we set out simply to look and enjoy the sights and sounds of what was practically a European city – streets and houses and cafés, girls in dresses, housewives and their husbands and to the fathers among us the joy of seeing children. Quietly we meandered through the town asking nothing but to feast quietly on this sight.

On its way from Tripoli to Tunis the regiment had acquired a large number of pets – stray dogs. The RMO, 'Doc' Wells, described to their owners not only the horrible symptoms of rabies but the equally horrible methods of treatment.

On 15 May 1943 22nd Armoured Brigade moved 50 miles south-west to Bou Arada and all the light squadrons handed in their old Crusader tanks and were re-equipped with diesel-engined Shermans, transported 1,500 miles from Cairo. The recce troops were re-equipped with Daimler scout cars and Bren-gun carriers. On 20 May a five-day journey, mainly by 3-tonners, took place, via Kairouan, Mahares, Skhirra, Gabes, through Tripoli and Castelverde to Homs.

The battalions of 131 Queens Brigade bivouacked on the sand between the palm trees and the sand to the east of the ruins of Leptis Magna with its classic Roman amphitheatre built by Septimus Severus. It was a superb camp site with excellent sea bathing on the golden sandy beaches. The padre of 1/6th Queens obtained prized NAAFI supplies from outside 'sources'.

Peter Hoggarth, an officer in the 1/7th Queens:

> The training phase was spent at Homs. When we arrived, my platoon found a large mound of sand on the beach, which we dug into to make a camouflaged area for our 15 cwt truck. To our surprise we found the remains of a Roman villa with a very fine tessellated floor. I think the design was a large snake. We lived in small tents close to the sea and went for a swim first thing every morning. Lt Col Gordon was the CO and Captain Francis was Adjutant. Shortly after arrival I became Assistant Adjutant.
>
> We had tents and held sand table exercises. I remember one officer trying, with success, to spot the exact place on the Italian mainland where we would land. There was emphasis

on weapon training, but there were no nearby rifle ranges, of course, for practice. Grenade throwing was practised with live grenades. As part of a toughening process there was a long, hard route march, lasting over a couple of days, which almost crippled some of us. There were also small scale tactical training exercises at platoon strength. An LST arrived at Homs Harbour and we practised climbing up the ropes on its side. The artillery paid us a visit and gave us a demonstration of firing 25 pounders. There was also a firing competition between our anti-tank platoon and some RTR tanks – not at each other, I hasten to add. The nearby ruins of the ancient city of Leptis Magna fascinated me. I obtained some notes on the city and took a party from the battalion on a conducted tour. Entertainment facilities were sparse. The Roman amphitheatre was used for ENSA concerts. I spent a short leave in Tripoli. The CO set general knowledge questions for the battalion and prizes were awarded.

A 'Jerboa' Club, a NAAFI club, cinemas and a theatre were opened in Homs. The amphitheatre was used as a large open-air theatre and Laurence Olivier, Vivien Leigh, George Formby and Leslie Henson took part in ENSA concert parties. 'We did nothing for weeks but sit in the sun, swim, read and eat,' wrote Jake Wardrop, 5 RTR. 'At night we'd sit around listening or go to Leptis to see a concert. There was some beer, most times two bottles per man.' Eight-day leave trips to Tunis were organised, and with some serious driving the 700-mile journey was reduced to a record twenty-five hours (in a 3-ton Ford with fifteen in the back). Recreational trips were also made to Djerba Island.

There were sports of all kinds: swimming competitions, water polo, boxing, cricket, football, athletics, and for some horse racing, and even lizard racing (crab racing was tried unsuccessfully). The divisional staff once provided an ex-Italian army brothel, but higher authority disapproved and the girls were sent back to Tripoli.

The CO of 1 RTR, Lieutenant-Colonel Michael Carver, had inherited two problems. His predecessor had promised that after the capture of Tunis, the regiment would be sent back to England and that everyone would be awarded a special medal in addition to the Africa Star. However, he later wrote: 'We did not know where we should be going next – Sicily, Sardinia, Italy or the Balkans.' For a time the powers that be – Winston Churchill and President Roosevelt – were not sure either. General Eisenhower, the supreme military commander, was against Sicily and preferred Sardinia and Corsica, if the real purpose (which it was) was to invade and defeat Italy. But the Casablanca Conference, in January 1943, decided to invade Sicily after the capture of Tunis, known by the codename Operation Husky.

The Queens Brigade settled into a routine at Homs, with bugle calls, muster parades, regular meal times. Brasses were cleaned, drill, weapon training, TEWTS for officers and NCOs and route marches on most days. Lieutenant Derek Watson, IO 1/5th Queens, recalls 'A 50-mile route march across the desert in full marching order over 3 days and nights.' With temperatures rising to over 100 degrees, training took place early or late in the day. There was an excellent rest camp on the cliffs overlooking the sea for four days 'local' leave.

Lieutenant-Colonel Mike Carver wrote afterwards 'In retrospect it is clear that we should have made a more basic change in our organisation, mixing tanks and infantry more closely together, instead of keeping the armoured and lorried infantry brigades separate.' Major-General Bobbie Erskine should have known that any of the four invasion possibilities required closer cooperation [but see Appendix B]. The Queens Brigade celebrated the 'Glorious First of June', their Regimental Day, with sports events and concerts. Brigadier 'Bolo' Whistler's brigade consisted of 1/5th Queens (CO Lieutenant-Colonel M. Elrington) 1/6th Queens (Lieutenant-Colonel M. Forrester) and 1/7th Queens (Lieutenant-Colonel D.S. Gordon). Brigadier 'Loony' Hinde still commanded 22nd Armoured Brigade. His 2 i/c was Lieutenant-Colonel Harry Scott, who had led 4 CLY in the hot pursuit to Tunis. Lieutenant-Colonel Viscount Cranley took command of 4 CLY. The extremely popular Lieutenant-Colonel 'Fearless Jim' Hutton left for the UK on 15 July to a tank-gun salute by 5 RTR and was succeeded by Lieutenant-Colonel R.N. Wilson. 'The Fighting Fifth' is a poem written by a member of 5 RTR; it was signed by the whole regiment – 420 of them – and presented to Hutton when he handed over command at Homs.

The Fighting Fifth

In the misty morning darkness, squat and ugly monsters rest
Heavy armoured, grim and deadly, with their guns all pointing west
Out behind them on the skyline, yet another morning breaks
For the past long shivering hour, every crew has been awake,
Awake and watching every movement ready for the show to start
It's the dreaded Fifth Battalion, once again they're taking part.
Swift and deadly this Battalion, pick of England's fighting chaps,
Hardy veterans of the desert, rightly named the desert rats.

As they sit there tensely waiting, silence changes into hell
And the earth is split and blasted by a hail of shot and shell,
Thick and heavy grows the barrage, till it's like a solid wall,
Flying steel, and orange flashes, shells a-shrieking as they fall.
See the cruisers gliding forward, slow at first then speeding fast,
Straight into that mad inferno, rocked and swayed by heavy blast;
On they go towards the Germans, probing, searching as they go,
Stopping now and then to batter with 6 pounder at the foe.

In and out they keep on creeping, keeping in a staggered line,
Then the air is split asunder as a cruiser hits a mine,
In the twinkling of a second all the crew are 'baling out',
They've been spotted by their comrades, watch that hornet wheel about.
Back he goes just like an arrow, stops while all his pals climb on,
Such a lightning piece of action, Jerry doesn't know they've gone.
One observant German gunner tries to strafe the helpless crew
But to hit that swerving cargo is as much as he can do.

Look now, are the lads retreating? No! It's just a bit of bluff,
They're trying now to draw the Germans, so the Grants can do their stuff,
True enough they've fallen for it, on they come into death's jaws,
See them lurching slowly forward, twenty of them all MkIVs.
Much too late they see their blunder, madly try to turn around,
But Grants and Shermans wait there ready, 75s begin to pound.

Deafening grows the noise of battle, fifteen Jerry tanks on fire,
See the others fleeing westward, smashing through their own barbed wire.

So once again we're moving forward, to establish our new lines,
Now we've got the job to hold it, while the engineers lay mines.
We know the Jerry panzer Div men, will not take it lying down,
And we expect at any moment, an attempt to take the ground.
But the Fighting Fifth is ready, morning, noon or dead of night,
And if Jerry wants his ground back, by the gods he'll have to fight.
So for now we'll go to leaguer for a short but hard-earned rest,
And the Hun will still remember, that our guns are pointing west.

VIPs visited Homs to inspect the Desert Rats. Monty came of course, so did their X Corps Commander, Lieutenant-General Brian Horrocks, who just before being wounded in Bizerta had lectured them on 'Lessons of the Desert Campaign'. King George VI inspected the division on 20 June, drove through lines of cheering troops and chatted (fairly informally) to his old regiment, the 11th Hussars.

After the capture of Tunis Lieutenant-Colonel M. Carver, CO 1 RTR, wrote a report on the lessons learned, and appropriate recommendations for an armoured regiment in desert and Algerian/Tunisian battlefields. The full report is in the Public Record Office, Ref. WO 169/9362 (1943). This is a brief summary:

Light Squadron The Sherman, Crusader MkII and the Stuart tanks are compared. The latter with improved range (miles per fuel tank) and improved gun (equivalent to 6 pdr) would fit admirably requirements of Light Squadron.
Recce Troop Dingoes, Bren carrier and small half track compared. Ideal would be composition ten Bren carriers plus intercom troop of 8 Dingoes with officer in command.
Heavy Squadron Shermans effective HE, MG fire, speed and accuracy is most effective weapon for dislodging A/Tk guns, mortars, MGs and OPs. A supporting RHA battery is essential to take on large calibre A/Tk guns such as 75mm or 88mm.
Tank v. Tank The new powerful Tiger Panzer MkVI, heavily armoured, can only be tackled by a tank with a 17-pdr gun.
Liaison Importance of recce troop providing information about progress of 'friendly' as well as enemy dispositions. The Intercom troop should have at least three wireless sets in addition to COs set in his HQ armoured car.
Mines Every man in armoured regiment should be trained to remove them. Every tank and scout car in 1 RTR equipped with six nails and fifty yards of old signal cable for mine removal.
Bombing 1 RTR bombed by 'our' light bombers on five occasions. Orange smoke not released *before* bombs released. Bombing of dispersed armoured vehicles ineffective. Light metal fragments do little damage. 'Noise is terrific, if prolonged has considerable effect on morale.'
Wireless Communications difficult, most frequencies had at least three other groups on it, bad discipline, chat all day.
Observation The description of targets generally bad. Better training needed at troop and squadron level. A 50,000 map should produce an approximate map reference (but not in the desert where landmarks were rare).
Road Work Appropriate tactics in tackling opposition on a road in close country. Against enemy in strength, locate his first post by recce troop, move up infantry, get tanks off the road. Against isolated A/Tk gun(s) lead with heavy Sherman squadron.

The armoured regiments soon had a full complement of diesel Shermans that had to be waterproofed at a later stage. Every item of equipment had to be checked: engines stripped down, weapons cleaned, aligned and tested, wireless sets tested in the field. The Cherry Pickers had an additional gun troop with 75mm guns mounted on White Scout cars.

The Queens battalions were now equipped with the new PIAT (Projectile Infantry, Anti-tank), a rocket-propelled and hand-held anti-tank weapon. It was effective at close quarters despite a risk of blow-back. The now well-tried 6-pounder anti-tank gun was the main protection against enemy armour. Each Queens battalion had an anti-tank platoon. Company and battalion exercises were carried out during ten-day visits to Tarhuna on the Jebel, 30 miles inland between Homs and Tripoli. There, in scorching heat, the bare hills were attacked with gusto and the anti-tank guns manhandled over impossible country. By contrast, amphibious training was a great relief – 'dryshod' lectures, getting in and out with full equipment and quickly, of 'mock-up' landing craft. 131 Brigade carried out 'wetshod' training at Homs. REME experts showed the tank crews how to waterproof a Sherman to drive in six feet of water. 3 RHA retained their towed 25-pounders and were now affiliated with the Queens Brigade. 'M' Battery (Major W.L.P.O. Fisher), with its three FOOs, had close links with 1/6th Queens, as did the other two batteries/battalions. 5 RHA was re-equipped with Sexton, 25 pounders on a tank chassis and each battery linked with an armoured regiment.

The invasion of Sicily took place on 10 July 1943. Clearly, 7th Armoured Division were not part of Operation Husky, but the GOC, 'Bobbie' Erskine, took a small TAC HQ and officers from all units to 'see the form'.

CHAPTER SIXTEEN

Black Jerboa in Operation Husky – the Invasion of Sicily

Major-General Erskine took with him a skeleton staff containing Operations, Intelligence, Supply, Medical and RASC representatives. They sailed from Sousse on 12 July 1943, sighted Sicily on the 14th, sailed towards Augusta, but landed instead in Syracuse harbour. The elaborately waterproofed vehicles drove straight off on to the quayside. After a fortnight in the Syracuse area 7th Armoured Division 'TAC' HQ (having enjoyed sixteen different varieties of Marsala wine, eaten the sweetest possible oranges and been entertained by some beautiful Italian 'ENSA' artistes) returned to Tripoli.

The purpose of the exercise was the possibility that the Independent Armoured Brigades might need to be welded together and used as an armoured division. General Patton's US Seventh Army included their 2nd Armored Division, which was very successful, and quickly helped mop up the Italian forces in the western part of the island. One of the independent armoured brigades was the 4th, proudly wearing the badge of the Black Jerboa Rat (its tail now above its head). This is, therefore, the story of their campaign in Operation Husky.

In the initial assault on Sicily there were 3,000 ships and landing craft carrying between them 160,000 men, 14,000 vehicles, 1,800 guns and 600 tanks. 4th Armoured Brigade landed with 95 diesel Sherman tanks, but with newcomers, 3rd CLY (Sharpshooters), and 44 RTR veterans, having fought in Crusaders, in the Knightsbridge battle and at Alamein as flail clearing tanks (the first regiment ever to be equipped with Scorpions); plus 'A' Squadron of the Royal Dragoons. Brigadier John Currie with Brigade HQ left Sfax on 21 May and returned to the Egyptian Delta. On 1 June the old title 'Light' Armoured was dropped and the brigade became part of XIII Corps under Lieutenant-General Miles Dempsey. Their initial task in Husky was to act as two independent tank regiments, 3 CLY usually supporting 5th British Division, 44 RTR, the 50th (Tyne-Tees) Division.

Lieutenant-Colonel Geoffrey Willis commanded 3 CLY and Lieutenant-Colonel E.D. Rash 44 RTR. After a peaceful sea journey starting from Port

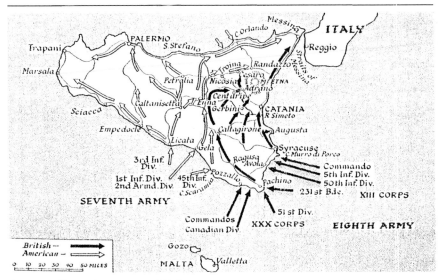

Operation Husky, the conquest of Sicily.

Said on 5 July, aboard HMS *Bulolo* and LSP *Dilwara*, they arrived off Sicily on the night of 9/10 July. Brigade TAC HQ were with HQ XIII Corps, the rest of Brigade HQ following on D + 28.

The 8th Army with XIII and XXX Corps consisted of four infantry divisions, part of 1st Airborne Division, 231st (Malta) Infantry Brigade, three commandos and 4th and 23rd Armoured Brigades. The enemy garrison in Sicily initially consisted of two German (one was armoured), four Italian infantry divisions and six low-grade Italian coastal divisions. General Patton's 2nd Corps had three infantry and one armoured division, part of 82nd Airborne and a battalion of Commando Rangers.

Models of the landing area had been prepared and thirty-seven different maps issued to each vehicle. The weather was rough on the night of the 9/10th. As the ships began to roll, the enthusiasm and keenness of many began to wane.

Airborne troops had been dropped just west of Syracuse to seize the Ponte Grande, an important bridge over the Anapo River. Many paratroops had been dropped too early and had been drowned. Casualties had been heavy and the gruesome wrecks of gliders on the coast were very depressing. Brigade HQ were not controlling the two regiments, so their stories are given separately.

The Sharpshooters in Sicily

Spitfires patrolled overhead and HMS *Erebus* was firing at shore batteries, their fire being returned. The water tower at Cassibile was spotted. The RN manned two DUKWs, known as Lily and Mary, and ferried the regiment ashore. 'A' and 'B' Squadrons were soon in action before Syracuse, dealing with the barracks and supporting 2nd Bn Northamptonshires. Mount Etna could be seen, but Hermann Goering's PZ Grenadiers ambushed the column and put five Shermans out of action. The next day, supporting 2nd Bn Royal Scots Fusiliers, the nine remaining 'B' Squadron tanks went through Priolo, but were held up by a natural tank obstacle. Brigadier Tarleton, commanding 17 Brigade of 5th Division, asked for help to get the 6th Seaforths into Augusta that night. Captain Woods fired at every pillbox or buildings seen in the half light until 0400 hrs when the last vital crossroads was taken. The RSF went in with the bayonet before dawn and took Augusta, but 3 CLY lost Second Lieutenant John Crews, killed by a 2.8cm 'needle' anti-tank gun.

'C' Squadron supported 24th Cameronians into Floridia, then Taverna and Solarino. An 88mm anti-tank gun knocked out two Shermans, but the 2nd Inniskillings and 2nd Wiltshires found Solarino deserted. 'A' Squadron supported 15th Brigade and the KOYLI near Villasmundo, where a strong counter-attack 'brewed up' four CLY Shermans causing twelve casualties. The lesson was learnt that in close country the tanks needed *very close* infantry support, totally unlike the desert tactics.

With the bridgehead now established a joint armour/infantry advance on Catania, with its port and airfields, was a prime objective. 3 CLY would lead 4th Armoured and 15th Infantry Brigade through Villasmundo, Carlentini, Lentini, capture the Primosole bridge spanning the River Simeto and on to

44 RTR Shermans approaching Leonardello, Sicily. *Imperial War Museum*

Catania. The first two villages were not defended, but the Korner Regiment with a strong screen of A/Tk guns, and the Luftwaffe out in force, were intent on defending the vital river bridge. On the 14th the Sharpshooters knocked out six well-sited 88mm guns, but several Shermans shed their tracks on the rough, hard going.

44 RTR in Sicily

The regiment under Lieutenant-Colonel E.D. Rash arrived in the *Orontes* to no apparent opposition, but the TULO (tank unloading liaison officer) party, who had landed at 0230 hrs on 10 July at Avolo, were destroyed by shellfire. The main body moved ashore on foot and 'married up' with their tanks and vehicles inland – which took thirty-six hours. During the afternoon of the 12th Lieutenant Ian Watkins's troop, supporting 60 Brigade of 50 Northumbrian Division, destroyed four guns and captured sixty rather timid prisoners beyond Palazzolo. The Luftwaffe was active, two ships were hit and nine Shermans of 'C' Squadron were lost on board ship. However, on the morning of the 13th, beyond Palazzalo Acreide, Sergeant Hampson, 5 Troop, supporting 6 DLI, knocked out an astonishing eight Italian R-35 tanks, six 105mm guns, twenty-nine trucks and much else, and put in the bag a divisional general, three brigadiers, four staff officers and fifty other ranks. Late that night 44 RTR halted just beyond Syracuse and came under brigade command for a 'lightning thrust' on Catania.

TAC Brigade now coordinated the advance from the 21st. The corps commander decided to concentrate the brigade on continuing the advance through Lentini towards Catania, led alternatively by 3 CLY or 44 RTR and 'A' Squadron of the Royals. Many of the invasion airborne troops had been dropped too far and too soon causing many casualties. A brigade of 1st Airborne Division were supposed to be dropped during the night to capture the Primosole Bridge. They weren't. Brigade HQ and a handful of men held the bridge, removed the detonating fuses of the explosive charges, but eventually violent counter-attacks forced them to leave the bridge. Four hundred German paratroops in a wood near Carlentini delayed 3 CLY, but 'A' Squadron, 44 RTR, just south of the Primosole Bridge, found many targets. The first attack to cross the bridge on the 15th by 151 Brigade and 44 RTR had failed, although Carlentini and Lentini were found to be unoccupied, except for crowds of cheering Italians. 'A' Squadron lost four tanks and eighteen captured in their assault; Lieutenant-Colonel Rash and the MO were killed on the same day. A night crossing over the bridge was planned for the 8 DLI, supported by 3 CLY, under a one-hour artillery barrage.

At 0500 hrs 'A' Squadron CLY crossed the long steel bridge with their five surviving Shermans, despite a desperate defence by German paratroops on the north side. They went left, 'C' Squadron followed and fanned out to the right and had four tanks knocked out. The CO, Lieutenant-Colonel

Geoffrey Willis, was sniped in his tank and killed, as were three other officers. Fighting to secure the bridgehead went on unrelentingly, with the Durham Light Infantry and German paratroops suffering heavy casualties. Eventually, the Sharpshooters extended the bridgehead and captured 150 prisoners from the Hermann Goering Parachute Division. 44 RTR had also sent 'B' Squadron to help the Wiltshires cross the Simeto River 2 miles west of Primosole Bridge. 'C' Squadron helped the Royal Berkshires who were nearly surrounded, but lost five tanks in the process. The contrast was clear to all now between the relatively easy-going Italian defences and the brave skilful German parachute troops. One witness wrote after the battle for the bridge. 'I've never seen such carnage.' The brigade had done well but with severe losses to officers and men and tanks.

For the rest of the month the brigade was in reserve in the estuary valley of the River Gorna Lunga. The enemy held the same line south of Catania, the infantry and armour on both sides sitting facing each other. A huge German naval gun on the slopes of Mount Etna shelled the bridge from time to time. The 44 RTR encountered the new, noisy multi-barrelled Nebelwerfer, and everybody suffered from mosquitoes which gave malaria to quite a few. One benefit was the arrival of 'Compo' rations. A tank crew now had a box full of goodies sufficient for three or four days – tins of stew, steak puddings, suet puddings, tinned fruit, sweets, cigarettes and ready-mixed tea, sugar and milk powder. The lava outcrop of Mount Etna played havoc with the rubber bogie wheels, so many tanks were repaired by the fitters. The brigade strength on landing was ninety-five, but no fewer than twenty-five had been knocked out. At one stage there were only fifty-five 'runners'.

The advance resumed on 1 August. Lieutenant-Colonel A.A. Cameron arrived from 4 CLY to take command of 3 CLY, and Lieutenant-Colonel F.R. Lindsay became the CO of 44 RTR. Catania was occupied on the 5th and the brigade harboured in Aci Castello, a pretty little seaside town 8 miles to the north. XXX Corps had made a left hook round the west side of Mount Etna, forcing the Germans to withdraw from the Catania region or risk being cut off. The 8th Army was putting on strong pressure from the south and the US 7th Army from the west. For a week XIII Corps followed the retreating enemy slowly and painfully northwards up the narrow strip between the mountains and the sea, constantly held up by skilful defensive rearguard actions – mines, road blocks, blown bridges, booby traps and occasional single Tiger tanks taking out the lead Shermans. 44 RTR fought through Aci Reale, Morgioni, Giarre and eventually Taormina. 3 CLY started from west of Nicolesi then Pedara, losing men and tanks each day. Movement was difficult along narrow roads, twisting and turning and dangerous at each bend.

Operation Blackcock was a seaborne operation to land No. 2 Commando 'C' Squadron, 3 CLY, a troop of SP guns and jeep-drawn 3.7 howitzers, a troop of anti-tank guns plus sappers near Cap d'Ali and bypass the German defences. On 14 August the Shermans were waterproofed and Brigadier

HQ 4 Armoured Brigade in Sicily. Brigadier John Curry, Lieutenant-Corporal Zolk, Sergeant Harris, Corporal Snow, Lieutenant-Corporal Close, Signaller Starkey, Lieutenant-Corporal Darroch, Sergeant Baxter, Corporal Wratten. *Imperial War Museum*

Currie and TAC Bde HQ set off in LSIs and LCTs from Catania, and the force sailed on the evening of the 15th. The GOC XXX Corps, Sir Oliver Leese, after this expedition had entered Messina on the 17th, wrote, 'I realise you were landed on the *wrong* beach. I knew how difficult your task was made by constant enemy demolitions and the shelling from the mainland. I congratulate you on forcing your way into Messina so quickly.' The force had loaded at Cap Scaletta, advanced north, found Messina to be empty of the enemy (except for much equipment) who had escaped to the mainland by ferry. American patrols arrived at the north end of town on the 17th and General Patton was received in front of the town hall. He was predictably unimpressed by 8th Army's speed of advance.

The brigade settled down for reorganisation and training near Fiumefreddo, with orchards, vineyards, sea bathing, ENSA concerts and an RTR band. On 29 and 30 August 1943 Brigadier John Currie inspected his brigade in great detail. Trooper Ken Morris remembers: 'We stood to for three hours, a detailed inspection, identity discs, field dressings, haversack contents.' On 7 September they moved to Paterno, 15 miles west of Catania. Trooper Morris, Brigade HQ, recalled that when they docked at Syracuse on 7 August (D-Day+28) they were greeted by a swarm of bum-boats whose owners were offering pears, grapes and tomatoes for sale. Brigade HQ stayed near the docks for another twelve days. Lieutenant-Colonel Cameron, CO 3 CLY, described the month of recuperation and rest in 'the shady groves of Misterbianco'. The DAQMG, Major E.B. Hambro, provided films, ENSA shows, band concerts among the olive groves and an officers' club was opened at Aci Reale. There was no shortage of Marsala and light local wines. The natives were now friendly, and when members of the brigade climbed and explored Mount Etna – all of 10,869 ft high – they found a notice posted, 'This volcano was captured by 13 Corps, 7 Aug 1943'.

The intrepid journalists Alan Moorehead, Alexander Clifford and Geoffrey Keating walked through Giardini just above Catania on the way to Taormina. They waded across the Torrente Rapido and the Fiumefreddo river up to the forward platoon. According to Moorehead 'Only an enemy rearguard was left behind. Of all the lovely towns of Sicily only Taormina remained untaken – the loveliest of all.' The journalists

> felt like jackals after the kill. There was the usual hush over this gap between the advancing army and the retreating enemy. Everything goes to earth. The road is clear and it is a little adventure to turn each corner. You smell the enemy. A house burns quietly . . . the discarded helmets and webbing of the enemy lie about. At the railway station, the bombing had carried black debris across the road and a stationary train full of some chemical threw out a strangely sickly smell.

They spotted the Teller mines lying just below the road surface and small craters caused by 'S' mines. They accepted the surrender of Italian MG posts and ordered them to throw their guns into a ravine.

At the end of the Sicilian campaign Brigadier Currie sent a message to his brigade. 'We were a scratch force drawn from all quarters of the army, yet everyone worked together. The dash and determination shown by all ranks was beyond praise.'

The total Allied casualties were 22,800. About 15,000 Axis troops were captured and another 5,000 killed or wounded, but Kesselring had fought brilliantly. No fewer than 40,000 Germans and 60,000 Italians crossed the Straits of Messina to fight another day.

Operation Husky was over – now for mainland Italy.

CHAPTER SEVENTEEN

Black Jerboa in Italy

The Italian Campaign – 'a damned good gallop'

On 3 September 1943 the 8th Army assaulted the toe of Italy, and in thirteen days had advanced 200 miles north to link up with the Anglo-American force breaking out of the Salerno bridgehead. The Italians gave up on the 8th, and the following day 1st Airborne Division landed unopposed to capture the airfields around Taranto and its port.

The 4th Armoured Brigade now had three more units under command, 46th and 50th RTR plus 111 Field Regiment RA. Orders were received on the 16th for a move by sea (tracked vehicles) and ferry (wheeled vehicles) from Messina to Taranto. The first move would be 30 miles north-east to Bari to come under command of 78 Division. On the 20th Lieutenant-General Sir Oliver Leese, XXX Corps Commander, addressed the brigade on the quayside and bade them farewell to Sicily. The convoys escorted by destroyers took thirty-six hours in fine weather, despite the threat of magnetic mines. In Taranto the docks were filled with the surrendered Italian fleet. On the 24th a very mixed composite force of Royals, Sharpshooters, two Recce Squadrons, Kensingtons, gunners, sappers and the more exotic SAS and 'Popski's Private Army' set off. The 4th Armoured Brigade became the spearhead of the 8th Army, advancing up the east coast of Italy.

Despite blown bridges and well placed rearguards armed with anti-tank guns, the brigade crossed the River Ofanto. The Sharpshooters had problems with their Shermans. Under a blazing sun and over melting tarmac roads the rubber bogie wheels soon deteriorated. 'B' Squadron limped into Bari with only 30 per cent effective runners. Inland the rest of the Sharpshooters moved north to Canosa to launch a serious attack against Foggia. Now that their war was over the Italians cheered on their liberators who were chasing the hated *Tedeschi*. The Royals occupied Canosa, and soon the SAS reported Cerignola clear of the enemy. Brigadier John Currie's plan to attack Foggia and secure its airfields was based on two mixed columns, 'Bakerforce' on the right and 'Cameronforce' on the left. The River Cervaro, 6 miles south of Foggia, was defended by the Germans in strength. Despite four bridges being blown, Cameronforce entered Foggia, which had been heavily bombed by the RAF, at 0800 hrs on 27 September. The Royals pressed on to Manfredonia and San Severo, and in Lucera, 56 Recce

Regiment freed scores of Allied POWs. Patrol bases were established at San Severo, Lucera, Troia Satriano and San Paulo.

The Sharpshooters had been in the fray non-stop. Lieutenant Dickie Roberts MM destroyed an enemy armoured car, and Lieutenant John Grimwade's troop lost a Sherman to an 88mm. Corporal Carter stalked and knocked out another 88mm A/Tk gun, and Lieutenant Kenneth Kiddles's troop of scout cars was ambushed and destroyed outside San Severo. The municipality gave a splendid funeral to the fallen Sharpshooters with crowds of thousands lining the route from church to cemetery.

The brigade was ahead of its echelons. The advance resumed again on 1 October when the Sharpshooters, with 5th Bn Northamptons of 11th Infantry Brigade under command, moved in column to San Paolo and forded the River Fortore, 7 miles south of Termoli, the brigade's objective. All went well, Serracapriola and Chieuti were taken, and despite heavy rainstorms the brigade reached the line San Martino–Portocannone by 2 October. The Sharpshooters' tanks had difficulties in the unaccustomed thick mud. Vehicles of the Recce Troop were temporarily abandoned; 'A' Echelon trucks stuck in the mud of their leaguer area. After their 200-mile advance from Taranto their Shermans needed intensive maintenance. By 5 October the whole brigade (with the Sharpshooters in reserve), now including 2nd Battalion KRRC, 98th Field Regiment RA, was concentrated near Lucera. 44 RTR arrived at Manfredonia that day and moved up through Bari to leaguer just south-west of Foggia.

The German High Command ordered 16 Panzer Division to move from the Salerno Front to capture the small but useful port of Termoli 4 miles north of the River Biferno. Commandos and SAS had seized Termoli on the night of 2/3 October, and were reinforced by infantry from 78th Division. The main bridge over the Biferno had been blown up, and on the night of 4th/5th two battalions of Panzer Grenadiers launched a ferocious attack on the Termoli garrison. Lieutenant-Colonel Cameron received urgent orders for the Sharpshooters to cross the river at dawn and come to the rescue of the beleaguered 11th and 36th Brigades of 78th Division.

After heavy casualties, the sappers completed a bridge over the River Biferno, and at 1430 hrs Major Bobby Gale led 'C' Squadron across to help sustain 11th Brigade's defence of the road into the port. The rest of the Sharpshooters headed for Difesne Grande to take on the enemy tanks threatening to engulf 36th Brigade. For thirty-six hours there was fierce fighting – Shermans v. German Mk IVs. Attack and counter-attack went on continuously. By the end of the battle 'C' Squadron had lost eight tanks, but knocked out six Mk IVs and killed scores of Panzer Grenadiers. In the follow up attack on Croce 'A' and 'B' Squadron lost another five Shermans supporting 38 Brigade (who had just arrived). But the victory was complete. The German positions were overrun and the Battle of Termoli had been won. The Sharpshooters had only eleven tanks in battleworthy condition; thirteen officers and men had been killed, another fourteen were wounded.

Brigadier John Currie wrote to Lieutenant-Colonel Cameron. 'You have had a damned good gallop and are far and away the best trained regiment in the Brigade.' Eight decorations were earned in this fine action. On the 9th, General Montgomery inspected 44 RTR and decorated five officers and men for their part in the Sicilian campaign. For two weeks the brigade was in reserve engaged in schemes, TEWTS range firings, map reading, even convoy driving practice in the Serracapriola area. Here solid farmhouses in the Massa Tronco gave warmth and shelter. Quartermasters issued battledress instead of khaki drill. Canteens were opened, one called *The Contented Penguin* in an old wine press. Foraging parties went out each day and Italian pigmeat proved popular.

The CLY armoured strength was down to twenty-nine tanks and four scout cars, but thirteen new Diesel-driven Shermans plus forty-six reinforcements arrived. RSM Holway reminded the Sharpshooters that guard mounting, saluting and ceremonial drill were still important even in the midst of a thoroughly unpleasant campaign. Sergeant C.E.S. Tirbutt had been in action in the desert in 1942 and had to have a mastoid operation, so he had spent much time in and out of hospital. On 16 October 1943 he joined 44 RTR at Foggia:

Met Captain Hales, the Adjutant. Their CO Gerry Hopkinson, a tall, genial very decent man interviewed me, agreed to take me on as a Sgt saying that I'd 'better make sure I earned my stripes'. 44th seem a decent crowd. A jolly crowd of officers, NCOs and men. Originally a Bristol Territorial unit with a good war record in desert and Sicily. Very fit, deliriously happy and spirits sky high. The feeling of being a new boy wearing off. The Sqn OC is Major Teddy Foster, tall, lithe, energetic, pipe-smoker, very keen and a stickler for details. The Sqn standing orders cover *four* pages, impossible to memorise!

A week later he noted:

Into battle again. Feel very confident. Went across to my troop this morning to get to know them. Rogers, the Tp Leader quiet, bespectacled, a nice chap. Philbrick, the Tp Sgt tall and pleasant, made me feel very welcome. One or two old 41st RTR men amongst them. Very decent crowd. In the spare crew of course.

The 2nd Battalion KRRC had spent five weeks west of Tripoli training, playing games and swimming. They arrived in American LSTs at Taranto on 25 September, moved on 8 October to Foggia and on the 28th to Termoli to defend the Forward Maintenance Area.

On 3 November the Battle of the River Trigno began. In a hard morning's fighting 46th RTR dealt with six enemy tanks and two SPs, but lost seven of their Shermans. Some officers of 44 RTR had a grandstand view of the battle in support of 78 Division from an Artillery OP on the high ground overlooking the River Trigno. There they saw twenty Mk IV tanks trundling briskly into battle down the road from Vasto towards the river where they knocked out the tanks of 46 RTR in very quick time. The army commander ordered 44 RTR forward, 30-odd miles from Serracapriola to take charge of the armoured battle. With tank headlights

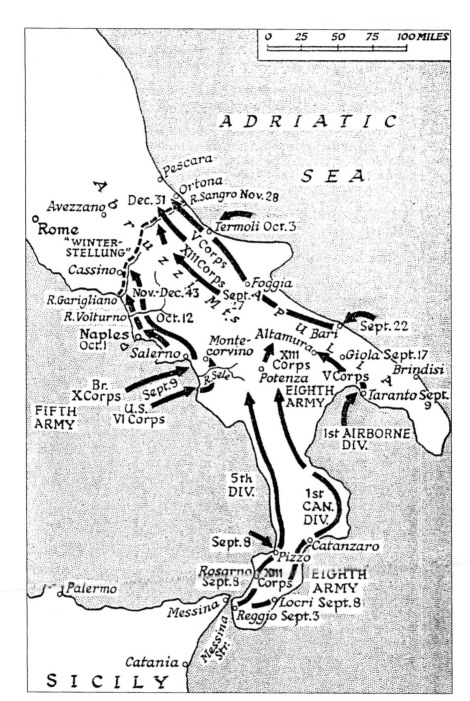

The invasion of Italy by the 8th Army.

switched on 44 RTR drove through the night, crossed the river at dawn, and moved up towards San Salvo. The going was heavy, mines and shelling held up the advance by 44, 46 and 50 RTR. Eventually, the high ridge south of Vasto was captured and the town was entered on the 5th. The next day 2nd KRRC helped 44 RTR get a bridgehead across the River Sinello. A full-scale attack to capture the village of Scerni, supported by three fieldgun regiments, was successful. Enemy Mk IVs were seen withdrawing and Casalbordino and the heights overlooking the River Osento were captured. The approach towards the River Sangro continued with stubborn German defences by SP guns, heavy shelling, occasional Mk IVs and 88mms taking their toll.

The Battle of the River Sangro

The German 65 Infantry Division held the main defensive position on the Li Colli Ridge with 26 Panzer Division and 90 Panzer Grenadier Division moving up in support. It was impossible to ford vehicles across the River Sangro. The British 78th Division had reached it on 8 November and established a bridgehead by the 19th. It was a wide, strongly flowing river and the northern defences were mined, wired and full of concrete pillboxes built by forced Italian labour. They ran westward from the sea to Fossalesia to the Li Colli Ridge and inland to Santa Maria and Mozzagrogna. The plan was for 8th Indian Division to take Mozzagrogna and then 4th Armoured Brigade and 78th Division to surprise the German defences by assaulting the Li Colli Ridge, although possibly too steep for armour to climb. The 4th Armoured Brigade would then sweep right flanking to the sea and open Route 16. A fortnight of detailed planning went into the assault, which was delayed by heavy rain, causing the level of the river to rise and fall. The sappers had built three bridges that were often submerged. The Indians, with great gallantry, battled for two days to reach Mozzagrogna and 50 RTR and the Gurkhas were counter-attacked by 26 Panzer Division and pushed back. The Sharpshooters made determined efforts, but had many tanks disabled by shelling and mud by the time they reached a difficult anti-tank ditch. For the first time Nebelwerfer multi-barrelled mortars were deployed by the German defenders.

The 2 KRRC were ordered to attack and seize Casa Casone, a strongpoint across the river, on the edge of the high escarpment overlooking the Sangro. 'We had a half hour concentration from four RA regiments [21 November]. The Casa stood out faintly in the moonlight and the escarpment looked as high and unclimbable as the cliffs of Dover', recalled Lieutenant J.F. Gammell, 'B' Company. The first attack failed, and on the 24th the Germans slipped away into thick country about two miles further back for yet another determined rearguard action. By 27 November, after five days of frustration, the floodwaters subsided and CLY were across, and the next day were

44 RTR at the River Sang-o with the Matella mountains in the background. *Imperial War Museum*

assembled beneath the northern escarpment. Behind the formidable barrage the full-scale attack started on the 29th, with CLY and 6th Royal Inniskilling Fusiliers leading. Seven tanks were lost in a minefield among the olive groves.

The sappers of 626 Field Squadron cleared the minefields under fire, and the Sharpshooters persevered, took out several anti-tank guns and advanced along the ridge to Santa Maria. At dawn on the 30th 44 RTR came up on the high ground on the left with the London Irish and another set-piece attack went in under a barrage from nine field and three medium regiments. By 1600 hrs all enemy resistance around Fossacesia ceased and 800 POWs were taken. The entire River Sangro position had been captured and route 16 to the Adriatic had been cut. 2 KRRC had played their part under command of the Indian Division. It was a considerable victory. Lieutenant-General Allfrey commanding 5 Corps wrote to Brigadier Currie. 'The success was mainly due to the dash and fighting qualities of your Brigade.'

The Battle of the River Moro

Ten miles beyond the Sangro lies the River Moro and the town of San Vito on the road to Pescara, which were planned to be the right-flank bastion of the Army's winter lines. 44 RTR led on 1 December 1943 in support of 38 (Irish) Brigade, through precipitous terrain with hairpin bends and blown bridges. The little villages of Rocca, Frisa and Apollinare were taken on the usual tit-for-tat basis: an enemy SP gun would knock out an RTR Sherman and the next Sherman would destroy the SP. 'B' Squadron took out two Mk IVs, one camouflaged as a haystack. Three Shermans were ditched and came under heavy MG and shellfire. On the 5th, the 2nd Canadian Brigade relieved the Irish Brigade. 44 RTR supported them on the next day *along* the river bed and then a steep climb up to Rualti. Despite Teller mines the RTR tanks struggled up to support the Canadians. Sergeant Tirbutt described the action:

> What a day we had. Moved off in the dark at 0530 hrs following the Moro river until we found a suitable crossing place. Then up a very steep slope to the village and only six tanks made it. Major Foster was grand going forward on foot repeatedly for personal Recce. We halted at the far end of the village, fanned out hull down to watch and wait. Suddenly the peace was shattered by Sgt Gray Boyce's voice over the air saying vehicles had been heard from the road. Next moment a Mark IV danced into view. Hell for leather, actions automatic, load, fire, reload. Hit it with probably third shot and pumped in a few more until it brewed up. Tug Wilson [operator/loader] was bloody good, a trifle excited but did not let it affect his judgment. Having disposed of one we were at once fired on by another and had to scuttle behind a house. Observation bad. AP and Browning flashing back and forth between two invisible opponents. He moved out. We fired together, felt a thud and the engine cut out. We were sitting meat. Tug had his Tommy gun, ordered me to take crew to safety. Our first shot had knocked out the Mark IV. We immobilised the guns in our tank. Tug looked for an ambulance for Captain Honniball and Hugh Bishop [who died of wounds]. We looked at Graham Boyce's tank one shot through the bottom of the driver's compartment, another through his headspace. Inspected the two Mk IVs. We re-organised, left a guard tank and leaguered at the top of the track.

'C' Squadron helped the Canadians defend Rualti against determined counter-attacks which went on non-stop until relief on the 10th by 50 RTR.

Meanwhile on the right flank, Lieutenant-Colonel Cameron commanded a composite force of CLY, 6th Royal Inniskilling Fusiliers, 98th Field Regiment RA and Sappers, tasked with the capture of San Vito. By 3 December the column advanced to within a mile of the town defended by the old adversary, 90th Light Division. Despite snipers in the town, shell and mortar fire San Vito was captured. Brigadier John Currie and the CLY CO enjoyed themselves firing from one of the houses at the retreating enemy. Major Woods captured an Italian opera singer.

Two days later CLY supporting the Canadians along the coastal sector had several tanks submerged in the ice-cold muddy River Moro. In all, eight Shermans were bogged and the remainder concentrated in torrential rain around the village of San Leonardo. They suffered casualties from German heavy artillery until they were relieved on the 7th and withdrew to Treglio. 'A' Squadron was lent to the 8th Indian Division, under command of 50 RTR for a five-day campaign from 13 December. Lieutenant Ted Dunn, who was awarded the MC, was heavily engaged on the 16th when his troop attacked Point 232 through vineyards and knocked out two 'special' Mk IVs.

Lieutenant Pat Brodie was detached after this action to act as one of General Montgomery's liaison officers. At the end of December Brigadier Currie left the brigade to go back to the UK, to become BRAC to the 1st Canadian Army. He was succeeded by Brigadier H.J.B. Cracroft, ex-CO 12 RTR.

Christmas was now at hand; for many of the brigade their third away from home. Foraging parties (the brigade was out of the line in reserve under 5 Corps) went out 'obtaining' food and wine, and on the 25th traditional meals were served as usual by the officers and NCOs. Major Oliver Woods was Santa Claus for the Sharpshooters, Corporal Lloyd Ponting trained a choir which sang carols round the various units, and the Revd Victor Pike, the Assistant Chaplain General, held a drumhead service.

44 RTR had been in action until 18 December, but spent Christmas in Martelli near Treglia. A piano was found in Lanciano and despite mud, cold and heavy rain the cooks excelled themselves. Sergeant Tirbutt noted that

Christmas passed very happily, very, very cold with biting wind. Christmas Eve drank too much of the local applejack and passed out. We celebrated New Year's Eve in style. Officers came into the Sgts Mess: Buck drunk but very funny. Gremlin got fighting drunk and had to be put to bed. Rumours abound about Regt going back to Blighty. On 8th January Medal ribbons issued. Africa stars twinkle on practically all breasts. Tuesday, 11th. Feeling rather dazed. Tug came up all beams told me I had won the MM; Gray Boyce also and Major Teddy Foster the MC. Good old 'C' Sqn. Four gongs for the Rualti ridge battle.

The rumours were correct. Blighty was on. The Sharpshooters handed their tanks over to 50 RTR, and by stages went back to Taranto where the Brigade Major, Miles Fitzalan Howard, visited them. Lieutenant-Colonel Cameron flew back to England to prepare for their arrival at Worthing.

The Sharpshooters sailed on 27 January 1944 on board MV *Tegelberg* and reached the Clyde on 8 February. The 44 RTR arrived in Taranto on 12 January; three days later they held a memorial service for the growing numbers killed in action in Africa, then Sicily and now Italy. On the 25th the regiment celebrated their last night on Italian soil in 'fairly rich style' and sailed for home on the good ship *Ranchi*. The 2nd Battalion KRRC – 31 officers and 639 ORs – embarked from Naples on HM *Almanzora* and docked at Glasgow on 9 February, two years since they encountered Rommel at Agedabia. A band greeted the brigade on arrival plus free tea, fags, buns and newspapers. The Royal Scots Greys rejoined the brigade and the Black Rats stepped ashore at the King George V Dock and went by train south to Worthing to join I Corps.

It soon became known that General Montgomery had specially asked for 4th Armoured Brigade to be part of the invasion team of the north-west European mainland – an honour – but a dangerous honour.

CHAPTER EIGHTEEN

The Desert Rats in Italy – Operation Avalanche

After machiavellian political manoeuvres involving Victor Emmanuel, Marshal Badoglio, General Ambrosio and Dino Grandi, Mussolini's twenty-one years of dictatorship in Italy ended on Sunday 25 July 1944. The king told the Duce 'Army morale is at rock bottom. . . . At this moment you are the most hated man in Italy.' Roosevelt and Churchill sent a proclamation, an ultimatum in effect, which was dropped by Allied aircraft over Italy on 17 July.

There were sixteen German divisions in Italy, eight in the north under Rommel, two near Rome and six further south under Kesselring. After the success of Husky, Baytown (the attack across the straits of Messina) and Avalanche (the attack on Naples via Salerno) were planned by Eisenhower and Alexander. Some time was spent by the 7th Armoured Divisional Staff (GSO1 Lieutenant-Colonel Pat Hobart) on Operation Buttress, the 8th Army's planned landing in south-west Italy (see Appendix B). Plans change, however, and the Desert Rats were to participate in Operation Avalanche, as part of X Corps (Lieutenant-General Dick McCreery) in General Mark Clark's 5th US Army. The two infantry divisions, 46th and 56th, were due to assault the northern sector in the landing area south of Salerno. The Desert Rats would pass through them and head north for Vesuvius and Naples.

The invasion of Italy began on 3 September when the 5th British and 1st Canadian divisions in Monty's 8th Army sailed across the Straits of Messina and took Reggio under an immense barrage. The German defenders had already left and the advance continued along the narrow, hilly roads of Calabria in the toe of Italy. Soon Locri and Rosarno were reached despite the usual small rearguard actions, demolished bridges and mines everywhere.

Peter Roach, 1 RTR, wrote

We drove 70 miles to Tripoli, loaded on to LCTs, journey to Salerno . . . The invasion had gone in and was now meeting trouble but well established inland. Obvious 1 RTR part of follow up. So it was goodbye to North Africa, to all the many races we had fought with and come to know with affection, to the desert which had been home for many of the men for some four years, no more the open vista, weirdly changing shapes under the heat of the desert sun, no more sleeping under great ripe stars, no more the understanding, ribaldry and irreverence of this magnificent army.

For Operation Avalanche Major-General Erskine commanded 22nd Armoured Brigade (1 RTR, 5 RTR, 4 CLY) and 131st Queens Brigade (1/5th, 1/6th, 1/7th Battalions). The 1st Rifle Brigade were the motor battalion for the armour and the Cherry Pickers were back (or rather in front) to lead the Desert Rats. Magnificent support would come from *seven* artillery regiments: 3 and 5 RHA, 24 and 146 Field Regiments RA, 15 LAA Regiment, 65th Norfolk Yeomanry A/Tk Regiment and 69th Medium Regiment, RA; as well as Sappers, RASC, RAMC, RAOC, REME and RMP. The staff worked frantically preparing loading tables so that the guns, tanks and vehicles would roll off the landing craft in the correct order on arrival at Salerno. Wireless sets had to be tuned. Vehicles were not the only equipment to be waterproofed; instruments and maps were treated similarly. The relative shortage of landing craft and the distance from Tripoli and other ports of embarkation limited the speed with which the invasion force could be built up. All the troops had to take Mepacrine tablets against malaria. Sergeant Jake Wardrop, 5 RTR, said on arrival 'The mosquitoes were bad. If anyone tells you that they only bite at night and sleep, don't believe it. The Italian brand are up all day long. They have a real party at sunset and for about two hours after that and then settle down.'

The MO of 1/6 Queens, Captain Jimmy Pretsell, enthusiastically directed the daily prescribed dose of Mepacrine. Lieutenant-Colonel Michael Forrester, CO 1/6 Queens, 'All embarkation camps were sealed [in the water-proofing areas near Tripoli]. Limited briefings included study of the terrain, of the enemy forces including the Hermann Goering Division [neatly escaped from Sicily] and our old friends from the Desert, 15 Panzer Grenadier Division.' The battalion IO, Humphrey Broad Davies, gave fuller briefings down to section level during the voyage to Salerno. Major-General Erskine was advised that the situation in the bridgehead might be sticky. The German troops had disarmed their Italian ex-Allies around the Salerno bridgehead. As ever Kesselring reacted quickly. He brought up most of the German forces in the south opposite the 8th Army, summoned three divisions down from the north and hauled in from the east a regiment of parachute troops. 'For three critical days the issue hung in the balance,' wrote Churchill. So the Queens Brigade would land first, 1/5 and 1/6 leading followed by 5 RTR, 3 RHA and a troop of sappers. Then came the 1 RTR and 4 CLY plus 1/7 Queens.

The 4 CLY embarked on 19 September. Lord Cranley, their CO, wrote

We slipped our moorings and set out for our destination, Salerno, in a four-day run through the smooth waters of the Mediterranean and the Straits of Messina. So at last we left North Africa for ever. I stood on the bridge with the Captain and looked back in the brilliant sunshine at the coast as it faded into the distance. I felt rather sorry to leave what had been for so long our nomad life with all its memories both sad and happy and those of our friends we had left buried there in the sand between Alamein and Tunis.

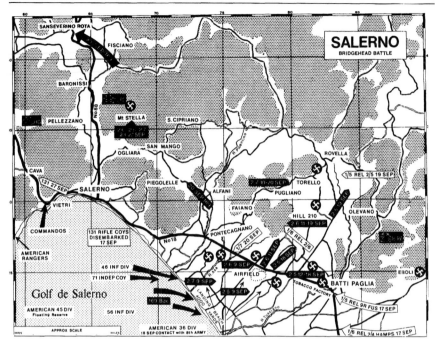

The Salerno bridgehead battle.

Brigadier 'Bolo' Whistler landed first in the bridgehead with unit advance parties on 15 September. The 1/5 and 1/6 Queens sailed on 13 September, and 1/7 four days later. 1 RTR's CO was on a LST with a very difficult naval commodore of the flotilla of LSTs. In their first run into Salerno Bay all the ships grounded on a sand bank. Later Lieutenant-Colonel Carver had to put the naval commodore under arrest at pistol point.

Divisional Intelligence reported that 16 Panzer Division was on the spot in the Battipaglia area, the Hermann Goering Division at Caserta, 3 Panzer Grenadier moving in from the Rome area and 26 and 29 Panzer Grenadier Divisions were coming up from the south. General Alexander cabled to the prime minister on 16 September 'First element of 7th Armoured arrive tonight but will take a few days to disembark and concentrate. One infantry brigade [The Queens] arrives tonight,' and on the 18th, '7th Armoured Division are getting ashore well.'

Churchill later wrote 'After six days of bitter fighting in which we suffered moments of grave hazard the Germans failed to throw us back into the sea . . . on the 16th the Fifth and 8th Armies joined hands. We had won.'

When the Desert Rats arrived, the harbour at Salerno could not be used; the town itself was no health resort and the whole of the bridgehead was under shellfire. Indeed, 2 Battalion 67 Panzer Grenadier Regiment put in a spirited counter-attack and Major-General Erskine's scout car only just escaped ignominious capture. Battipaglia, 8 miles inland, was captured, but then recaptured by 26 Panzer Division. At the height of the crisis 1,600 paratroopers of the US 82nd Airborne Division were flown in. The Royal Navy sent in *Warspite* and *Valiant* to bombard the strongpoints and FUPs of Kesselring's troops. Churchill wrote to General Eisenhower on the 21st. 'As the Duke of Wellington said of the Battle of Waterloo, "It was a damned close-run thing".'

Eventually the division was concentrated by 27 September, and 23rd Armoured Brigade came under command of the 7th, just the Royal Scots Greys in Shermans, the King's Dragoon Guards' armoured cars, as well as gunners and sappers. The plan was for 46th British Division to clear the Vietri gap west of Salerno, as far as Camerelle. The American Rangers would form a bridgehead, 23rd Armoured Brigade (ie the Royal Scots Greys) could debouch on to the plain of Naples, and the Desert Rats and the 23rd would converge on Scafati 15 miles north-west on the River Sarno. After that 23rd Armoured Brigade would advance on Naples along the coastal road between Mount Vesuvius and the sea. The rest of the division would pass the inland side of Vesuvius and move north towards the River Volturno in the Capua area. The roads were few and narrow, the country close and small; thick orchards and difficult mountainous country made the going very difficult.

The Desert Rats leading group for the breakout were 1/7 Queens, a squadron of 5 RTR Shermans, a battery of 3 RHA, a troop of sappers and all the Queens rifle companies in Troop Carrying Transport. Their night leaguer was near Cava. At 0515 hrs on 28th (D + 19) they set off. They passed through 46 Division, cleared Nocera, seized a hill feature and took some of the Hermann Goering Division as prisoners. Brigadier Whistler then unleashed his 1/6 Queens group with the same 5 RTR/3 RHA mix. Captain W.C. Johnson, OC 'A' Company:

> It was like being lined up ready for a race waiting for the word 'Go'. My orders were to get to Scafati and try to find a suitable crossing for the Div. over the Sarno. The CO [Lieutenant-Colonel Michael Forrester] appreciated that if we really got cracking we might get the bridge intact. . . . We went batting along that road like nobody's business. The tanks were off the flanks mostly, not too happy about the going – one troop got into Scafati.

An 88mm A/Tk gun and an enemy half-track caused trouble. Johnson led 'A' Company of the Queens over a wooden footbridge, and outflanked and captured the anti-tank gun crew. Lieutenant-Colonel Forrester and his two reliable RHA FOOs (Major Bill Fisher and Captain Harry Oulton) quickly entered the town and climbed the campanile (bell tower). 5 RHA regimental fire persuaded 2nd Hermann Goering Panzer Grenadier Regiment, which provided the bridge guard, to leave hurriedly with bridge intact. 'B' and 'C' Companies of 1/6 Queens crossed the bridge just in time to fend off repeated counter-attacks. The sappers cleared the bridge of explosives and the many cleverly concealed mines.

Lieutenant Nick Nice brought his anti-tank troop of 6-pounders up from Pagani to deal with four Mk IV Panzer tanks holding up the Queens advance: 'That night was violent in the extreme. Not only were enemy guns and mortars firing, but coincidental with their explosions was a severe thunder storm, brilliant lightning, crashes of thunder, torrential rain.' The CO was awarded the DSO and Harry Oulton the MC. The campanile, an obvious OP, had heavy fire directed on it from enemy tanks, MGs and mortars which killed Oulton's signallers. The enemy attacked again and again with tank support to try to regain the bridge.

The third of the Queens groups, Lieutenant-Colonel Elrington's 1/5, moved up through the pass behind 1/6, and struck northwards from Nocera towards San Mazzano. Major Borrett, OC 'D' Company, was held up by three Mk IV Panzer tanks but worked round them to capture the canal bridge intact – ready for the advance on San Valentino. The Queens Brigade had a splendid day: an advance of 10 miles, capture of the communications centre at Nocera and two bridgeheads over the Sarno and the canal. The following day 1/5 Queens moved on from Mazzano to San Valentino on the right flank, 1/7 Queens from Scafati north to Poggiomarino and San Gennaro. 1/6th Queens were to head north-west from Scafati to Passani, San Giuseppe and Ottaviano. The plain ahead was criss-crossed with waterways, dangerous country for tanks. Sergeant Jake Wardrop, 5 RTR: 'We drove up the road to Vesuvius . . . the Luftwaffe had been very quiet. Each day three MEs would slip in from the sea with a bomb each, drop it

5 RTR tank action in Scafati. *Imperial War Museum*

and run. Everybody laced them, Bofors, tanks, rifles and Bren guns. Up above the Spits and Lightnings were hanging around.'

Jake Wardrop noted that 'B' Squadron got across the bridge at Scafati before it could be blown, that 'A' had exploited to the north and that three newspapermen were killed by fire from a German tank. He and his tank crew spent a night in a jam factory, where they found sacks of sugar, tins of tomatoes and peaches. Trooper George Harvey was killed by a self-propelled gun at short range:

> We got it and carried on to a place called Poggiomarino which was being held by the Boches. They had quite a lot of guns, some tanks and a few 'Moaning Minnies'. We got all around the place by night and the Queens went in with the bayonet and the Tommy gun. We watched a bunch of them going up the road on a night fighting patrol. There were ten of them dressed in shirt and slacks, no equipment, rubber soles, black faces and armed with Tommy guns and grenades – did they look tough! As they passed the tank one big rangy lad looked up and said 'I'll bring you an 88 in the morning.' The Queens went through the village in the night 'and sorted out everything in it. They are very smooth workers.'
>
> Major Bill Griffiths was Vanguard commander of the 1/7 Queens Group who had passed through 1/6th Queens in Scafati still drying themselves out after the storms. After several kilometres an anti-tank gun knocked out a 5 RTR Sherman.

Major Griffiths wrote 'The enemy rearguards were difficult to locate. They fired bursts of spandau fire down the road, and occasionally anti-tank weapons and then retired as we deployed to engage them.' On 29 September in the village of Marra 'Italian villagers were cheering us on at the south side. From the north the enemy were firing solid shot straight down the road. The Sherman near "C" Company HQ was hit, caught fire. CSM 'Porky' West, Pte Dafter and I did a rescue act.'

The Hermann Goering staff planned their rearguard actions brilliantly. The Goering Engineer Battalion destroyed roads, bridges, stations, water, gas and electricity installations, mills and factories; roads would be mined, large trees felled across the roads and then booby trapped. Nebelwerfer mortars, troops of guns, a couple of well-sited anti-tank guns made progress slow and very dangerous. Meanwhile 1/5th Queens Group cleared San Valentino and 1/6th Queens took the well defended Pasanti, then moved astride roads to the Sarno, San Giuseppe and Torre Annunziata.

On the far left flank 23rd Armoured Brigade, led by the Royal Scots Greys, had reached Castellamare (south-west of Scafati on the coast) and were joined by Captain Peter Freeman's 'D' Company, 1/7 Queens, on 28 September. From Piedimonte, a height above Nocera, he could see all over the plain ahead. 'As we watched there were explosions as the enemy blew bridges over the River Sarno,' and the conical Vesuvius mountain sent up plumes of smoke and a red glow at night. 'The night was terrible, very black, torrential rain and a terrific thunderstorm.' The following morning the Queens in TCVs followed the Greys' Shermans across the Sarno at Scafati, moving left on the coast road to Pompeii. The column went through Torre Annunziata, where the Greys met light opposition, to Torre Del Greco,

A 5 RTR Sherman tank on the road to Aversa, north of Naples. *Imperial War Museum*

where Greys and the Queens met heavy opposition, which continued the next day. Then American Rangers took over.

For the Queens, 30 September was a hard slog. Deep drainage ditches meant tracked vehicles could not get off the roads and tracks. 1/6th Queens group advanced four kilometres, but were pinned down a mile from Passanti. Lieutenant Nick Nice brought his 6-pounder anti-tank guns up to help 'D' Company. Under constant fire, the CO, Lieutenant-Colonel Michael Forrester

strode casually up the middle of the road towards Major Ted Kilshaw and myself . . . Hoping he would share my comfortable safe ditch I smiled winningly. No, it was one of his unnerving moments. I had to join him there in full view of the whole German Army. I stood there, a cringing, miserable fellow, waiting for the inevitable Bang Whisssh – Crash of the 88mm. After 10 years off my life I was counselled to get my guns in before dark if I could.

Poggiomarino was occupied by 1/7 Queens quite peacefully, but met strong resistance north of the town. On 1 October 1/5 Queens and 1/6 Queens cleared San Giuseppe where the green-leaded dome and galleried cupola of the church dominated the countryside. The inhabitants of Ottavio, who had been hiding on the wooded slopes of Vesuvius, came down into the main square and – hundreds of them – overwhelmed 'A' Company 1/6 Queens 'with hugs and kisses, gifts of fruit and flowers. It was gorgeous,' recalled Lieutenant-Colonel Forrester, 'spontaneous and tumultuous', but they had to press on to Somma Vesuviana. Captain Peter Freeman led the advance guard of 1/7 Queens Group to cut the main road from Poggiomarino to San Giuseppe to Striano. He and Lieutenant Gordon Courchee, his 2 i/c, without any sappers, found and lifted twenty anti-tank Teller mines. 'Luckily they were all plain mines hastily laid without any anti-lifting devices.' 'A' Company, under Captain Carver with a 5 RTR troop, reached San Gennaro Vesuviano at 1300 hrs. At dusk 1/6 Queens were firmly in Piazolla and 1/7th at Gennaro. Sergeant Jake Wardrop, 5 RTR:

On the 1st we hit San Gennaro, caught some Boche lorries baling out to the north. Jimmy did some very sweet shooting, two in two shots, one went on fire. From the other we collected pairs of shoes, two sacks of sugar and a sack of potatoes. The Boches had machine gunned all the cows and horses and shot a 14-year-old lad. We handed over POWs of Hermann Goering division to the RBs who led them away and 'looked after them'.

The armoured cars of the King's Dragoon Guards entered Naples at 0930 hrs on 1 October. German demolition squads had done their worst, and great columns of smoke rose from many parts of the city. General McCreery sent a message on 1 October to General Clark. 'Today has given us one of the highlights of the campaign and Naples has fallen to X Corps. Armoured patrols of the First King's Dragoon Guards, followed by the Scots Greys were the first to enter the city, later reinforced by troops of US 82 Airborne Division.'

Alan Moorehead had followed Montgomery's 8th Army into Calabria, but with the drama unfolding on a huge scale around Salerno, bravely (or

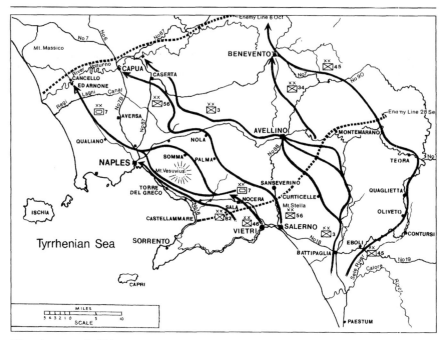

The advance to the Volturno.

rashly) drove in a 15-cwt truck from Reggio to Naples. It was a journey of 240 miles through enemy-held territory. He wrote:

> Driving through Castellamare and Pompeii the crowd thickened steadily along the road. On the outskirts of Naples it was one tumultuous mob of screaming, hysterical people and this continued all the way into the centre of the city. They had been cruelly bombed. There had been spasmodic street fighting for a week. And now they stood on the pavement and leaned out of the balcony windows screaming at the Allied soldiers and the passing trucks. They screamed in relief and in pure hysteria.

5 RTR had done well, and on 2 October 1 RTR took the lead. Peter Roach, the CO's driver, wrote of

> the fields dense with crops, blocking the view, dead bodies lay undiscovered amongst tall tobacco plants, arms and ammunition amongst the tomatoes. All was lush and voluptuous, fat and greedy, soon to decay, to rot, to stink, , , . In the small villages we were liberating heroes, big calm men, fearless and competent. As we drove out we shrunk to our normal diminutive size!

Major General Bobbie Erskine handed the lead over to 22nd Armoured Brigade, who found Somma Vesuviana a mass of rubble and demolitions. With 4 CLY on the left flank, 1 RTR on the right, with the Cherry Pickers ahead (but less mobile in this close countryside), the brigade pushed ahead against a spirited defence. Melito di Napoli, Afragola, Cardito and Aversa were captured. 'B' Squadron, 4 CLY, had to rescue a troop of Cherry

Pickers trapped in a village near Somma Vesuviana; the following day outside Arzano Lieutenant McKenzie was killed by sniper fire. Albanova was reached by 4 CLY at dusk on the 4th, the route through Grumo, Giugliano, Prete and Trentola was heavily mined with extensive demolitions all the way. Lieutenant-Colonel Carver, 'There could not have been a greater contrast to the desert. We struggled forward, blown bridges and muddy vineyards causing more delay than opposition from the enemy.' At Caserta a 75mm SP gun held up Major Pedraza's 'B' Squadron. It was dark and pouring with rain, so 1 RTR leaguered nose to tail north of Afragola. 'Every movement or noise brought down a burst of enemy artillery or mortar fire on us. It was one of the most unpleasant nights I experienced in the whole war.' Brigadier 'Loony' Hinde ordered 1 RTR on the 2nd to get going towards Caserta.

Cardito lies 10 miles due north of Naples. The German defenders caused problems and 1 RTR lost six tanks in a day's fighting. Lieutenant-Colonel Victor Paley, CO 1st RB:

The tanks were held up south of Cardito by unlocated enemy anti-tank guns well concealed in vineyards and standing maize. Desmond Pritty's 'C' Company lost one third of their strength on their start line from heavy shell fire. 1 RTR had lost tanks both to the left and to the right of the village and could not get on.

Sherman tanks of 22nd Armoured Brigade resting by the side of the main road to Naples. *Imperial War Museum*

Lieutenant-Colonel Peter Gregson, CO 5th RHA, brought down the fire of his twenty-four 25-pdrs plus a battery of 69th Medium Regiment RA. Eventually 'B' Squadron, 1 RTR and the RBs cleared the village.

Sergeant Wardrop:

> The CLY had taken the lead and we followed on behind. The previous day 1st Tanks had captured Cardito after a terrific scrap in which they had lost eight Shermans of one squadron and six in the other. They had pushed through the vineyards and bumped some well camouflaged SP guns. They knocked a couple out and we had a look at them – 105mm guns firing solid shot mounted on a tank chassis. They were very low and hard to spot in the trees, they are pretty bad medicine. The CLY were scrapping around Aversa. . . . the large American heavy guns moving up for the Volturno crossing battle – 7.2 inch and 155 mms being towed at a great pace. The mediums from Africa, the 4.5 and 5.5 inch were going up to the front, also loads of the 46 and 56th [division] lads.

The sappers of 4th Field Squadron worked hard at mine clearance. 1 RTR's recce troop tried out every possible road and track (the maps were excellent), and 1 RTR managed to effect a crossing over the Regi Lagni Canal. By the end of 5 October they were on the outskirts of Capua. Lieutenant Bob Stedman, 'C' Squadron, on foot, discovered and reported a footbridge at Grazzanise. Under fire from mortars MGs and a SP gun he sketched the wooden bridge. The area between the Regi Lagni Canal and the River Volturno was then cleared. On the other side – waiting – were 15 Panzer Grenadier Division. Oberst Grell had prepared all the bridges over the River Volturno for efficient demolition. The town of Capua was held in strength, and the river, swollen by the heavy winter rains, was wide, high-banked and very fast flowing. On the left flank 23rd Armoured Brigade had pushed north and west of Naples, and by 5 October had reached the line of the Volturno opposite Cancello Ed Arnone.

Major-General Erskine, GOC 7th Armoured, entrusted to the Queens Brigade the difficult task of getting across the Volturno and forming a bridgehead. Brigadier Bolo Whistler had 4 CLY, all of the divisional artillery and sappers under his command. On 5 October carrier patrols of 1/5 Queens penetrated to the outskirts of Capua and to Santa Maria Capua Vetere without contact with the enemy who had withdrawn all his forces north of the river. The next day 1/5 Queens closed up to the river line at Santa Maria La Fossa.

The village of Grazzanise, 7 miles west of Capua, had been chosen for the Desert Rat river crossing. There the wooden bridge had been partly demolished, but the 80-foot centre span was still intact. Sappers brought up Bailey bridges to span the gaps in the bridge. Tanks would have to find a ford for their crossing in about six feet of water. The 56 (London) Division were making the main crossing at Capua with the Queens Brigade making a 'diversionary' attack to distract the enemy. 'B' Squadron, 4 CLY, on the south bank would give direct supporting fire, and 3 RHA indirect covering fire.

The Queens had an unfortunate start, as Major Bill Griffiths, OC 'C' Company 1/7 Queens, reported. The brigade was heavily shelled by its 'own' barrage at 2100 hours on the night of 12/13th. Five men were killed and ten wounded. 'Then we were subject to intense shell fire for an hour.' An attempt to cross by boat at 0200 hrs failed under heavy airburst barrage. Griffiths asked Lieutenant-Colonel Gordon if they could try again. At 0400 hrs this effort was successful. By 0530 hrs two platoons were across, and by daylight the rest of the sorely battered company were over. Many assault boats were holed by shrapnel or MG fire, or were carried downstream in the current. 1/7 Queens, with their anti-tank guns, were across and dug in by the 14th.

1/5 Queens cleared the banks by vigorous patrolling and Brezzia was occupied by 1/7 Queens patrols early on the 16th. Their 2-in mortars fired more mortar bombs during the Volturno crossing than in the *entire* African campaign. The construction of the bridge was delayed by heavy shellfire, but was completed, working only at night, on the 15th. The river flow suddenly dropped and revealed a possible ford for the 4 CLY Shermans. Major Dick Sutton lined up the seventeen Shermans of 'C' Squadron behind a 20-foot anti-tank bank 200 yards from the river. He climbed a poplar tree near 1/7 Queens Bn HQ and brought down three rounds per gun of HE on every German mortar he spotted. Lieutenant Peter Hoggarth was wounded by the 'friendly' barrage, evacuated to Naples in an American Friends Ambulance, and later rejoined 1/7 Queens at Mondragone.

Major Dick Sutton, 4 CLY, was determined to get his squadron across the river:

> I reconnoitred the river bed just upstream of the Santa Maria la Fossa bridge which the REs were repairing. The river was 70 yards wide and 6–7 feet deep with a gravel bottom. We might get the tanks across if we could carry the exhausts to turret level and bung up the more obvious holes. I left Peter MacColl in charge and spent a day with REME. We fixed the exhausts with an open 40 gallon drum and a flexible tube to the exhaust outlet. We made a mixture of tar, clay and sand which we smeared round the turrets and other openings. The tow-rope was attached to the further shore.

The river bank was shovelled away and a bulldozer got across and made a gap in the far bank – and the CLY tanks got across and with 1/5 and 1/6 Queens set out to clear the area about 3,000 yards ahead. San Andrea and Pizzone were soon taken with only slight opposition.

The armoured regiments withdrew, after contact had been made with 56th (London) Division. It was back to Albanova and Aversa in reserve. Sergeant Jake Wardrop soon found the wine shops in Aversa. 'They sold Vermouth, Muscatel and an egg and brandy mixture called Baton.' He then visited Naples, saw the cathedral of San Gennaro and the Castel Nuovo, and the town overlooked and dominated by Vesuvius, 'always smoking, sometimes thick black smoke'.

7th Armoured Division resumed their advance along the low ground moving along Highway 7. Peter Roach, 1 RTR:

> A toilsome dreary, desolate advance through a tract of earth with tree lined roads that stretched soullessly past squalid little towns of timeless dreariness. And all the time it rained. The fields turned into mud and the water dropped in the [tank] turret chilling the crews and leaving nowhere dry to fight, to cook or to rest. Beneath the leaden skies the bombed rubble of the towns gave an impression of drab misery which the Italians themselves in their habitual black did nothing to alleviate.

The enemy was withdrawing slowly to his next line of defences along the River Garigliano (and Monte Cassino) demolishing bridges and culverts as he went. In the south-west the Cherry Pickers made good progress, but their CO, Lieutenant-Colonel Small, was badly injured in a jeep accident, so Major Wainman took command. Cancello was captured on the 15th. The enemy abandoned the line of the River Volturno and fell back on the little River Savone holding a mountainous line around Francolise and Sparanise. 5 RTR found themselves in Santa Maria, 10 miles east of Capua on the 17th and the next day moved into the village and camped in an old Italian barracks. Lieutenant Heywood, OC No. 9 troop, found crates of Peroni's Italian beer. 'We had a little session around the tank, got quite lit up.'

The 5 RTR led an operation two days later back to Capua over the repaired bridge to capture two villages, Sparanise and Francolise, supporting the Hampshires of 56th (London) Division. Lieutenant Heywood, Sergeants 'Snowy' Harris and Jake Wardrop encountered bunches of enemy infantry, and by use of Brownings and Tommy guns destroyed many, capturing 'white, thin Poles' and a Panzer Grenadier. 'I' Company, 1st Rifle Battalion, cleared enemy OPs in the hills above Sparanise, and by the 26th the division was firmly established on the line of the River Savone. At the end of the month the Desert Rats made a 30-mile night march, south-west through flattened Concello to take over the line of the Regi Agnena near the sea. 1st Rifle Brigade took over the front of the line patrolling by night in woods and along the banks of dykes. Ahead lay the small town of Mondragone, dwarfed by the bulk of Monte Massico three miles beyond. 1 RTR in their approach march towards Mondragone had fifteen tanks bogged (but retrievable), four disabled by mines and one broke down. However, 1/6 Queens, aided by 5 RTR, cleared the small port at dawn on 1 November A few tanks were lost on mines near the beach, but the group pushed on to the high ground and took the Massico ridge at little cost. The 1/6 Queens spent an unpleasant night, cold, under mortar fire, and their echelons, with dixies full of *hot* nourishing bully beef stew could not find their front-line comrades. Sergeant Jake Wardrop, 5 RTR, 'There were streams running into the sea, and in every case the bridge was blown. Mines had been laid and there was a gun or two to hold us up. We moved forward steadily [towards Cicola and Sessa Alrunca] until we got to the Garigliano River. To the north was Cassino and Rome.'

The division was withdrawn into reserve behind the Massico feature early in November leaving the Cherry Pickers, 1st Rifle Brigade and a squadron of 5 RTR to hold a 4,000-yard front. Most units had heard rumours, but these were confirmed between the 5th and the 10th when COs read out a message that their beat-up equipment was to be handed over to (indignant) Canadian tankless regiments arriving from England. The division would then move to concentrate on the northern side of the Sorrento Peninsula to await transport home. Corporal Peter Roach, 1 RTR:

> The Canadian unit [of 5th Canadian Armoured Division] was horrified at the old wrecks. Then to Castelmare, south of Naples, looked across the bay to Capri. Our home was in a spaghetti factory. We met the locals and made friends. We did find a house where we could eat spaghetti napolitan and sing Italian songs round the piano with our hosts . . . we visited Pompeii and toured the ruins. We visited Naples in search of anything to buy but either there was nothing or the price was exorbitant . . . we watched the sea for ships, swapped rumours and stuffed our packs with lemons and our minds with dreams.

Sergeant Wardrop, 5 RTR, and 'C' Squadron were camped in a red jam factory:

> At that time there were seventeen of us sleeping in one room, Busty the Sergeant Major, Nippy the Quartermaster, Len, Dusty, Joe, Ted, Cliff, Sam, Jerry, Digger, Pickes, Stan, Ernie, Jack, Snowy, Dixie and myself.

Wardrop met some RHA men:

> hard cases in this crowd, been abroad for six years and were quite mad. Many a night they would sing the English county songs 'Lincolnshire Poacher', 'Ilkley Moor', 'Bladon Races', and 'Here's good luck to the Barley Mow'. I liked these gunners, they were sun bleached blond-haired killers and great guys.

3 and 5 RHA were the Desert Rats' usual gunner regiments, but in the early desert days 4 RHA joined in the fun. The Royal Navy arranged some trips to Capri, Ravello and Amalfi. There were cinemas, the NAAFI of course, lacklustre dances (the ladies were scarce and well-chaperoned). Advance parties arrived at the docks to supervise the loading of the three ships in the convoy. Early on 20 December, after a short night's rest in Casoria, they marched – rather slowly – through the streets of Naples. On board the *Cameronia* were 1 and 5 RTR, 4th CLY, 11th Hussars and 1st RBs. The fortunate advance party flew via Algiers to Marrakesh to Prestwick in Scotland.

Monty had been brought back to England to help mastermind Overlord, the invasion of north-west Europe. Of course, he wanted his faithful desert legions – 50th Tyne-Tees, 51st Highland and the Desert Rats – to be the spearhead into the Third Reich.

On 7 January 1944 7th Armoured Division docked at Glasgow. Some of them had been away for five or six years from the time when the great 'Hobo' (Major-General Percy Hobart) trained and welded them into the British Army's best formation.

The D-Day Dodgers
(to the tune of Lili Marlene)

Oh, We're the D-Day dodgers, out in Italy
Always on the vino, always on the spree
Eighth Army scroungers, and our tanks
We live in Rome, amongst the Yanks
We are the D-Day dodgers in sunny Italy.

We landed at Salerno, a holiday with pay
The Jerries brought the bands out to greet us on our way
Showed us the sights and gave us tea
We all sang songs, the beer was free
To welcome D-Day dodgers to sunny Italy.

Naples and Cassino were taken in our stride
We didn't come to fight here, we just came for the ride
Anzio and Sangro were just names
We only came to look for dames
The randy D-Day dodgers in sunny Italy.

On the way to Florence we had a lovely time
We ran a bus to Rimini, right through the Gothic line
Soon to Bologna we will go
and after that we'll cross the Po
We'll still be D-Day dodging in sunny Italy.

Dear Lady Astor, you think you know a lot
Standing on your platform and talking tommyrot
You, England's sweetheart and its pride
We think your mouth's too bleedin' wide
That's from your D-day dodgers in sunny Italy.

Look around the mountains in the mud and rain
See the scattered crosses, there's some that have no names
Heartache and sorrow are all gone
The boys beneath them slumber on
They are the D-Day dodgers who'll stay in Italy.

Voices in the UK, possibly inspired by Lady Astor MP, implied that the troops left in Italy to battle their way northwards had taken the easy option.

CHAPTER NINETEEN

Green Jerboa Rats in Iraq, Syria and Italy

The two formations of 7th Armoured Brigade, 7th Hussars and 2 RTR without tanks were last seen recuperating in India after their heroic struggles in the Burma campaign in early 1942. In June of that year the brigade came under command of the 32nd Indian Armoured Division. After casualties and sickness their strength had dwindled to 1,500 men. The next month they were inspected by the Duke of Gloucester at Dhond and some General Grant tanks, Bren-carriers and armoured cars arrived. By September the brigade had absorbed reinforcements, was reasonably proficient with its new equipment and then they started on a curious odyssey. It would be another two years before they fought again. On 21 September the brigade set sail from Alexandria docks in Bombay on HMT *Neuralia*, with their tanks aboard HMT *Risalder* and HMT *Belray*. Nine days later they reached the mouth of the Shat el Arab, moved upstream to Margil, disembarked on 2 October and travelled by train to Zubair. Tactical exercises were carried out between Hammadiya and Latafiya. During the exercises 2 RTR code names were used, stuck and have been used ever since: HQ Squadron – Nero; 'A' Squadron – Ajax; 'B' Squadron – Badger; 'C' Squadron – Cyclops; and Recce Troop – Huntsman.

For six long unhappy months the Green Jerboa Rats exercised, fired on ranges and organised wireless schemes amid occasional sand storms south of Baghdad. In that hot, dusty, colourless station in Iraq, hockey and soccer were played, and in April 1943, in the severe heat, cricket was played. Tank crews familiarised themselves with ageing General Grant tanks and the lighter Stuarts. General Sir H. (Jumbo) Maitland-Wilson, GOC Paiforce, visited the brigade on 11 December, and the GOC, 5th Indian Division, welcomed the brigade on Christmas Day and presented medal ribbons for actions in Burma. Smaller composite squadrons trained with 21 Corps in Mosul, 200 miles north of Baghdad. Sandfly fever or malaria claimed a hundred or so victims from the brigade. Exercise Scotter took place in March and April in the Karbala area.

On 6 May the brigade sent their tracked vehicles by rail to Basra for embarkation and the two tank regiments began a six-day march by road and desert.

A café owner and family with Lieutenant-Colonel George Yule, CO 2 RTR (2nd from right); Major R. Brotherton, OC 'C' Squadron; Major H. Dumas, OC 'A' Squadron. *Lieutenant-Colonel Peter Dey, 2 RTR*

When they entered Transjordania they came once more under Middle East Forces command. Turning north in Palestine the brigade crossed the Syrian frontier on 12 May and went into camp at Insurriya. Then followed three idle and relaxing weeks beside the seaside. On 1 June the Green Rat brigade set out on the 300-mile journey to Aleppo and came under command of 10th Armoured Division. 7th Hussars were now commanded by Lieutenant-Colonel F.G.G. Jayne (who had commanded 'C' Squadron in Libya with a DSO after Beda Fomm) and Lieutenant-Colonel H.A. Lascelles was CO 2 RTR. Aleppo is 20 miles from the Turkish frontier and their army officers attended 7th Armoured Brigade exercises and training (practice convoy driving in hilly country, passage of defiles, minefield clearance). The brigade had a few much-travelled Sherman tanks and a number of Crusaders. Leave camp at Beirut 300 miles south was popular, but sand fly fever was still very prevalent. In early July at camp at Baalbek (east of Beirut on the Syrian border) Stuart tanks arrived and were allocated to the light squadrons. One small excitement occurred when, in the summer of 1943, 7th Armoured Brigade with some fighting, had to disarm the Greek Brigade. Their Moscow-led ELAS group were at loggerheads with the Republican anti-Communist group. They squabbled so violently that no Allied commander would have them under his command.

Lieutenant Peter Dey joined 2 RTR at the end of August 1943 and commanded 1 Troop 'C' Squadron. 'Shermans and Stuart tanks started to arrive. TEWTS and field firing took place at Slennfe on the Turkish border. The Baalbek valley was covered with sharp rocks and carpeted with a layer

'Red Devil' whirlwind hits 2 RTR camp, Baalbek, Syria, August 1942. *Lieutenant-Colonel Peter Dey, 2RTR*

Sergeants Clothier, Lane and Basham, Corporals Wright and Snelson, and Lieutenant Moulder at Fayid. *Lieutenant-Colonel Peter Dey, 2 RTR*

of fine red dust which periodically blew up into a whirlwind and swept through the tented camp, felling tents and distributing paperwork from regimental and squadron offices all over the valley.' Dey took his troop on 'a delightful excursion up the Orontes river, living off the abundant fruit trees growing wild along the river bank and bartering some of our issue rations for milk, eggs and other products.' The brigade was visited by ubiquitous ENSA parties, and excursions were made to see the Roman remains, to Beirut and the Bain Militaire for a swim in the lagoon.

In September 1943 7th Armoured Brigade left Syria for Egypt. Their march through Palestine needed very careful security measures as the Jewish terrorist organisation was active. The terrorists raided the British forces armouries – if they could – to steal arms and ammunition. On arrival in the Delta on 2 October both regiments were brought up to strength at Fanara in men and equipment – including new Shermans, Stuarts and Daimler scout cars. In November 7th Hussars became, for a time, the reconnaissance regiment of 10th Armoured Division. 6 RTR, under command of Lieutenant-Colonel A.C. Jackson, rejoined the brigade as did 1 RHA and 2 RB. Each troop now consisted of two Shermans and two Stuart tanks. Out of the fray now for eighteen months, having absorbed many new recruits and unfamiliar equipment, the brigade had a strenuous Egyptian winter. New tactics of direct fire as forward artillery in support of infantry had to be learned. The desert arena was not of much help since the brigade's eventual destination would be somewhere in Europe. Desert colouring on tanks and vehicles were painted over for the sombre hues needed for the close, green battlefields to come. A 'dry-shod' combined operation armour with infantry took place at Fayid followed by a 'wet-shod' fortnight's course at Kabrit.

By 31 October the brigade, commanded by Brigadier O.L. 'Minnow' Prior-Palmer, was up to strength with 52 Sherman M4A4 tanks and new Daimler scout cars for the recce troops for each armoured requirement. The brigadier was a stickler for turn-out and discipline and imported a Guards drill instructor. The drill courses and daily parades were not popular, but General 'Jumbo' Maitland-Wilson approved the divisional parade turn-out on 22 December.

One exercise was carried out with 84 Anti-Tank Regiment RA to prove the effectiveness of self-propelled guns to reinforce static anti-tank defences against tanks. Another tactic practised was the avoidance of ground attack by enemy aircraft in desert conditions without cover by turning tanks in tight circles at maximum speed to create a dust cloud. Sergeants Brooks and Basham taught 2 RTR mine and booby-trap clearing at courses at Fayid.

After Christmas 1943, exercises took place at Bir Beida near Jebel Ataqa: 'Fig Picker', 'Octopus', 'Kipper' and 'Tussle' (10th Armoured Division against 6th South African Division). In February, wet-shod combined operations training started at Kabrit: wading, loading and unloading landing craft. Major Morrell of the Lancashire Fusiliers lectured about operating in Italy – clearly the next campaign. On 18 March Exercise 'Formidable' was a full-scale assault; it was based on a D + 1 landing on a beach and live ammunition was used. 1 RHA fired their 105mm field guns. Some shells dropped on to 2 RTR and 6 RTR Shermans without causing casualties.

In the spring of 1944 the brigade had for the second time to disarm a Greek detachment – a naval one – at Kabrit on the Suez Canal.

In April, training now over, the brigade moved to Muhaggara on the coast of the Gulf of Suez to await embarkation. From Suez on 27 April the Green Desert Rat brigade – three regiments, artillery and sappers – sailed on the *Reina Del Pacifico* and *Champollion*, north, then west through the Suez Canal to Taranto, on the heel of Italy. They landed on 4 May moved up by rail and road, via Bari, Foggia, Termoli to just south of Pescara in the Lanciano area. Detachments from the three armoured regiments were allotted to support 4th and 10th Indian Divisions in V British Corps.

Apart from occasional shelling the Adriatic front was quiet and peaceful. Squadrons were harboured among olive groves and oak woodlands. The Central Mediterranean Training Centre at Benevento (between Naples and Foggia) was valuable for COs and squadron commanders to bring newcomers up to date on 'required' tactics for the Italian front. Target spotting, working with and without infantry, and range practices were on the agenda.

On 11 May the 5th and 8th Armies opened the battle for Rome and the beleaguered Allied beachhead forces in the Anzio pocket would break out. Kesselring had now fortified the 'Caesar', 'Hitler', 'Gothic' and 'Gustav' lines of defences. The Allied strength, of many nationalities, after the withdrawal of three divisions for Overlord and seven for Anvil, was twenty-eight divisions compared to the Germans' twenty-three. General Alexander wanted a local superiority at the point of attack of 3.1 in order to succeed, since the four 'lines' were well structured, well defended. In the middle of June, 7th Hussars were placed under command of 2nd Polish Corps (Lieutenant-General Anders). Supporting 3rd Carpathian Division at the mouth of the River Tronto, Major Richard Thornton and three others were blown to pieces when their jeep hit a mine.

Not a single Hussar knew a word of Polish, but many Poles had a smattering of English. Colonel Bobinski, OC of 6th Armoured Regiment and 6th Carpathian Infantry Battalion, spoke excellent English. Interpreters were provided at squadron level, below that basic hand gestures were used. On 7 July the Hussars lost Captain R. Nickels who was killed in a jeep accident. 'A' and 'C' Squadrons supported Polish attacks towards the Gothic line until, on 2 September, they rejoined 7th Armoured Brigade. 'B' Squadron remained with Cavforce, commanded by Colonel Bobinski, in their advance through the Gothic line.

Lieutenant Peter Dey, 2 RTR:

We were now under command of 4th Indian Division at the eastern end of the 'Hitler Line', stuck in mountainous ground covered in undergrowth while the battle raged for Cassino at the western end. Limited success was achieved by all three squadrons supporting infantry attacks

2 RTR inspect knocked out German Panther tank near Cassino, July 1944. *Lieutenant-Colonel Peter Dey, 2 RTR*

at Lepione and Guardiagrele but no real progress was made until Cassino fell and the Germans fell back to their next line of defence north of Rome. The Germans on the east coast now fell back to conform and C Squadron followed up without resistance as far as Chieti in what became nicknamed the 'Vino Hunt' because of the tremendous reception they received in every village along the way. In the meantime A Squadron advanced to try and cut the Rome–Pescara road. The road had been demolished in a number of places but diversions were being created by Italian engineers and A Squadron was able to advance to the Pescara River. They were now placed under command of the Utile Division with the task of protecting the Italian engineers. In the meantime the rest of the Regiment had concentrated at Castel Frenato and on 27th June it moved to join 6 RTR and 8 RTR at Venafro north of Naples. At the same time Lt Col George Yule handed over command of 2 RTR to Lt Col Lascelles.

On 1st July the Brigade, now concentrated at Venafro was visited by GOC 5 Corps, Lt Gen Allfrey, and over the next two weeks there was a demonstration of bridge laying followed by practice at crossing obstacles and a number of TEWTS. On 18th July the Regiment moved to Fiuggi via Cassino and Ferentino. Sadly, Tom Kirkbride, the Adjutant was trapped under his tank when it overturned on the journey and his arm had to be amputated. On arrival there was a Brigade exercise followed by a demonstration of Duplex Drive Valentine tanks swimming on Lake Bracciano. At the time Churchill was thinking of an assault on southern France, no doubt using DD tanks which operated splendidly on the smooth water of the lake but none of us fancied using them in rough water.

The decision to switch the main thrust by 8th Army to the east coast and to do so without alerting the Germans meant that the move across the Appenines had to take place in darkness and all vehicles had to be leaguered up and camouflaged by first light. Wireless silence was strictly enforced and no movement was allowed in the open. For the tanks this involved three night moves starting on 14th August. The roads over the mountains were narrow, dusty and tortuous and drivers were restricted to shaded front and rear lights.

The brigade was joined by 8 RTR under Lieutenant-Colonel G. FitzTalbot, and usually supported the 56th (London) Division. Commanded by

Brigadier OL Prior-Palmer, the brigade of four regiments were now to be organised as an all-arm pursuit force, debouching across the Foglia River into the plains north of the Marecchia and left flank protection for 1st Armoured Division.

The attack on the Gothic Line – between Pesaro and Rimini on the Adriatic coast running south inland following the river banks of the Foglia, Conca and Marecchia – started on 25 August. The Metauro River defences had first to be breached. 6 RTR under Lieutenant-Colonel Sturdee supported 4th Indian Division across the Foglia in the severe Croce battle, then captured Montecalvo on 31 August; there was a fierce fight for Tavoleto, which fell on 5 September. Captain S.C. Hadley wrote this account of the Tavoleto battle:

> At 0500 hrs we were up, packed our blankets and slowly moved out on to the road and, as shelling was heavy, on into a field. Directly in front of us was a two-storey shed with three haystacks standing nearby. Suddenly a machine-gun opened up, not at us but at the infantry on our right; it was coming from the shed only about a hundred yards away. I put my 75 on and told the lap gunner to look after the ricks. A white flag appeared around the corner, and two badly wounded enemy came in to surrender.
>
> We quickly decided upon our next action; Corporal Dobson and I started shooting our 75s as we thought it would scare the enemy more. It certainly did; from the cemetery the infantry collected about thirty of them.

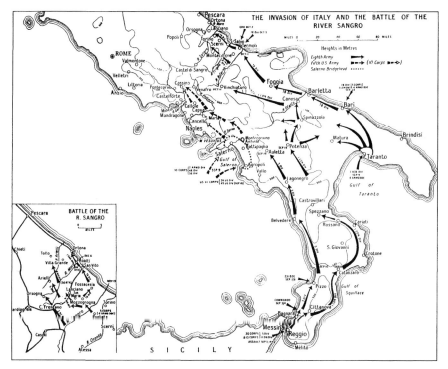

The invasion of Italy and the Battle of the River Sangro.

After a day of spasmodic fighting and a sleepless night we moved on to take up hull-down positions just in front of the infantry and engaged the enemy in a valley on the far side of Pian de Castello. . . . It was a difficult target and it wasn't long before we were caught in a shocking stonk which I thought had fixed us. . . . We were hit on the front, side and on the front of the turret; but as the dust cleared I checked the crew and everyone was found to be all right, although a little shaken.

The infantry now dug in all around us, and we waited for the attack we knew would come. . . . They soon came in. We let everything go; the FOO brought counter-fire down all along the reverse slope, just in front of our infantry and the attack collapsed. . . . Things went on like this for four days and three nights and we repulsed seven counter-attacks. During this time the crews did not get out of their tanks. . . . On the fourth night our ammo. was nearly out and about 8 p.m. the enemy came on again. Fortunately two more troops came up to help us, and arrived just in time. Soon afterwards we were relieved.

The enemy were holding Tavoleto and Auditore on the northern side of the Foglia in strength. The little republic of San Marino lay 15 miles ahead. On 3 September 8 RTR had hard fighting and heavy losses at Saludecio (partly owing to frequent changes of plans by 56th Division). However, on joining the pursuit 8 RTR pushed the enemy across the River Marano (south-west of Rimini). At Morciano 8 RTR and 6 RTR were withdrawn into reserve having helped the Canadian Corps. 6 RTR next supported 4th Indian Division in its advance north of San Marino to the Cesena–Rimini road.

On the morning of the 3rd, 7th Hussars were on the western slopes of Monte Fabbri in harbour, when it was suddenly heavily shelled at 1300 hrs. 'A' Squadron suffered severely (eleven casualties) as did 2 RTR. At dusk the brigade crossed the river, turned left at San Giorgio and harboured at El Casino tucked away in the deep Foglia valley. It was now working with the Canadian Corps again. Plans were made for an advance to the Marano, the next river north of the Conca. This took place on the 5 September as far as Mondaino to a line of hills. Now under 56 Division command, the objective was to seize the crossings over the River Uso between Santarcangelo and Poggio Berni. But as the villages of San Savino and Croce were still in enemy hands, the brigade was ordered to evict them. 2 RTR led and found Croce empty, but 8 RTR lost eighteen tanks as the first attack on Gemmano failed, against three troops of enemy 88mm anti-tank guns. Enemy OPs on the hills overlooking the Conca valley brought down heavy artillery and mortar fire. For three days 2 RTR, 8 RTR and 7th Hussars attacked, were counter-attacked, and attacked again in the Croce, Gemmano and Monte Colombo areas; Croce was taken, retaken and finally taken again. The enemy had deployed several SP guns with success. Both 2 RTR and 8 RTR lost heavily in men and tanks. The 8th Army now launched a major attack synchronised with Fifth Army assault on the Gothic Line in the centre of Italy, with the brigade still supporting 56 Division tasked with clearing the Fabbri ridge.

The following is an account by Captain S.R.F. Elmslie, 2 RTR:

After the opening of the battle of the Gothic Line, the Germans had fallen back to a defensive position, at the southern end of which was the village of Croce. From Croce a second ridge, the Fabbri Ridge, ran north for about a mile.

On 13th September the infantry were attacking due west, their start line being along the Coriano Ridge. The slopes were too steep and the country too thick for tanks. 'A' Squadron therefore started from a separate position to the south and advanced round the head of the valley to join them on the objective whilst 'C' Squadron gave fire support.

The start was slightly delayed by the fact that there were still enemy on the infantry start line to the right, but we moved off just after first light. There was a very heavy concentration of artillery fire in the valley, together with a smoke-screen to shield us from observation from San Savino. This together with the half light, made it very difficult to see more than a few yards, and we were worried by the fact that we had no infantry with us and would have to manoeuvre amongst enemy positions without being able to see them until we were well within bazooka range. But we had no casualties from this cause, and found out later that we had very good reason to be thankful for the poor light. Three tanks stuck in the ploughed land within a few yards of the start line, but these were the only casualties we had in getting up on to the objective. The right leading troop was hung up by bad country in the valley, and the two remaining tanks of the other leading troop got up on to the ridge completely by themselves. They had come right through the main infantry positions and then had to turn and fire backwards among the tanks of the rest of the squadron in order to help them to get forward, which they soon did. We found afterwards that the route by which we had travelled was occupied by more than 300 enemy infantry, who were taken completely by surprise.

In about ten minutes from the start of the attack, the nine remaining tanks of the squadron were all concentrated at the northern end of the Fabbri Ridge. As the light grew and the smoke cleared, we saw that we were splendidly placed: looking back at the whole of the enemy's reserve positions, along the Coriano Ridge, and overlooking any movement that he made. The main positions had been attacked during the night, and most of them, including San Savino, should have been cleared by dawn; but all the ground we could see behind us was still in enemy hands. No one else had had the success that we had. We were actually on Fabbri Ridge for about two hours before any infantry joined us; they had run into enemy infantry as soon as they had moved off from the start line: 'C' Squadron being unable because of the steep ground to support them closely, and we equally unable because we should have been firing back towards them and did not know their positions well enough to do so safely.

We had a number of excellent shoots at enemy moving about in and behind San Savino, and during the morning an enemy MkIV tank appeared moving down the hill. We must have fired about 80 or 100 rounds from all the tanks in the squadron at it, and hit it repeatedly. The crew abandoned it. We also brewed up a half-track near some haystacks which caught fire, revealing two enemy 88mm anti-tank guns concealed in them.

Suddenly an enemy anti-tank gun (probably an SP) concealed in one of the farmhouses to the north opened up and with his first round hit Corporal Jenkins' tank and set it on fire. The rest of us moved back to dead ground where the infantry were digging in.

By now the area had been cleared of enemy fairly well and our troops were established on the reverse slope. At the top of the ridge was a house which we shot up and a number of enemy in it surrendered. About every half an hour thereafter throughout the afternoon the same thing happened so that by the end of the day we had got about fifty prisoners from this one place.

Enemy along the hedgerow at the top of the ridge and from mortar positions over the far side kept causing trouble. We bounced delayed action shells on the crest and put 2 in mortar bombs over it, but none of our infantry actually got to the crest so we were unable to get observation of the enemy mortars. We remained to help the infantry consolidate and were relieved about 3am by which time, nearly twenty four hours since we started, every man in the squadron had fallen asleep.

8 RTR had to deal with enemy counter-attacks to recapture Gemmano between the 12th and 14th, in which considerable casualties were incurred with little to show for them. 2 RTR again took up the advance, crossing the River Marano and helping capture Mulazzano and Cerasolo and in the subsequent fighting on Monte Olivo.

'C' Squadron 2 RTR Sherman tank in Forli area, December 1944. Herb Staines (on turret), Babs Manning, Ray Rider, George Thornalley and Paddy Walsh. *Lieutenant-Colonel Peter Dey, 2 RTR*

On 18 September 8 RTR carried out two brilliant attacks in the Cerasolo area well ahead of the infantry. Close-range hand-held bazookas caused much damage. SSM P. Cleere, DCM, 'C' Squadron 7th Hussars, was advancing on Casa di San Marco clearing up the enemy positions. For a time the tanks had all their own way, when suddenly a bazooka man fired three shots at Cleere's tank. They all missed. His machine-gun jammed. The 75mm gun could not depress enough to engage, so Cleeve shot the bazooka man with his tommy-gun. By the 19th the Hussars, under strength in tanks and tank crews due to casualties, had to merge 'A' and 'C' Squadrons. The result was five troops each of two Shermans and two Stuarts. However, a week later the Hussars handed in their tanks and 'marched' to Lake Bracciano to become an amphibious D-D (Dual-Duplex) regiment.

Brigadier George Davy, 7th Hussar historian, wrote:

> In the autumn of 1944 the armies in Italy were faced with a particular problem which had never confronted them on such a scale before – the crossing of large rivers and extensive flooded areas. Training in DD (duplex-drive) tanks was a novel experience. When waterborne, the drive was transferred to two propellers and the tracks again came into play when the tank reached a depth of about nine feet of water on the opposite bank. Buoyancy was obtained by the watertight structure of the hull and canvas screen wich was erected before entering the water. Steering was the main difficulty and a good deal of practice was needed before a straight course could be kept. The tanks could only swim Lake Bracciano when the lake was calm. Great things were expected of the DD tank and many senior commanders faced with the problems of crossing the watery plains of the Po and the Adige came to see – and steer – for themselves. 'A' and 'B' Squadrons of 7th Hussars were equipped with DD Valentines, 'C' retained their Shermans, but became expert in rafting with Class 40 rafts capable of carrying a Sherman tank.

Another amphibious craft to appear was an armoured troop carrier designed for operating in shallow water and mud. In north-west Europe it was called a 'Buffalo' and in Italy a 'Fantail'. It could carry both troops and guns and a 25-pounder could be mounted to fire from it both ashore and afloat. DUKWS (DUCKS) were unarmoured load-carrying vehicles with a 2½-ton load. When waterborne they were driven by a propellor and on reaching the shore wheels took the ground and drove them inland.

2 RTR took part in four days of fighting from the 26th, driving the enemy north of the Rubicon. 6 RTR fought with 4th Indian Division through Monte Colombo and Pian de Castello over a five-week period, clearing the theoretically neutral republic of San Marino. Two squadrons of 6 RTR fought with 56th Division in its advance by Mulazzano and Coriano to the Marecchia River and finally in unsuccessful attacks on the Longiano Ridge.

Major John Warner led two troops of 6 RTR in the battles for Monte Calvo and Castelnuovo. He reccied the river crossings of Conca and Marecchia, and on 22 September, on foot, led his squadron up steep slopes of a hilltop near Scorticata to support the infantry under heavy mortar and MG fire.

It rained on most days in September and October, the fields were boggy traps, the tracks had crumbled and the roads were usually pinpointed by enemy OPs. In December, 8 RTR helped the Indians across the Senio, and 2 RTR, on 3 January 1945, eliminated a bridgehead west of Furli. The Python scheme started and large drafts of 'time-expired' men and officers returned to the UK, including Lieutenant-Colonel R.F.G. Jaynes, CO 7th Hussars, with a DSO earned in the Italian campaign.

Captain S.R.F. Elmslie, 2 RTR, describes one such attack with two new activities involved:

Tracked, armoured personnel carriers called Kangaroos were involved bringing infantry more quickly and more safely into action. The Tactical Air Force had honed their skills to pinpointing individual pill boxes and houses known or suspected to contain the enemy.

The tank units started 'Two Up' and advanced through thick smoke without casualties for about a mile, moving across country and thereby avoiding enemy mines.

'C' Squadron 2nd RTR cleared the start line successfully on their sector of the front, and 'A' and 'B' moved forward through them. The tanks had to advance for about a mile through very thick smoke. But this was got through successfully without casualties.

Air support was called down on practically every house, which was bombed only a hundred or two hundred yards ahead of the tanks as the latter moved forward.

After the RAF had shot up or bombed each house the tanks fired a few rounds into it and then moved on to the next, leaving the infantry to mop up. The enemy opposition was negligible because of the demoralising effect of the air and tank bombardment, until about 2pm when the tanks reached a line of houses about a mile from the river bank. Mopping up and remounting into Kangaroos had delayed the two companies of infantry and, as it took some hours to collect them and arrange plans, the last houses were not cleared till it was getting dark. The tanks were thus unable to get forward on to the river that day, and the enemy dug in along the banks. He remained there for the rest of the winter.

The Hussars, after training with DD tanks, spent two months dismounted. Their tanks were left at Ostra with the technical staff. In between two dismounted Lancer regiments they held the line at Madonna del Albero and Molinaccio, a few miles south of Ravenna. Patrols went out day and night across the Lamone river held by 114th Jaeger Division. On 1 February 1945 they left the Lamone marshland and brimming dykes around the Senio and returned to Lake Bracciano. On 14 April they fitted Platypus Grousers to all 54 DD tanks (metal fins attached to tracks to give a better grip in deep going).

Lieutenant Peter Dey, 2 RTR, wrote:

On 7 October, 7th Armoured Brigade withdrew to Porto Recanati to be refitted. By the end of September we had cleared the last of the ridges and were now faced with the totally different terrain of the Po valley: flat open country crossed by numerous narrow but fast flowing rivers, each reinforced with flood banks. In the first week of October 2 RTR was placed under command of 43 Gurkha Brigade who had the task of crossing the Fuimicina River and capturing Gatteo. Rains descended making tank movement imposible.

In early January 1945 two pockets of land on the east side of Senio River had to be eliminated – the Cassanigo pocket – before the big spring offensive could start, Operation 'Cygnet' was led by 2 RTR, followed by 2/6th Queens infantry in Kangaroos, and then by the rest of 169 Brigade. In thick fog, over waterlooged but now frozen ground the Germans were taken by surprise, as they had never encountered infantry operating from kangaroos. Over 200 prisoners were taken and a number of tanks and SP guns were captured. During February 2 RTR had a static role on the Senio and did their best to dislodge the enemy by firing armour-piercing shells into the flood banks. At the end of the month we came again under command of 43 Gurkha Brigade for operational planning in a pursuit role.

The appalling winter eventually came to an end, and the 'campaigning season' started again in April 1945. General McCreery's 8th Army was ordered to push the Vth Corps through the Argenta Gap (on its right flank) with the Polish Corps forcing the lines of the Senio and Santerno. The US

5th Army, under General Mark Clark, would endeavour to capture Bologna and Verona and possibly bring the Italian campaign to an end. Kesselring still had ten German divisions established in his 'Genghis Khan' Line, heavily mined, well wired. It was sited along the northern Apennines south of Bologna, along the line of the Senio and across the lower Po Valley. 7th Armoured Brigade, now commanded by Brigadier K.C. Cooper, consisted of 2nd RTR (Lieutenant-Colonel H.A. Lascelles), 6th RTR (Lieutenant-Colonel A.C. Jackson) and 8th RTR (Lieutenant-Colonel S.D.W. Seaver).

In early April 1945, the 8th Army was holding its winter line on the Senio River from Lake Commacchio in the north to Brisighella in the south. The Allied forces now included Indians, New Zealanders, Poles, a Jewish Brigade and Italian troops. 7th Armoured Brigade, less 2 RTR, was under command of 2 Polish Corps for the initial breaking of the Senio River position. 2 RTR, having fought the battle of the Cassanigo pocket in January and February and then rested in the Forli area, was now under command of 43 (Gurkha) Lorried Infantry Brigade. Opposite 2 Polish Corps were German units with forty Tigers, thirty-five Panthers, forty Mk IV Special tanks and a brigade of SP guns. 29 Panzer Grenadier Division were in reserve and the famous 90th Light Division were in the Budrio area. 7th Armoured Brigade were part of the 'pursuit' force, and each tank troop was now equipped with the new 17-pounder and two 76mm Shermans; Squadron HQ was equipped with two 105 mm guns carrying hollow charge anti-tank ammunition.

In the campaign in north-west Europe 'Hobart's Funnies', 79th Armoured Division, had been an outstanding success. A fearsome array of specialised armoured products, crewed in the main by Royal Engineers, had broken through every defensive line including the D-Day invasion defences. Some of these machines were available in the Italian campaign: Sherman (bull)dozers and tracked Kangaroos carrying infantry (14th/20th Hussars had recently joined 7th Armoured Brigade for this purpose). For crossing anti-tank ditches, two options were available. Cribs were man-made steel frames with baulks, wooden railway sleepers, placed on top. The completed effect was excellent provided the working party was not killed in the process of completion. Fascines, or circular bundles of wooden staves, could be lashed to the front or rear and could be dropped 'in situ' into the obstacle without the crew dismounting. Lieutenant-Colonel P.H. Hordern, CO 2 RTR, was naturally keener on the use of fascines, which were then used in the forthcoming battle. Also Churchill tanks (AVREs), turretless and carrying metal bridge ramps from each end, with a bit of luck and considerable skill, when driven into an anti-tank ditch, formed a hump-backed bridge. The Wasp (a miniature Crocodile) flame-thrower mounted in a Bren-gun carrier was also available.

The main offensive started on 9 April. 8th Indian Division would be supported by the brigade on their crossing of the Senio on either side of Lugo (due west of Ravenna). The battlefields here were on a large flat plain with hamlets, farmhouses and vineyards. Apart from the enemy strongpoints the irrigation system was perfect for the farmers, but usually presented, by way of ditches, streams and canals, very tricky obstacles. They usually ran south-west to north-east across the line of advance. The larger canals and rivers (and the Po was very wide and fast-flowing) needed major bridging and/or rafting operations. General Vietinghoff was now in command of the German forces, as Kesselring had been promoted to Commander-in-Chief West. He had no fewer than twenty-three German and, rather surprisingly, four Italian Divisions, thus outnumbering the Allies. The RAF/USAAF dominated the skies, and the German armour were restricted by a shortage of fuel.

With 6 RTR on the right, 8 RTR on the left crossed over the Lugo Canal helping in the capture of Solarolo. Both reached the Santerno on 11 April giving much help to the hard-pressed infantry. 2 RTR followed up with the 43rd (Gurkha) Lorried Brigade. A week later they were across the Sillaro, had occupied Medicina and had reached the Qualderna Canal south of Budrio (just east of Bologna).

Captain S.R.F. Elmslie, 2 RTR, described the regiment's last action in Italy:

The enemy was definitely in retreat, but rearguards of their 1st and 4th Parachute Divisions were putting up strong resistance in well-chosen positions. The ground in this area is cut up by a series of rivers, canals and ditches and heavily planted with tall vines. At intervals there are unexpected patches of completely open ground, across which an enemy anti-tank gun could kill as the tank emerged suddenly from the vines.

At first light on 16th April 'A' Squadron, 2 RTR (PS Hunter) acted as advanced guard to 14/20 Hussars (half tanks, half Kangaroos), carrying 2/6 Gurkha Rifles in a ten mile advance to Medicina.

At 6am 'A' Squadron led across the Sillaro, which though practically dry had very steep banks. Two Arks had been put in one on top of the other, but the ramps were still at an extremely sharp angle. The leading tank slipped and the driver stalled his engine leaving the tank at a sideways angle half way up the exit ramp. At this moment an accurate enemy salvo arrived slap on the crossing, but the driver managed to straighten up and drive forward off the ramp.

The squadron commander decided to go straight across country and avoid all roads, which were expected to be heavily mined. As a result there were no tank casualties from mines or anti-tank guns the whole day. The 14/20 Hussars on the other hand followed the main road, and suffered considerably, as every small bridge was blown and mined and often covered by anti-tank fire.

The squadron advanced on the left of the axis with two troops up. At La Palazza, the leading tank bogged in a deep ditch. A German armed with a bazooka who crawled up the ditch to snipe the tank was killed before he could fire. An SP gun flashed out of the houses, fired twice at one tank, missed it, and disappeared northwards. No. 1 Troop Commander (G.C. Sansom, MC) by following its tracks was able to cross the ditch, and throughout the whole day the track marks of this troop of hostile SPs which paid as much attention, also saved as much reconnaissance time in finding crossing places.

'A' Squadron received orders from OC 14/20 Hussars to hold back in Medicina. No 1 Troop, however, was too fully occupied shooting up enemy held houses at point-blank range, and co-operating with a platoon of Gurkhas against barricaded and sandbagged houses. Wireless messages did, however, eventually penetrate through the fog of battle, and No 1 Troop also unwillingly withdrew.

8 RTR were in action on the 15th in the attack on Imola and the advance to the Sillaro, and on the 19th took part, with the Poles, to the line of the

'B' Squadron, 7th Hussars, carrying infantry of 8th Indian Division on the way to Venice, 30 April 1945. *Imperial War Museum*

'B' Squadron, 7th Hussars (DD Tanks), in Piazzale Roma, Venice, 30 April 1945. *Imperial War Museum*

Bologna-Ferrara high road. 6 RTR arrived at Minerbio (north-east of Bologna) on 23 April, having supported 10th Indian Division across the Sillaro. 'A' Squadron had a determined action at the Galana Canal completely surprising the enemy who made off for the Idice River line which fell on the 21st.

Brigadier George Davy, historian of the 7th Hussars:

The crossing of the Po was carried out on a wide frontage and the 7th Hussars played a leading part on the whole front of the 8th Army. Lieutenant-Colonel Congreve and his RHQ directed the technical side of the river crossing on one sector of the front. 'A' Squadron, under Major M.V. Argyle, was placed under command of 56th (London) Division, 'B' Squadron went to 8th Indian Division and 'C' to 6th Armoured Division. A troop of 'C' was detached to 2nd New Zealand Division. The Squadrons did not meet again until the pursuit was over. Within a week the regiment was spread around the head of the Adriatic with its extremities 150 miles apart.

'A' Squadron crossed the Po on the evening of 25 April, Sergeant Johnson's DD led, then Lieutenant Agnew, Captain Barton, Lieutenant Argue and Lieutenant Iles. There were no casualties, but one tank hit an underwater obstruction and sank like a stone. 2/6 Queens infantry then crossed in Fantails. After desultory resistance a bridge over the Tartaro was captured, and then another over the Adige at Anguillara. The village of Mardimago needed combined Queens and Hussars to clear. At 11 p.m. on the 27th at Pioppe, five DD Shermans swam the River Adige, followed by 2/7 Queens in Fantails. The hot pursuit continued and by 9 p.m. on 28 April the Queens/Hussars column was held up near the canal bridge at Brenta only three miles from the great Venice lagoon. The next day at the canal bridge at Dolo the column met the New Zealanders arriving from Padua. A half-hour argument ensued – who should lead into Venice? The New Zealanders had maps of the area and also had wireless contact with divisional (or higher) formations. At Mestre the New Zealanders kept straight ahead and the Queens/Hussars turned off down the causeway into Venice. The port authorities surrendered and 'A' Squadron moved into leaguer in the docks area. An hour later 'B' Squadron arrived having supported the Royal Fusiliers and 5th Gurkhas across the same three rivers starting from near Ferrara to Canale Bianco and Roverdicre. Major Murray Smith's seventeen DD Shermans loaded up a company of Mahrattas and set off along Route 16 to Battaglia, sped through Padua along the autostrada into Venice. there they harboured in the Piazzale Roma instead of the docks. Major Marcus Fox led 'C' Squadron initially with the 3rd Grenadier Guards, then the Welsh Guards, a New Zealand formation and 2nd Rifle Brigade, but after the Po and Adige crossing, the 6th Armoured Division were held in check as the New Zealanders had road priority. Lieutenant Rawlings' 4th Troop of 'C' Squadron allied to 20th New Zealand Armoured Regiment drove via Padua, Musile and Route 14 straight for Trieste, where Sergeant Edwards, having covered 97 miles in one day, entered the city and met a patrol of the Long Range Desert Group there. Fifty-seven Piazzale Hussar DD tanks had set off and eighteen were still fit for swimming at the end (Venice lagoon or Trieste). All of the rest except one were recoverable. By the time the capitulation was signed 7th Hussars were concentrated at Mestre. First equal into Venice and Trieste – what a satisfactory way to end a war.

CHAPTER TWENTY

In at the Death

They were all there helping to end the Third Reich. The Green Jerboa Rats of 7th Armoured Brigade had helped smash through the last German defence line – the Genghis Khan – and had hounded the last German troops out of Venice and Trieste.

The Black Jerboa Rats of 4th Armoured Brigade – Monty's Marauders – under the redoubtable Brigadier Michael Carver, helped take Bremen and met the Russians at Wismar on the Baltic. The original Jerboa Desert Rats of 7th Armoured Division, after difficulties in Normandy, took part in the armoured charge in September 1944 across northern France, into Belgium and Holland, known as the 'Great Swan'; then hot pursuit over half a dozen well-defended water barriers in the Rhineland to the capture of Hamburg.

General G.L. Verney wrote after the great Victory Parade in Berlin:

> What thoughts must have passed through the minds of the veterans as they saluted their great war leader [Churchill]. Of that first venture through the wire of the Egyptian frontier and the overwhelming victory of Beda Fomm and Sidi Saleh; of Sidi Rezegh in November 1941 and the desperate fighting in that same area a few months later. Alam Halfa and Alamein; Tripoli and Tunis; the crossing of the Volturno. . . . So many scenes, good times and bad, savage heat and extreme cold, sand storms and snow, rain and sunshine and perhaps too so many names – O'Connor and Creagh, the first architects of victory: Gott and Campbell, Pinney, Ward Gunn and Beeley; Halliman and Wainman and all those others whose names have no written records but who gave their whole endeavours to their comrades and their Regiments and who died in battle.

FLOREAT JERBOA

Acknowledgements

Many thanks to Lieutenant-Colonel (Retd) G. Forty OBE and Colonel (Retd) John Longman, Regimental Colonel Royal Tank Regiment, for allowing me to quote extracts from *Tanks Across the Desert – The War Diary of Jake Wardrop*. Also to the Trustees and Museum Archivist of 7th Queen's Own Hussars for permission to quote extracts from Brigadier G.M.O. Davy's book *The Seventh and Three Enemies*. To Lieutenant-Colonel (Retd) Peter Dey MBE and Major (Retd) Norman Plough for permission to quote from their 2 RTR journals and notes and to use several of their photographs which have greatly enhanced this book – very many thanks. To Major (Retd) Derrick Watson 1/5th Queens Regiment for his campaign notes. To the late Field Marshal Lord Michael Carver for permission to quote extracts from his campaign articles of 1 RTR in North Africa and Italy. To Major (Retd) Bill Close MC for permission to quote from his book *A View from the Turret*. To Pen & Sword Books for permission to use extracts from Peter Roach's *8.15 to War*. To the late Major-General G.P.B. Roberts for permission to use extracts from his book *From the Desert to the Baltic*, and to the late Lieutenant-Colonel Cyril Joly for permission to quote from his book *Take these Men*. Also thanks must go to C.E.S. (Ted) Tirbutt for allowing me to quote from his journal.

A Speech to the Men of the 8th Army at Tripoli

3 February 1943

by Prime Minister Winston Churchill

General Montgomery and men of the Joint Headquarters of the 8th Army:

The last time I saw this army was in the closing days of August on those sandy and rocky bluffs near Alamein and the Ruweisat Ridge, when it was apparent from all the signs that Rommel was about to make his final thrust on Alexandria and Cairo. Then all was to be won or lost. Now I come to you a long way from Alamein, and I find this army and its famous commander with a record of victory behind it which has undoubtedly played a decisive part in altering the whole character of the war.

The fierce and well fought battle of Alamein, the blasting through of the enemy's seaward flank, and the thunderbolt of the armoured attack, irretrievably broke the army which Rommel had boasted would conquer Egypt, and upon which the German and Italian peoples had set their hopes. Thereafter and since, in these remorseless three months, you have chased this hostile army and driven it from pillar to post over a distance of more than 1,400 miles – in fact, as far as from London to Moscow. You have altered the face of the war in a most remarkable way.

What it has meant in the skill and organisation of movement and manoeuvres, what it has meant in the tireless endurance and self-denial of the troops and in the fearless leadership displayed in action, can be appreciated only by those who were actually on the spot. But I must tell you that the fame of the Desert Army has spread throughout the world.

After the surrender of Tobruk, there was a dark period when many people, not knowing us, not knowing the British and the nations of the British Empire, were ready to take a disparaging view. But now everywhere your work is spoken of with respect and admiration. When I was with the Chief of the Imperial General Staff at Casablanca and with the President of the United States, the arrival of the Desert Army in Tripoli was a new factor which influenced the course of our discussions and opened up hopeful vistas for the future. You are entitled to know these things, and to dwell upon them with that satisfaction which men in all modesty feel when a great work has been finally done. You have rendered a high service to your country and the common cause.

It must have been a tremendous experience driving forward day after day over this desert which it has taken me this morning more than six hours to fly at 200 miles an hour. You were pursuing a broken enemy, dragging on behind you this ever-lengthening line of communications, carrying the whole art of desert warfare to perfection. In the words of the old hymn, you have 'nightly pitched your moving tents a day's march nearer home'. Yes, not only in the march of the army but in the progress of the war you have brought home nearer. I am here to thank you on behalf of His Majesty's Government of the British Isles and of all our friends the world over.

Hard struggles lie ahead. Rommel, the fugitive of Egypt, Cyrenaica, and Tripolitania, in a non-stop race of 1,400 miles, is now trying to present himself as the deliverer of Tunisia. Along the eastern coast of Tunisia are large numbers of German and Italian troops, not yet equipped to their previous standard, but growing stronger. On the other side, another great operation, planned in conjunction with your advance, has carried the First British Army, our American comrades, and the French armies to within 30 or 40 miles of Bizerta and Tunis. Therefrom a military situation arises which everyone can understand.

The days of your victories are by no means at an end, and with forces which march from different quarters we may hope to achieve the final destruction or expulsion from the shores of Africa of every armed German or Italian. You must have felt relief when, after those many a hundred miles of desert, you came once more into a green land with trees and grass and I do not think you will lose that advantage. As you go forward on further missions that will fall to your lot, you will fight in countries which will present undoubtedly serious tactical difficulties, but which none the less will not have that grim character of desert war which you have known how to endure and how to overcome.

Let me then assure you, soldiers and airmen, that your fellow-countrymen regard your joint work with admiration and gratitude, and that after the war when a man is asked what he did it will be quite sufficient for him to say, 'I marched and fought with the Desert Army.' And when history is written and all the facts are known, our feats will gleam and glow and will be a source of song and story long after we who are gathered here have passed away.

7th Armoured Division Training Memorandum for Italy

Major Patrick Hobart, GSO2 issued on Major General Bobbie Erskine's behalf the 'Most Secret' 7th Armoured Division Training Memorandum No 1 to establish tactics in the forthcoming Italian campaign – dated July 1943.

MOST SECRET

Main HQ 7 Armd Div
6 July 43
Copy No . . . . . .

7 Armd Div Training Memorandum No. 1

Future operations will take place in mountainous country where movement off the roads will be very restricted and frequently quite impossible. A paper on topography will be issued shortly by this HQ to all concerned. I wish the following aspects of training to be studied carefully forthwith.

1.   Use of Armour
Armoured Regts must be prepared to support inf through restricted and mountainous country. This may often work out as one Armd Regt in sp of an Inf Bde moving on a single road. The leading tps might be one Inf Bn with the sp of one sqn tks and one RHA (SP) Bty. The Forward Body of such a force is dealt with below.

2.   Forward Body (see diagram at Appx A).
This might consist of:
>   One sqn tks
>   One sec or more of armd recce tp
>   One coy inf (lorry borne)
>   Carrier pl of inf bn (less one or more secs)
>   One tp RHA
>   RE recce party.

This Forward Body should be commanded by the TK Sqn Ldr, who has better comns than the inf coy comd; he can have a wireless link with the inf bn comd.

Such a Forward Body may not be always suitable, but it has speed and punch and may be taken as a reasonable standard. Comds will study the problems of the employment of a body of such nature and tk tp and sqn tactics down a road with restricted country on either side will be practiced. The HOMS–MISURATA road is suitable for this trg.

3.   Infantry

I cannot stress too much the importance of physical fitness. Tps MUST be able to undertake long marches carrying heavy weights and be able to fight at the end of such marches. The Motor bn must be just as fit as the other inf bns. We must be prepared to march and fight up to 90 miles in 6 days.

4.   Traffic Control and Road Discipline.

Road discipline and traffic control has assumed an importance never before experienced in this war. Roads are few, narrow, bounded by walls, and in many places it is quite impossible for any wheeled vehicles to get off the roads at all.

First class march discipline is absolutely vital and this is a matter for each individual driver. A very high standard of driving is required. Drivers must be able to manoeuvre through narrow gaps, they must be prepared to get out instantly and tear down walls or widen gaps for turning off the road, and they must all realise the vital importance of keeping moving and keeping the road open.

During all moves all available MCs will be ridden by officers who will patrol unceasingly up and down their columns taking immediate action to rectify any checks or blocks that may occur. In the past some officers have ridden in their own vehicles and taken no action to ensure the smooth passage of their units on road moves. This practice will never occur again.

Dispersal areas are few and movement will often be by bounds from one dispersal area to the next. Recce ahead and a drill for dispersing off the road on arrival are essential, and during actual moves from one dispersal area to another there must be no checks or halts.

The clear marking of axes (Div and Bdes), sign-posting and marking of HQs will be very important and formations and units will ensure that the necessary signs are available and that the drill for marking axes and HQs is clearly laid down. Axis signs will be placed on the offside of the road facing down towards the enemy and turnings will be marked by two axis signs one upright and one inclined in the direction of the turn.

The Div Pro Coy will frequently not be sufficient to control large-scale moves and formations and units will be required to assist by the provision of Sector controls, TPs and pointsmen. Each arty regt, motor and inf bn will train and maintain two Sector controls. Attention is drawn to MTP No. 47 of 1941 'Movement by Road'.

Good road movement depends upon the co-operation and initiative of each individual driver and the energy of each officer.

5.   Protection

We shall be fighting for the first time in enemy country and must be prepared against attack by civilians, fifth columnists and agents as well as by parachutists dropped in the rear areas. This means that all units and HQs, administrative as well as fighting, must be prepared for attack at all times. In the past, in the desert, we have always relied on our mobility to escape from attack in the rear areas. In the new theatre of operations movement will not be possible so we must fight to protect ourselves.

Although the principle of picqueting as used on the North-West Frontier should not be necessary adequate steps must be taken to safeguard the flanks of our axis of advance. Where there are suitable positions for the enemy to conceal himself for attack on the flanks of our advance, formations and units must be prepared to protect themselves by recce to prevent counter-attack on the column after the head has passed. Generally speaking ground up to a mile each side of the road must be cleared by infantry, but the advance of the Forward Body need not wait for this. Side roads must be blocked with small arms fire and A.Tk guns.

6.   Mines and Demolitions

The type of country we shall be operating in lends itself to defence and we must be prepared to meet mines in large quantities and many demolitions. All arms must be prepared to deal with both mines and demolitions themselves to maintain the speed of advance which is so important, and must not always wait for the RE to deal with such obstacles.

The removal of demolition charges is most important and must always be done at the earliest opportunity, since bridges and obstacles are liable to change hands several times.

Further training memoranda will be issued from time to time in the near future.

Maj Gen.
Cmd.

PRCH/aw
DISTRIBUTION

	Copy Nos		Copy Nos
HQ 22 Armd Bde	1–5	A/Q	22
131 Bde	6–9	OC Div Sigs	23
OC 11 H	10	CRASC	24–29
CRA	11–17	ADMS	30–33
CRE	18–21	CREME	34–37
		APOS	38–39

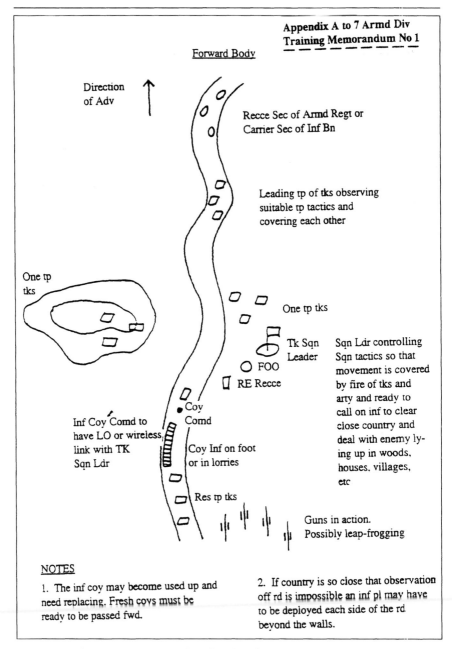

Appendix A of the 7th Armoured Division Training Memorandum No. 1.

	APM	40
Copy to:	OC HQ Sqn	41
HQ 8 Armd Bde 42–46	OC Royals	47

Appendix A to 7 Armd Div
Training Memorandum No 1

Notes

1.   The inf coy may become used up and need replacing. Fresh coys must be ready to be passed fwd.

2.   If country is so close that observations off rd are impossible an inf pl may have to be deployed each side of the rd beyond the walls.

Types of Tanks in service with 7th Armoured Division

Mark VI light tank crew 3, weight 5½ tons, developed from Carden-Lloyd series of light tanks and carriers. Maximum speed 35 mph, range 130 miles. Armament 1 x .5 in Vickers MG, 1 x .303 Vickers MG. Engine Meadows 89 bhp. Period 1936–41.

Cruiser Mark I (A–9) crew 6, weight 12.8 tons, maximum speed 25 mph, range 150 miles. Armament 1 x 2 pdr (close support type had 3.7 inch mortar) and 3 x .303 in Vickers MG. Engine AEC 6 cylinders 150 bhp. Period 1937–42.

Cruiser Mark II (A–10) crew 5, weight 14 tons, maximum speed 16 mph, range 100 miles. Armament 1 x 2 pdr (close support version with 3.7 inch mortar) and 1 x .303 in Vickers MG. Engine AEC 6 cylinders 150 bhp. Period 1938–42.

Cruiser Mark III (A–13) crew 4, weight 14 tons, maximum speed 30 mph, range 90 miles. Armament 1 x 2 pdr. 1 x .303 in Vickers MG. Engine Nuffield Liberty 1 340 bhp. Limited numbers produced. Period 1939–42.

Cruiser Mk VI (A–15 Crusader) crew 4, then 3, weight 19 tons, maximum speed 27 mph, range 100 miles. Armament 1 x 2 pdr (1 x 6 pdr on Crusader III) 2 x 7.92 in Besa MG. Engine Nuffield Liberty 340 bhp. Period 1941–44.

Stuart I (Light tank US M-3) 'Honey' crew 4, weight 12½ tons, maximum speed 36 mph, range 70 miles. Armament 1 x 37mm, 2 x .30 Browning MG. Engine Continental 7 cylinder radial 250 bhp. Period 1941–44.

Grant I (Medium tank US M-3) crew 6, weight 28½ tons, maximum speed 26 mph, range 144 miles. Armament 1 x 75mm (in hull), 1 x 37mm (in turret), 1 x .30 Browning MG. Engine Continental 9 cylinder radial 340 bhp. Period 1942–44.

Sherman I and II (Medium tank US M-4) crew 5, weight 30 tons, maximum speed 24 mph, range 85 miles. Armament 1 x 75mm, 2 x .30 Browning MG. Engine Continental 9 cylinder radial 400 bhp. Period 1942–45. (Diesel version preferred to petrol, less likely to catch fire.)

Armoured Cars

Rolls-Royce crew 4, weight 3.8 tons, maximum speed 50 mph, range 150 miles. Armament 1 x MG. Period 1940–41.

Morris CS9/LAC crew 4, weight 4.2 tons, maximum speed 45 mph, range 240 miles. Armament 1 x Boys, 1 x Bren LMG. Period 1936–42.

Bibliography

Allen, W.D. and Cawston, F.R.H., *Carpiquet Bound*, Chiavari, 1997
Churchill, W., *The Second World War*, Cassell, 1956
Clarke, D., *The Eleventh at War*, Michael Joseph, 1952
Close, W.H., *A View from the Turret*, Dell & Breden, 1998
Curtis, G., *Salerno Remembered*, Bredon, Queen's Royal Surrey Museum, 1988
Davy, G.M.O., *The Seventh and Three Enemies*, Heffer, 1953
Delaforce, P., *Monty's Marauders*, Tom Donovan, 1999
Draper, A., *Retreat from Burma*, Leo Cooper, 1987
Farran, R., *Winged Dagger*, Cassell, 1998
Forty, G., *Desert Rats at War*, Purnell Book Services, 1977
——, *Wardrop of the Fifth*, William Kimber, 1981
Hart, B.L., *The Tanks* (Vol 2), Cassell, 1959
Johnson, R.B., *The Queens in the Middle East and North Africa*, Queens Royal Surrey Museum, 1996
Joly, C., *Take these Men*, Buchan & Enright, 1985
Lunt, J., *Hell of a Licking*, Collins, 1986
Masters, D., *With Pennants Flying*, Eyre Spottiswoode, 1943
Moorehead, A., *African Trilogy*, Hamish Hamilton, 1944
Perrett, B., *Tank Tracks to Rangoon*, Arms & Armour, 1995
——, *Iron Fist*
Pitt, B., *Crucible of War (1941–1942)*, Macmillan, 1986
——, *Year of Alamein, 1942*
Roach, P., *The 8.15 to War*, Leo Cooper, 1953
Roberts, G.P.B., *From the Desert to the Baltic*, William Kimber, 1987
1 RTR War Diary, Public Record Office
2RTR War Diary, Public Record Office
7th Armoured Division War Diary, Public Record Office

Index